Graphing Calculator Manual

College Algebra and
Algebra and Trigonometry

Graphing Calculator Manual

College Algebra and Algebra and Trigonometry

Marvin L. Bittinger
Indiana University - Purdue University at Indianapolis

Judith A. Beecher
Indiana University - Purdue University at Indianapolis

David Ellenbogen
St. Michael's College

Judith A. Penna

Judith A. Penna

▲ ADDISON-WESLEY

An imprint of Addison Wesley Longman, Inc.

Reading, Massachusetts • Menlo Park, California • New York • Harlow, England
Don Mills, Ontario • Sydney • Mexico City • Madrid • Amsterdam

Reprinted with corrections, May 1997.

Reproduced by Addison Wesley Longman from camera-ready copy supplied by the author.

ISBN   0-201-87360-5

2 3 4 5 6 7 8 9 10 CRS 999897

Table of Contents

The TI-82 and TI-83
Graphics Calculators

Preliminaries

Press ON to turn on the TI-82 or TI-83 graphing calculator. (ON is the key at the bottom left-hand corner of the keypad.) The display contrast can be adjusted by first pressing 2nd . (2nd is the blue key on the TI-82 and the yellow key on the TI-83 in the left column of the keypad.) Then press and hold △ to increase the contrast or ▽ to decrease the contrast. To turn the grapher off, press 2nd OFF . (OFF is the second operation associated with the ON key.) The grapher will turn itself off automatically after about five minutes without any activity.

It will be helpful to read the Getting Started section of your grapher Guidebook before proceeding. See pages 1 - 14 of the TI-82 Guidebook or pages 1 - 18 of the TI-83 Guidebook.

Press MODE to display the MODE settings. Initially you should select the settings on the left side of the display.

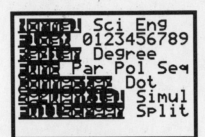

To change a setting use ▽ or △ to move the cursor to the line of that setting. Then use ▷ or ◁ to move the blinking cursor to the desired setting and press ENTER . Press CLEAR or 2nd QUIT to leave the MODE screen. (QUIT is the second operation associated with the MODE key.)

Chapter G
Introduction to Graphs and Graphers

SETTING THE VIEWING WINDOW

The viewing window is the portion of the coordinate plane that appears on the grapher's screen. It is defined by the minimum and maximum values of x and y: Xmin, Xmax, Ymin, and Ymax. The notation [Xmin, Xmax, Ymin, Ymax] is used in the text to represent these window settings or dimensions. For example, $[-12, 12, -8, 8]$ denotes a window that displays the portion of the x-axis from -12 to 12 and the portion of the y-axis from -8 to 8. In addition, the distance between tick marks on the axes is defined by the settings Xscl and Yscl. The TI-83 includes an additional setting, Xres, which sets the pixel resolution. We usually select Xres = 1. The window corresponding to the settings $[-20, 30, -12, 20]$, Xscl = 5, Yscl = 2, (Xres = 1), is shown below.

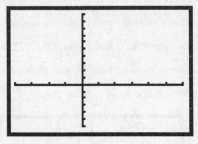

Press the WINDOW key on the top row of the keypad to display the current window settings on your grapher. The standard settings are shown below.

```
███████ FORMAT
 Xmin=-10
 Xmax=10
 Xscl=1
 Ymin=-10
 Ymax=10
 Yscl=1
```

To change a setting press ▽ to move the cursor to the setting you wish to change and enter the new value. For example, to change from the standard settings to $[-20, 30, -12, 20]$, Xscl = 5, Yscl = 2, on the TI-82 press ▽ (−) 2 0 ENTER 3 0 ENTER 5 ENTER (−) 1 2 ENTER 2 0 ENTER 2 ENTER. You must use the gray (−) key on the bottom row of the keypad rather than the dark blue − key in the right-hand column to enter a negative number. (−) represents "the opposite of" or "the additive inverse of" whereas − is the subtraction key. The ▽ key may be used instead of ENTER after typing each window setting. On the TI-83, the cursor appears at Xmin after WINDOW is pressed, so the ▽ preceding −20 above should be omitted.

To return quickly to the standard window setting $[-10, 10, -10, 10]$, Xscl = 1, Yscl = 1, press $\boxed{\text{ZOOM}}$ 6.

GRAPHING EQUATIONS

An equation must be solved for y before it can be graphed on the TI-82 and the TI-83.

Example 8 (a), page 8 (Page numbers refer to pages in the textbook.): To graph $2x + 3y = 18$, first solve for y, obtaining $y = \dfrac{18 - 2x}{3}$. Then press $\boxed{\text{Y} =}$, the key at the top left-hand corner of the keypad. If there is currently an expression displayed for Y_1, press $\boxed{\text{CLEAR}}$ to delete it. Do the same for expressions that appear on all other lines by using $\boxed{\nabla}$ to move to a line and then pressing $\boxed{\text{CLEAR}}$. Then use $\boxed{\triangle}$ to move the cursor to the top line beside "$Y_1 =$." Now press $\boxed{(}$ 18 $\boxed{-}$ 2 $\boxed{\text{X, T, }\Theta}$ $\boxed{)}$ $\boxed{\div}$ 3 to enter the right-hand side of the equation. (The key that produces the X on the TI-83 is marked $\boxed{\text{X, T, }\Theta\text{, }n}$.) Note that without the parentheses the expression $18 - \dfrac{2x}{3}$ would have been entered.

You can edit your entry if necessary. If, for instance, you pressed 5 instead of 8, use the $\boxed{\triangleleft}$ key to move the cursor to 5 and then press 8 to overwrite it. If you forgot to type the right parenthesis, move the cursor to the division symbol /; then press $\boxed{\text{2nd}}$ $\boxed{\text{INS}}$ $\boxed{)}$ to insert the parenthesis before the division symbol. ($\boxed{\text{INS}}$ is the second operation associated with the $\boxed{\text{DEL}}$ key.) You can continue to insert symbols immediately after the first insertion without pressing $\boxed{\text{2nd}}$ $\boxed{\text{INS}}$ again. If you typed 25 instead of 2, move the cursor to 5 and press $\boxed{\text{DEL}}$. This will delete the 5.

Once the equation is entered correctly, select a viewing window and then press $\boxed{\text{GRAPH}}$ to display the graph. You may change the viewing window as desired to reveal more or less of the graph. The standard window is shown here.

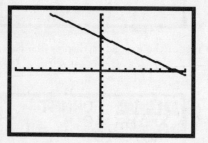

Example 8(c), page 8: To graph $x = y^2 + 1$, first solve the equation for y : $y = \pm\sqrt{x - 1}$. To obtain the entire graph of $x = y^2 + 1$, you must graph $y_1 = \sqrt{x - 1}$ and $y_2 = -\sqrt{x - 1}$ on the same screen. Press $\boxed{\text{Y} =}$ and clear any expressions that currently appear. With the cursor beside "$Y_1 =$" press $\boxed{\text{2nd}}$ $\boxed{\sqrt{}}$ $\boxed{(}$ $\boxed{\text{X, T, }\Theta}$ $\boxed{-}$ 1 $\boxed{)}$. ($\boxed{\sqrt{}}$ is the second operation associated with the $\boxed{x^2}$ key.) Note that if the parentheses had not been used, the equation entered would have been $y_1 = \sqrt{x} - 1$. On the TI-83, the left parenthesis appears along with the radical symbol, so a separate keystroke is not necessary to introduce it.

Now use $\boxed{\nabla}$ to move the cursor beside "$Y2 =$." There are two ways to enter $y_2 = -\sqrt{x - 1}$. One is to enter the expression $-\sqrt{x - 1}$ directly by pressing $\boxed{(-)}$ $\boxed{\text{2nd}}$ $\boxed{\sqrt{}}$ $\boxed{(}$ $\boxed{\text{X, T, }\Theta}$ $\boxed{-}$ 1 $\boxed{)}$.

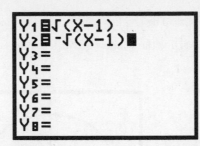

The other method of entering y_2 is based on the observation that $-\sqrt{x-1}$ is the opposite of the expression for y_1. That is, $y_2 = -y_1$. To enter this on the TI-82, place the cursor beside "Y2 =" and press $\boxed{(-)}$ $\boxed{\text{2nd}}$ $\boxed{\text{Y-VARS}}$ 1 1. (Y-VARS is the second operation associated with the $\boxed{\text{VARS}}$ key.) This enters the opposite of y_1 as the expression for y_2. On the TI-83, press $\boxed{(-)}$ $\boxed{\text{VARS}}$ $\boxed{\triangleright}$ to select Y-Vars. Then press 1 1 to select y_1.

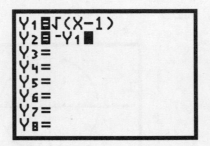

Select a viewing window and press $\boxed{\text{GRAPH}}$ to display the graph. The window shown here is $[-2, 5, -5, 5]$, Xscl $= 1$, Yscl $= 1$.

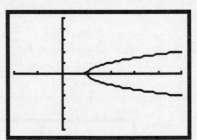

The top half is the graph of y_1, the bottom half is the graph of y_2, and together they yield the graph of $x = y^2 + 1$.

SQUARING THE VIEWING WINDOW

In the standard window, the distance between tick marks on the y-axis is about 2/3 the distance between tick marks on the x-axis. It is often desirable to choose window dimensions for which these distances are the same, creating a "square" window. Any window in which the ratio of the length of the y-axis to the length of the x-axis is 2/3 will produce this effect.

This can be accomplished by selecting dimensions for which $\text{Ymax} - \text{Ymin} = \dfrac{2}{3}(\text{Xmax} - \text{Xmin})$. For example, the windows $[-12, 12, -8, 8]$ and $[-6, 6, -4, 4]$ are square. To illustrate this, graph the circle $x^2 + y^2 = 49$ in the standard window by first entering $y_1 = \sqrt{49 - x^2}$ and $y_2 = -\sqrt{49 - x^2}$ or $y_2 = -y_1$. Note that x^2 can be entered either by pressing

X, T, Θ $\boxed{x^2}$ or by pressing $\boxed{X, T, \Theta}$ $\boxed{\wedge}$ 2. The $\boxed{\wedge}$ key can be used to enter any exponent, but for the exponent 2 the $\boxed{x^2}$ key is more efficient. Select $\boxed{\text{ZOOM}}$ 6 if the window settings are not already standard or press $\boxed{\text{GRAPH}}$ if the standard settings have previously been entered.

Note that the graph does not appear to be a circle.

Now change the window dimensions to $[-12, 12, -8, 8]$, Xscl $= 1$, Yscl $= 1$, and press $\boxed{\text{GRAPH}}$.

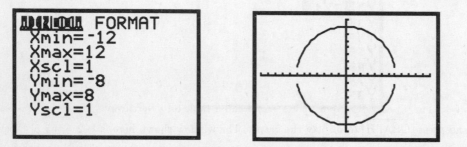

Observe that the distance between tick marks appears to be the same on both axes and that the graph appears to be a circle.

The window can also be squared using the grapher's ZSquare feature. Press $\boxed{\text{ZOOM}}$ 6 to return to the graph of $x^2 + y^2 = 49$ in the standard window. Now press $\boxed{\text{ZOOM}}$ 5 to select the ZSquare feature. The resulting window dimensions and graph are shown below. Note that the graph also appears to be a circle in this window.

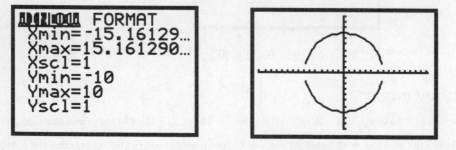

THE TABLE FEATURE

For an equation entered in the "Y =" screen, a table of x-and y-values can be displayed. For example, on the "Y =" screen enter $y_1 = 3x^3 - 5x^2 + 2x - 1$ by positioning the cursor beside "Y₁ =" and pressing 3 $\boxed{X, T, \Theta}$ $\boxed{\wedge}$ 3 $\boxed{-}$ 5 $\boxed{X, T, \Theta}$ $\boxed{x^2}$ $\boxed{+}$ 2 $\boxed{X, T, \Theta}$ $\boxed{-}$ 1. Then press $\boxed{\text{2nd}}$ $\boxed{\text{TblSet}}$ to display the table set-up screen. (TblSet is the second function associated with the $\boxed{\text{WINDOW}}$ key.) A minimum value of x can be chosen along with an increment for the x-values. Press $-5 \boxed{\triangledown} .1$ to select a minimum x-value of -5 and an increment of 0.1. The "Indpnt" and "Depend" settings should both be "Auto." If either is not, use the $\boxed{\triangledown}$ key to position the blinking cursor over "Auto" on that line and then press $\boxed{\text{ENTER}}$. To display the table press $\boxed{\text{2nd}}$ $\boxed{\text{TABLE}}$. (TABLE is the second function associated with the $\boxed{\text{GRAPH}}$ key.)

Use the $\boxed{\triangledown}$ and $\boxed{\triangle}$ keys to scroll through the table. For example, by using $\boxed{\triangledown}$ to scroll down we can see that $y_1 = -213$ when $x = -3.6$. Using $\boxed{\triangle}$ to scroll up, observe that $y_1 = -2530$ when $x = -8.9$.

THE SPLIT SCREEN

A horizontally split screen can be used on both the TI-82 and the TI-83 to display the graph of an equation along with its corresponding table of values. The TI-83 will also display a graph and a table on a vertically split screen. To produce a split screen, we first use the MODE menu. For instance, for the table settings and the equation $y = 3x^3 - 5x^2 + 2x - 1$ entered as above, select a viewing window. Then on the TI-82 press $\boxed{\text{MODE}}$ $\boxed{\triangledown}$ $\boxed{\triangledown}$ $\boxed{\triangledown}$ $\boxed{\triangledown}$ $\boxed{\triangledown}$ $\boxed{\triangledown}$ $\boxed{\triangleright}$ $\boxed{\text{ENTER}}$. This selects the split screen option.

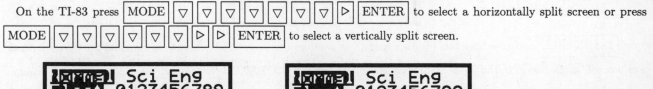

On the TI-83 press $\boxed{\text{MODE}}$ $\boxed{\triangledown}$ $\boxed{\triangledown}$ $\boxed{\triangledown}$ $\boxed{\triangledown}$ $\boxed{\triangledown}$ $\boxed{\triangledown}$ $\boxed{\triangledown}$ $\boxed{\triangleright}$ $\boxed{\text{ENTER}}$ to select a horizontally split screen or press $\boxed{\text{MODE}}$ $\boxed{\triangledown}$ $\boxed{\triangledown}$ $\boxed{\triangledown}$ $\boxed{\triangledown}$ $\boxed{\triangledown}$ $\boxed{\triangledown}$ $\boxed{\triangleright}$ $\boxed{\triangleright}$ $\boxed{\text{ENTER}}$ to select a vertically split screen.

Now press $\boxed{\text{2nd}}$ $\boxed{\text{TABLE}}$. In the horizontal mode the result is a split screen displaying the graph at the top with two rows of the table below it. In the vertical mode the graph is displayed on the left with seven rows of the table to its right. The $\boxed{\triangledown}$ and $\boxed{\triangle}$ keys can be used to scroll through the table as before.

Return the TI-82 to full screen mode by pressing $\boxed{\text{MODE}}$ $\boxed{\triangledown}$ $\boxed{\triangledown}$ $\boxed{\triangledown}$ $\boxed{\triangledown}$ $\boxed{\triangledown}$ $\boxed{\triangledown}$ $\boxed{\text{ENTER}}$. On the TI-83 press $\boxed{\text{MODE}}$ $\boxed{\triangledown}$ $\boxed{\triangledown}$ $\boxed{\triangledown}$ $\boxed{\triangledown}$ $\boxed{\triangledown}$ $\boxed{\triangledown}$ $\boxed{\triangledown}$ $\boxed{\text{ENTER}}$.

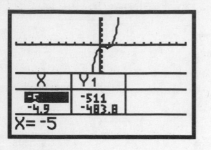

The TABLE feature can also be used to evaluate an expression. Enter $y_1 = 5x^4 - 6x^2 + 4$ in the "Y =" screen. Then press $\boxed{\text{2nd}}$ $\boxed{\text{TblSet}}$ $\boxed{\triangledown}$ $\boxed{\triangledown}$ $\boxed{\triangleright}$ $\boxed{\text{ENTER}}$ to set the table in ASK mode. In ASK mode the grapher disregards the values of TblMin and Δ Tbl.

```
TABLE SETUP
 TblMin=-5
 ∆Tbl=.1
Indpnt: Auto Ask
Depend: Auto Ask
```

Press $\boxed{\text{2nd}}$ $\boxed{\text{TABLE}}$ and an empty table is displayed. Now x-values can be entered in the X-column and the corresponding y-values will be displayed in the Y_1-column. For example, when $\boxed{(-)}$ 9 $\boxed{\text{ENTER}}$ is pressed, -9 appears in the X-column and the grapher computes and enters 32323 in the Y_1-column. This is the value of $5x^4 - 6x^2 + 4$ when $x = -9$, or $5(-9)^4 - 6(-9)^2 + 4$. Press 16 $\boxed{\text{ENTER}}$ and 326148 appears in the Y_1-column. This is the value of the expression when $x = 16$. You can continue to enter x-values as desired.

X	Y₁	
-9	32323	
16	326148	

X=

IDENTITIES

An equation that is true for every possible real-number substitution for the variable is an identity. The grapher can be used to provide a partial check whether an equation is an identity. Either a graph or a table can be used to do this.

Example 9 (a), page 11: Determine whether $(x^2)^3 = x^6$ appears to be an identity.

To determine whether this equation appears to be an identity, graph $y_1 = (x^2)^3$ and $y_2 = x^6$. Examine the graphs in several viewing windows. The graphs appear to coincide no matter what the window. Thus, although there is a possibility that the graphs fail to coincide outside the windows that were examined, the equation appears to be an identity.

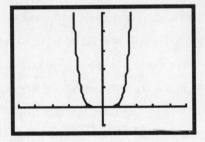

A table will also confirm this. Scroll through a table of values for y_1 and y_2 and observe that y_1 and y_2 appear to have the same value for a given value of x. Again, although the y-values could differ for an x-value that was not observed, the equation appears to be an identity.

X	Y₁	Y₂
-3	729	729
-2	64	64
	1	1
0	0	0
1	1	1
2	64	64
3	729	729

X = -1

Example 9 (b), page 11: Determine whether $\sqrt{x+4} = \sqrt{x} + 2$ appears to be an identity.

To determine whether this equation appears to be an identity, graph $y_1 = \sqrt{x+4}$ and $y_2 = \sqrt{x}+2$. Note that parentheses must be used on the TI-82 when entering $\sqrt{x+4}$: $\boxed{\text{2nd}}$ $\boxed{\sqrt{\ }}$ $\boxed{(}$ $\boxed{\text{X, T, }\Theta}$ $\boxed{+}$ $\boxed{4}$ $\boxed{)}$. Without parentheses the expression entered would be $\sqrt{x}+4$. (Although the right parenthesis is optional, we include it for completeness.) The TI-83 forces the use of parentheses by producing "$\sqrt{}($" when $\boxed{\text{2nd}}$ $\boxed{\sqrt{}}$ is pressed and assumes a right parenthesis at the end of the expression if none is entered earlier. Thus, although it is not necessary to type parentheses when entering $\sqrt{x+4}$ on the TI-83, it is necessary to enter a right parenthesis in $y_2 = \sqrt{x} + 2$. Press $\boxed{\text{2nd}}$ $\boxed{\sqrt{}}$ $\boxed{\text{X, T, }\Theta}$ $\boxed{)}$ $\boxed{+}$ 2. If the right parenthesis is omitted, the expression becomes $\sqrt{x+2}$ rather than $\sqrt{x} + 2$.

Any window that includes a portion of the first quadrant will show that the graphs differ. Thus, the equation is not an identity.

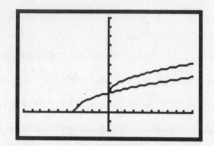

On the TI-83 different graph styles can be selected to allow us to differentiate visually between two or more graphs. Here, for example, we could have selected a solid line for y_1 and a dotted or thick line for y_2. Page 3-9 of the TI-83 Guidebook illustrates the available graph styles and their icons. The original settings of the TI-83 call for all equations to be graphed with a solid line. To change the style of a graph, begin by pressing $\boxed{\text{Y}=}$ to display the "Y =" screen. To graph $y_2 = \sqrt{x}+2$ using a thick line, for example, we would first press $\boxed{\text{Y}=}$. Then press $\boxed{\triangledown}$ to move the cursor to y_2. Now press $\boxed{\triangleleft}$ $\boxed{\triangleleft}$ to move the cursor to the graph style icon in the far left-hand column beside y_2. Press $\boxed{\text{ENTER}}$ repeatedly to rotate through the graph styles. These styles rotate in the same order in which they appear in the table on page 3-9 of the TI-83 Guidebook. When the thick line icon appears beside y_2, press $\boxed{\text{GRAPH}}$ to display the graphs of y_1 and y_2.

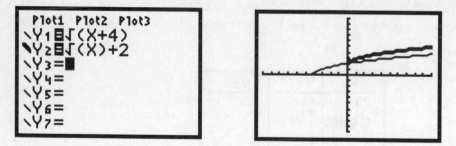

A table will also show that y_1 and y_2 do not always have the same value for a given x-value.

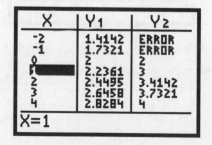

Note that y_1 and y_2 have the same value for $x = 0$ but not for the other possible substitutions shown. (The ERROR entries in the Y_2-column show that $x = -2$ and $x = -1$ cannot be substituted in $\sqrt{x} + 2$ to obtain a real number.)

Both the graph and the table demonstrate that the equation is not an identity.

SOLVING EQUATIONS USING TRACE AND ZOOM

There are several techniques that can be used to solve equations with a grapher. One uses the grapher's TRACE and ZOOM features.

Example 10, page 13: Solve $x^3 - 3x + 1 = 0$. Approximate the solutions to three decimal places.

The solutions of this equation are the first coordinates of the x-intercepts of the graph of $y = x^3 - 3x + 1$. To find these coordinates we first graph $y = x^3 - 3x + 1$ in a viewing window that shows all of the x-intercepts. Here we use the standard window, $[-10, 10, -10, 10]$.

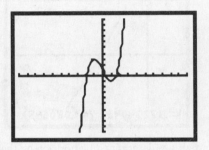

We see that x-intercepts occur near $x = -2$, $x = 0$, and $x = 2$. A portion of the viewing window can be enlarged near each of these values in order to find the desired three decimal place approximation. For example, let's examine the graph near $x = 0$.

Press ⎡TRACE⎤. The TRACE cursor appears on the graph at the middle x-value of the window, in this case at $x = 0$. On the TI-82 the number 1 appears in the upper right-hand corner of the screen indicating that the cursor is on the graph of equation y_1. The equation of the curve being traced appears at the top of the screen on the TI-83. The x-and y-values at the bottom of the screen indicate the coordinates of the point where the cursor is positioned, in this case at $x = 0$, $y = 1$.

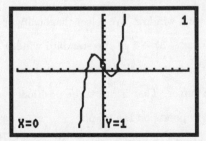
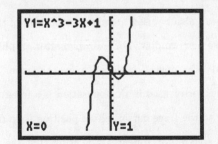

Pressing ◁ or ▷ moves the cursor to the left or right along the curve. Note that the TRACE cursor always remains on the curve.

In order to find the middle x-intercept, we enlarge the portion of the graph near $x = 0$ by first positioning the cursor as close to this intercept as possible. That is, near $x = 0$, position the cursor as close as possible to $y = 0$. Then press ZOOM 2 ENTER to zoom in on the graph near $x = 0$.

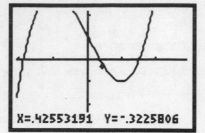

X=.42553191   Y=⁻.3225806

Press TRACE again and move the cursor as close as possible to $y = 0$ near $x = 0$. Now press ZOOM 2 ENTER again to enlarge this portion of the graph further.

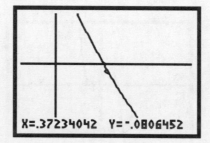

X=.37234042   Y=⁻.0806452

Continue tracing and zooming in until the x-values determined by positioning the cursor just to the left and just to the right of the x-intercept are the same when rounded to three decimal places. We find that $x \approx 0.347$ at the middle x-intercept. This is one solution of the equation $x^3 - 3x + 1 = 0$.

To find a second solution of the equation press ZOOM 6 to return to the standard window; then trace to a position on the curve near another x-intercept and zoom in as described above. Continue to trace and zoom in until the desired accuracy is obtained. Repeat this process to find the third solution. The other two solutions are about -1.879 and 1.532.

At any point in this process, we can zoom out to the previous window by pressing ZOOM 3 ENTER. This can be repeated as many times as desired.

The ZOOM BOX operation can also be used to enlarge a portion of the viewing window. We select diagonally opposed corners of a box that defines the new window. For example, after graphing $y = x^3 - 3x + 1$ in the standard window press ZOOM 1 to access the ZOOM BOX operation. Then move the cursor from the center of the screen to any corner of the box to be defined. Note that the cursor used in this operation is a free-moving cursor. That is, it can be positioned at any point on the screen as opposed to the trace cursor whose position is restricted to points on the graph.

Press ENTER and a small square dot appears, indicating that the first corner has been selected. Now use ◁, ▷, △, and/or ▽ to move the cursor to the corner of the box diagonally opposite this one. As you move the cursor away from the first corner the boundaries of the box appear on the screen and change as the position of the cursor changes.

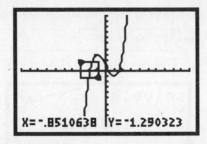

X=-.8510638   Y=-1.290323

When the box is defined as you want it, press ENTER to show only the portion of the graph in the box.

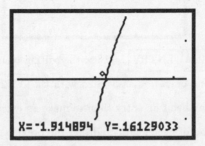

X=-1.914894   Y=.16129033

Now we can zoom in or use ZOOM BOX again to further enlarge a portion of the graph.

SOLVING EQUATIONS USING SOLVE OR SOLVER

The SOLVE operation on both the TI-82 and the TI-83 or the SOLVER operation on the TI-83 can also be used to solve equations. It is important to note that an equation must be written with 0 on one side of the equals sign when this operation is used.

Example 10, page 13: Solve $x^3 - 3x + 1 = 0$. Approximate the solutions to three decimal places.

Begin as in the procedure described above for using TRACE and ZOOM by graphing $y = x^3 - 3x + 1$ in a window that shows all of the x-intercepts. Note again that the x-intercepts occur near $x = -2$, $x = 0$, and $x = 2$. We will first find the solution near $x = -2$.

The TI-82's SOLVE operation is item 0 on the MATH menu. It follows item 9 and is not immediately visible when the MATH menu is selected. Access it by pressing MATH 0 or by pressing MATH, then using ▽ to scroll down and position the cursor over "0:" and finally pressing ENTER. The TI-83's SOLVE operation must be accessed through the CATALOG, an alphabetical list of all functions and instructions available on the TI-83. Select the CATALOG by pressing 2nd CATALOG. (CATALOG is the second operation associated with the 0 key.) Press ▽ to scroll down until the triangular selection cursor in the left-hand column is beside "solve(." Now press ENTER. To find SOLVE more quickly in the CATALOG, press S (by pressing the LN key) after 2nd CATALOG to skip to the first item beginning with the letter S. Then use ▽ to scroll down to "solve(."

On either grapher, the notation "solve(" appears on the screen with the blinking cursor positioned to the right of the parenthesis. We enter the left-hand side of the equation, the variable used in the equation, and a guess for the solution.

These entries must be separated by commas and a right parenthesis must follow the guess. Since we are seeking the solution near $x = -2$, we use this for the guess. Press $\boxed{\text{X, T, }\Theta}$ $\boxed{\wedge}$ 3 $\boxed{-}$ 3 $\boxed{\text{X, T, }\Theta}$ $\boxed{+}$ 1 $\boxed{,}$ $\boxed{\text{X, T, }\Theta}$ $\boxed{,}$ $\boxed{(-)}$ 2 $\boxed{)}$ $\boxed{\text{ENTER}}$. The grapher returns the value -1.879385242. Thus one solution is about -1.879.

```
solve(X^3-3X+1,X
,-2)
         -1.879385242
```

To find the solution near $x = 0$ press $\boxed{\text{2nd}}$ $\boxed{\text{ENTRY}}$ and use the editing techniques described on page 6 of this manual to change -2 to 0. (ENTRY is the second operation associated with the $\boxed{\text{ENTER}}$ key. It is used to recall the previous entry. Often it is more efficient to recall and edit an entry than to make an entirely new entry.) Then press $\boxed{\text{ENTER}}$ and the value $.3472963553$ is returned. Instead of recalling and editing the previous entry, we could have selected the SOLVE operation from the MATH menu again and reentered the left-hand side of the equation, the variable, and the new guess. To find the solution near $x = 2$, repeat the previous process, changing 0 to 2. Thus, as we saw before, the other two solutions are about 0.347 and 1.532.

```
solve(X^3-3X+1,X
,0)
          .3472963553
solve(X^3-3X+1,X
,2)
         1.532088886
```

Since $y_1 = x^3 - 3x + 1$ has been entered in the "Y =" screen, we can enter Y_1 instead of $x^3 - 3x + 1$ in the SOLVE operation. To do this on the TI-82 press $\boxed{\text{2nd}}$ $\boxed{\text{Y-VARS}}$ 1 1 instead of $\boxed{\text{X, T, }\Theta}$ $\boxed{\wedge}$ 3 $\boxed{-}$ 3 $\boxed{\text{X, T, }\Theta}$ $\boxed{+}$ 1. On the TI-83, press $\boxed{\text{VARS}}$ $\boxed{\triangleright}$ 1 1.

```
solve(Y₁,X, -2)
         -1.879385242
solve(Y₁,X,0)
          .3472963553
solve(Y₁,X,2)
         1.532088886
```

The TI-83's SOLVER operation is item 0 on the MATH menu. It follows item 9 and is not immediately visible when the MATH menu is selected. Access it by pressing $\boxed{\text{MATH}}$ 0 or by pressing $\boxed{\text{MATH}}$, then using $\boxed{\bigtriangledown}$ to scroll down and position the cursor over "0:" and finally pressing ENTER . When this is done the EQUATION SOLVER screen is displayed. If SOLVER has previously been used, it will be necessary to press △ after MATH 0 to display the EQUATION SOLVER screen. Then press CLEAR to delete the previously entered equation. The cursor appears beside "eqn: 0 =."

```
EQUATION SOLVER
eqn:0=■
```

We can type $x^3 - 3x + 1$ followed by ENTER or, since $y_1 = x^3 - 3x + 1$ has been entered in the "Y =" screen, we can enter Y_1 by pressing VARS ▷ 1 1 ENTER . Now the interactive solver editor is displayed. To find the solution of the equation near $x = -2$, type the initial guess (−) 2 beside "X =." It is not necessary to change the "bound =" setting, although since we know that all of the solutions of this equation are between -3 and 3 we could move the cursor to this line and edit the entry there to $\{-3, 3\}$. This is optional, but it could help find the solution more quickly. Move the cursor to the line on which the variable X appears and press ALPHA SOLVE . (SOLVE is the Alpha operation associated with the ENTER key.) The solution X = −1.879385241... is displayed, so $x \approx -1.879$.

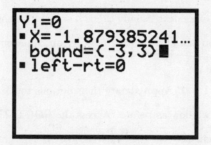

```
Y₁=0
■X=-1.879385241…
 bound=(-3,3)■
■left-rt=0
```

To find the solution near $x = 0$, simply edit X = −1.879385241... to X = 0 on the screen in which the first solution appeared, followed by ALPHA SOLVE . Find the solution near $x = 2$ similarly. We see that the other two solutions are about 0.347 and 1.532.

Example 12, page 15: Solve: $\frac{2}{3}x - 7 = 5$.

Since the SOLVE and SOLVER operations require an equation to be written with 0 on one side of the equals sign, we write this equation as $\frac{2}{3}x - 7 - 5 = 0$, or $\frac{2}{3}x - 12 = 0$. Then graph $y = \frac{2}{3}x - 12$ in a window that shows the x-intercept. Here we use $[-5, 35, -10, 10]$, Xscl = 5, Yscl = 2. Observe that the x-intercept is near $x = 20$. This is the value we will use as a guess for the solution.

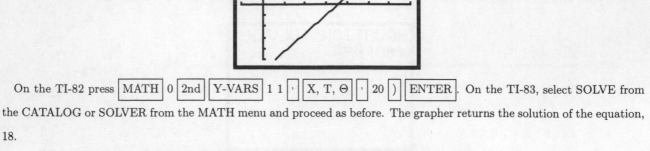

On the TI-82 press [MATH] 0 [2nd] [Y-VARS] 1 1 [,] [X, T, Θ] [,] 20 [)] [ENTER]. On the TI-83, select SOLVE from the CATALOG or SOLVER from the MATH menu and proceed as before. The grapher returns the solution of the equation, 18.

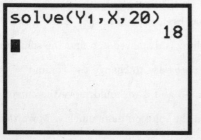

SOLVING EQUATIONS USING ROOT OR ZERO

A solution of an equation with zero on one side is usually called a zero, but is sometimes called a root. The TI-82's ROOT operation or the TI-83's ZERO operation can also be used to solve an equation. (These are actually the same operation but with different names.)

Example 10, page 13: Solve $x^3 - 3x + 1 = 0$. Approximate the solutions to three decimal places.

Graph $y = x^3 - 3x + 1$ in the standard window as before. Access the ROOT/ZERO operation by pressing [2nd] [CALC] 2. (CALC is the second operation associated with the [TRACE] key.) The grapher prompts us to select, in succession, lower and upper bounds as well as a guess for the zero. We will illustrate by using ROOT/ZERO to find the solution of $x^3 - 3x + 1 = 0$ near $x = 0$.

After [2nd] [CALC] 2 is pressed, the prompt "Lower Bound?" appears on the TI-82 screen below the graph. The TI-83 displays the prompt "Left Bound?" in the same location. Position the cursor just to the left of the x-intercept near 0 and press [ENTER]. The TI-82 prompt "Upper Bound?" or the TI-83 prompt "Right Bound?" then appears. Position the cursor just to the right of the intercept and press [ENTER] again. Now the prompt "Guess?" appears. Move the cursor as close to the x-intercept as possible and press [ENTER]. On the TI-83 we can also use the keypad to enter numbers for the left and right bounds and for the guess instead of using the cursor. Here we might enter 0, 1, and 0.5, respectively. The x-value that the grapher returns is the solution. We see again that the solution is about 0.347.

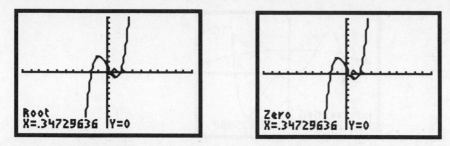

The other two solutions of the equation can be found by using the ROOT/ZERO operation two more times.

FINDING POINTS OF INTERSECTION

There are several ways in which the grapher can be used to determine the point(s) of intersection of two graphs.

Example 11, page 14: Find the point of intersection of the graphs of the equations $y_1 = 3x^5 - 20x^3$ and $y_2 = 34.7 - 1.28x^2$. Approximate the coordinates to three decimal places.

First graph the equations in a window that shows all of the points of intersection. We use $[-4, 4, -80, 80]$, Xscl = 1, Yscl = 20 here.

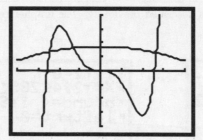

There are three points of intersection. One way to find their coordinates is to use TRACE and ZOOM. (See "Solving Equations Using Trace and Zoom" on page 13 of this manual.) Another method is to use the INTERSECT operation. We will illustrate its use by finding the point of intersection at the far left. After graphing y_1 and y_2 as above, access INTERSECT by pressing $\boxed{\text{2nd}}$ $\boxed{\text{CALC}}$ 5. The prompt "First curve?" appears on the screen below the graph. Move the cursor to the graph of y_1 and press $\boxed{\text{ENTER}}$. (If the cursor is positioned on the graph of y_1 when the prompt appears, simply press $\boxed{\text{ENTER}}$.) Now the prompt "Second curve?" appears. Position the cursor on the graph of y_2 and press $\boxed{\text{ENTER}}$. The prompt "Guess?" then appears. Move the cursor as close as possible to the point of intersection and press $\boxed{\text{ENTER}}$ again. On the TI-83 we can also use the keypad to enter a number for the guess, say -2.5. The grapher returns the coordinates of the point of intersection. We see that they are about $(-2.463, 26.936)$.

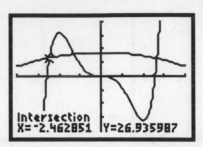

The coordinates of the other two points of intersection can be found by using the INTERSECT operation two more times.

The SOLVE or SOLVER operation can also be used to find the x-coordinates of the points of intersection by finding solutions of $y_1 = y_2$, or $y_1 - y_2 = 0$. Since the SOLVE and SOLVER operations require an equation to be written with 0 on one side of the equals sign, we must use the form $y_1 - y_2 = 0$.

Again it is necessary to graph y_1 and y_2 in order to find guesses for the solutions. To find the point of intersection on the far left, first note that its x-coordinate is about -2.5. This is the value we will use for the guess. On the TI-82 press $\boxed{\text{MATH}}$ 0 $\boxed{\text{2nd}}$ $\boxed{\text{Y-VARS}}$ 1 1 $\boxed{-}$ $\boxed{\text{2nd}}$ $\boxed{\text{Y-VARS}}$ 1 2 $\boxed{,}$ $\boxed{\text{X, T, }\Theta}$ $\boxed{,}$ $\boxed{(-)}$ 2 $\boxed{.}$ 5 $\boxed{)}$ $\boxed{\text{ENTER}}$. Either SOLVE or SOLVER could be used on the TI-83 as described previously. The grapher returns the value -2.462851032. This is the first coordinate of the point of intersection.

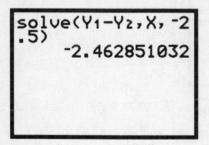

This value must be substituted into either y_1 or y_2 to find the second coordinate. To substitute in y_1 after using SOLVE press 3 $\boxed{\text{2nd}}$ $\boxed{\text{ANS}}$ $\boxed{\wedge}$ 5 $\boxed{-}$ 20 $\boxed{\text{2nd}}$ $\boxed{\text{ANS}}$ $\boxed{\wedge}$ 3 $\boxed{\text{ENTER}}$. (ANS is the second operation associated with the $\boxed{(-)}$ key. This operation recalls the answer to the previous computation, thus allowing it to be used in a new computation.) To substitute in y_1 after using SOLVER on the TI-83 first exit the SOLVER screen by pressing $\boxed{\text{2nd}}$ $\boxed{\text{QUIT}}$. Then press 3 $\boxed{\text{X, T, }\Theta, n}$ $\boxed{\wedge}$ 5 $\boxed{-}$ 2 0 $\boxed{\text{X, T, }\Theta, n}$ $\boxed{\wedge}$ 3 $\boxed{\text{ENTER}}$. The value 26.93598694 is returned.

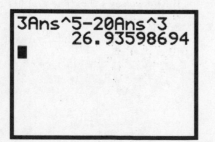

```
3X^5-20X^3
           26.93598694
```

Thus, we see that the coordinates of the point of intersection are about $(-2.463, 26.936)$. If we had used the rounded x-value of -2.463 in y_1 to compute the corresponding y-value, the result would have been 26.908. If we had used the rounded x-value in y_2, the resulting y-value would have been 26.935. To achieve the greatest accuracy, then, it is important to use the unrounded x-value in this computation.

A table set in ASK mode can be used to find the second coordinate more quickly. After performing the SOLVE operation, press 2nd TABLE 2nd ANS ENTER . After using SOLVER, simply press 2nd TABLE X, T, Θ, n ENTER . The value 26.936 appears in both Y-columns.

X	Y₁	Y₂
-2.463	26.936	26.936

X=

Note that, although the table shows the rounded x-value of -2.463, the unrounded x-value resulting from the SOLVE or SOLVER operation was actually used to compute the y-value. Confirm this by entering the rounded value -2.463 in the table. The table shows different values in the Y_1- and Y_2-columns, demonstrating that a less accurate result is produced with the rounded number and that the y-value computed depends on which equation is used.

X	Y₁	Y₂
-2.463	26.908	26.935

X=

SOLVING EQUATIONS USING INTERSECT

The INTERSECT operation can also be used to solve equations.

Example 12, page 15: Solve: $\frac{2}{3}x - 7 = 5$.

The solution of this equation is the first coordinate of the point of intersection of the graphs of $y_1 = \frac{2}{3}x - 7$ and $y_2 = 5$. Thus, we graph these equations in a window that shows the point of intersection and use INTERSECT as described in "Finding Points of Intersection," page 19 of this manual. The x-coordinate of the point of intersection is 18. This is the solution of the equation.

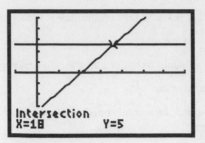

SELECTING DOT MODE

When graphing an equation in which a variable appears in a denominator, DOT mode should be used. To select DOT mode press $\boxed{\text{MODE}}$ and use $\boxed{\triangledown}$ and $\boxed{\triangleright}$ to position the blinking cursor over "Dot."" Then press $\boxed{\text{ENTER}}$.

See page 16 in the text for further explanation of why DOT mode is used in certain cases and for an illustration of an equation graphed in both CONNECTED and DOT modes.

Chapter R
Basic Concepts of Algebra

SCIENTIFIC NOTATION

To enter a number in scientific notation, first type the decimal portion of the number; then press 2nd EE (EE is the second operation associated with the · key.); finally type the exponent, which can be at most two digits. For example, to enter 1.789×10^{-11} in scientific notation, press 1 · 7 8 9 2nd EE (−) 1 1. To enter 6.084×10^{23} in scientific notation, press 6 · 0 8 4 2nd EE 2 3. The decimal portion of each number appears before a small E while the exponent follows the E.

To use the grapher to convert from decimal notation to scientific notation, first select Scientific mode by pressing MODE ▷ ENTER.

Example 3, page 28 (Page numbers refer to pages in the textbook.): Convert 38,500,000,000 to scientific notation.

With the grapher in Scientific mode, type 38500000000 followed by ENTER. The grapher returns 3.85E10, indicating that the scientific notation is 3.85×10^{10}.

Example 4, page 28: Convert 0.00000000000000000000000000167 to scientific notation.

With the grapher in Scientific mode, type .00000000000000000000000000167 ENTER. The grapher returns 1.67E−27, indicating that the scientific notation is 1.67×10^{-27}.

 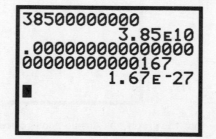

Even if Normal mode is selected for a computation, the TI-82 and TI-83 will display results less than 0.001 or greater than or equal to 9,999,999,999.5 in scientific notation. Thus, the only numbers that can be converted to decimal notation using the TI-82 and TI-83 are those within this range.

To use the grapher to convert from scientific notation to decimal notation, first set the grapher in Normal mode. Then type a number using scientific notation as described above, followed by ENTER .

Example 5 (a), page 28: Convert 7.632×10^{-4} to decimal notation.

Since $7.632 \times 10^{-4} < 0.001$, the grapher cannot be used for this conversion. To confirm this, with the grapher set in Normal mode, press 7.632 2nd EE (−) 4 ENTER . The grapher returns scientific notation rather than decimal notation.

Example 5 (b), page 28: Convert 9.4×10^5 to decimal notation.

Since $0.001 \leq 9.4 \times 10^5 \leq 9,999,999,999.5$, the grapher can be used to make this conversion. With the grapher set in Normal mode, press 9.4 2nd EE 5 ENTER . The grapher returns decimal notation, 940000.

To express the result of a computation in scientific notation, set the grapher in Scientific mode before performing the computation.

EXPRESSIONS WITH RATIONAL EXPONENTS

When using the TI-82 to find rational roots of the form $a^{m/n}$, where $a < 0$, m and n are natural numbers with no common factors other than 1, and $m > 1$, we must enter the expression as $((a)^m)^{1/n}$ or $((a)^{1/n})^m$. Similarly, to graph $y = x^{m/n}$, enter $y = ((x)^m)^{1/n}$ or $y = ((x)^{1/n})^m$. To illustrate this, first enter $(-8)^{4/3}$. The TI-82 returns the message ERR:DOMAIN. Now enter $((-8)^4)^{1/3}$ and $((-8)^{1/3})^4$. In each case the result is 16.

```
((-8)^4)^(1/3)
                16
((-8)^(1/3))^4
                16
```

Now graph $y_1 = x^{4/3}$. Notice that the graph contains no points corresponding to negative x-values.

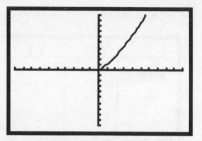

Then graph $y_1 = (x^4)^{1/3}$. This graph includes negative as well as nonnegative x-values. The same result is obtained for $y_1 = (x^{1/3})^4$.

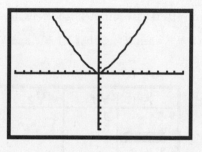

CHECKING SOLUTIONS USING A TABLE

The grapher's TABLE feature can be used to check solutions of equations. In this situation it is most efficient to select "Ask" for the Indpnt setting in the TABLE SETUP screen. To do this, press $\boxed{\text{2nd}}$ $\boxed{\text{TblSet}}$ $\boxed{\triangledown}$ $\boxed{\triangledown}$ $\boxed{\triangleright}$ $\boxed{\text{ENTER}}$. (The values of TblMin and ΔTbl are irrelevant in Ask mode.)

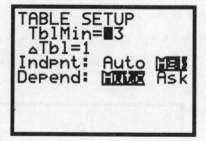

Now press $\boxed{\text{2nd}}$ $\boxed{\text{TABLE}}$. The grapher displays a table that allows us to enter values for the independent variable. We can then enter the left-hand side of an equation as y_1 and the right-hand side as y_2 in the "Y =" screen and use the TABLE feature to evaluate each side for any values that are possible solutions of the equation. For a given value of x, when $y_1 = y_2$ the equation is true and the given x-value is a solution . When $y_1 \neq y_2$ the equation is false and the given x-value is not a solution.

Example 1, page 59: The possible solution of $3(7 - 2x) = 14 - 8(x - 1)$ is 1/2. Use a table to check.

Enter $y_1 = 3(7 - 2x)$ and $y_2 = 14 - 8(x - 1)$ in the "Y =" screen. Now, with the table set in Ask mode, press $\boxed{\text{2nd}}$ $\boxed{\text{TABLE}}$ to display the empty table and then press 1 $\boxed{\div}$ 2 $\boxed{\text{ENTER}}$ or .5 $\boxed{\text{ENTER}}$. We see that Y1 = Y2 = 18, so the equation is true when X = 1/2 and thus the solution is 1/2.

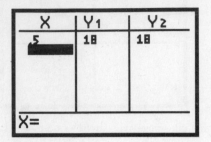

Example 4, page 62: The possible solutions of $5 + \sqrt{x+7} = x$ are 9 and 2. Use a table to check.

Enter $y_1 = 5 + \sqrt{x+7}$ and $y_2 = x$. With the table set in Ask mode, display the TABLE screen and press 9 $\boxed{\text{ENTER}}$ 2 $\boxed{\text{ENTER}}$ The table shows that Y1 = Y2 = 9 when X = 9, but Y1 = 8 and Y2 = 2 when X = 2. Thus, 9 is a solution of the equation, but 2 is not.

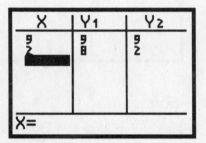

CHECKING SOLUTIONS OF INEQUALITIES

Solutions of inequalities can be checked graphically.

Example 1 (b), page 67: The possible solution set of $13 - 7y \geq 10y - 4$ is $\{y | y \leq 1\}$. Check with a grapher.

Replace y with x and graph $y_1 = 13 - 7x$ and $y_2 = 10x - 4$ in a window that shows the point of intersection of the graphs. The standard window is shown here.

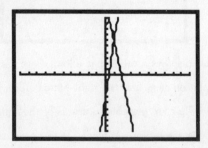

Now use INTERSECT or TRACE and ZOOM to find the first coordinate of the point of intersection, 1. Then observe that the graph of y_1 lies on or above the graph of y_2 at the point of intersection and to its left. That is, $y_1 \geq y_2$, or $13 - 7x \geq 10x - 4$, for $\{x | x \leq 1\}$. Thus, the solution set of the original inequality, $13 - 7y \geq 10y - 4$, is $\{y | y \leq 1\}$.

Example 4, page 70: The possible solution set of $2x - 5 \leq -7$ *or* $2x - 5 > 1$ is $(-\infty, -1] \cup (3, \infty)$. Check with a grapher.

Graph $y_1 = 2x - 5$, $y_2 = -7$, and $y_3 = 1$ in a window that shows the points of intersection of the graphs. The standard window is shown here.

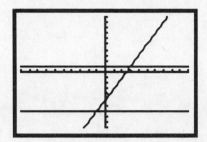

Now use INTERSECT or TRACE and ZOOM to find the first coordinates of the points of intersection. When $x = -1$, y_1 and y_2 intersect, and y_1 and y_3 intersect when $x = 3$. Now observe that the graph of y_1 lies on or below the graph of y_2 at their point of intersection and to its left. Thus, $y_1 \leq y_2$, or $2x - 5 \leq -7$, on $(-\infty, -1]$. Also observe that the graph of y_1 lies above the graph of y_3 to the right of their point of intersection. That is, $y_1 > y_3$, or $2x - 5 > 1$, on $(3, \infty)$. Then the solution set of the inequality is $(-\infty, -1] \cup (3, \infty)$.

Chapter 1
Graphs, Functions, and Models

FINDING FUNCTION VALUES

When a formula for a function is given, function values for real-numbered inputs can be found in several ways on a grapher.

Example 4 (a), (b), page 87 (Page numbers refer to pages in the text.): For $f(x) = 2x^2 - x + 3$, find $f(0)$ and $f(-7)$.

Method 1: Substitute the inputs directly in the formula. For example, to find $f(0)$ press 2 $\boxed{\times}$ 0 $\boxed{x^2}$ $\boxed{-}$ 0 $\boxed{+}$ 3 $\boxed{\text{ENTER}}$. To find $f(-7)$ press 2 $\boxed{(}$ $\boxed{(-)}$ 7 $\boxed{)}$ $\boxed{x^2}$ $\boxed{-}$ $\boxed{(}$ $\boxed{(-)}$ 7 $\boxed{)}$ $\boxed{+}$ 3 $\boxed{\text{ENTER}}$.

```
2*0²-0+3
                    3
2( -7)²-( -7)+3
                  108
```

Method 2: Enter $y_1 = 2x^2 - x + 3$ in the "Y =" screen. Then press $\boxed{\text{2nd}}$ $\boxed{\text{QUIT}}$ to go to the home screen. (QUIT is the second operation associated with the $\boxed{\text{MODE}}$ key.) Now to use the TI-82 to find $f(0)$, the value of y_1 when $x = 0$, press 0 $\boxed{\text{STO} \triangleright}$ $\boxed{\text{X, T, } \Theta}$ $\boxed{\text{2nd}}$ $\boxed{:}$ $\boxed{\text{2nd}}$ $\boxed{\text{Y-VARS}}$ 1 1 $\boxed{\text{ENTER}}$. (: is the second operation associated with the $\boxed{.}$ key.) This series of keystrokes stores 0 as the value of x and then substitutes it in the function y_1. To find the function value at $x = -7$ on the TI-82, repeat this process, using -7 in place of 0 or press $\boxed{\text{2nd}}$ $\boxed{\text{ENTRY}}$ to recall the previous entry, move the cursor to 0, and replace 0 with -7. Note that since two keystrokes are required to enter -7, it is necessary to use $\boxed{\text{2nd}}$ $\boxed{\text{INS}}$ to change 0 to -7. That is, with the cursor on 0 press $\boxed{(-)}$ $\boxed{\text{2nd}}$ $\boxed{\text{INS}}$ 7 $\boxed{\text{ENTER}}$ to make this change.

To use the TI-83 to find $f(0)$ using this method press 0 $\boxed{\text{STO} \triangleright}$ $\boxed{\text{X, T, } \Theta, n}$ $\boxed{\text{ALPHA}}$ $\boxed{:}$ $\boxed{\text{VARS}}$ $\boxed{\triangleright}$ 1 1 $\boxed{\text{ENTER}}$. (: is the ALPHA operation associated with the $\boxed{.}$ key.) To find $f(-7)$ either repeat this process using -7 in place of 0 or recall and edit the first entry as described above.

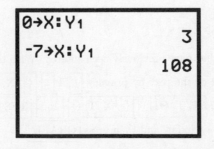

```
0→X:Y₁
                    3
-7→X:Y₁
                  108
```

Method 3: Enter $y_1 = 2x^2 - x + 3$ in the "Y =" screen and press $\boxed{\text{2nd}}$ $\boxed{\text{QUIT}}$ to go to the home screen. Then, to find $f(0)$ on the the TI-82 press $\boxed{\text{2nd}}$ $\boxed{\text{Y-VARS}}$ 1 1 $\boxed{(}$ $\boxed{0}$ $\boxed{)}$ $\boxed{\text{ENTER}}$. On the TI-83 press $\boxed{\text{VARS}}$ $\boxed{\triangleright}$ 1 1 $\boxed{(}$ $\boxed{0}$ $\boxed{)}$ $\boxed{\text{ENTER}}$. Note that these entries closely resemble function notation. To find $f(-7)$ either repeat this process entering -7 in place of 0 or recall the first entry and replace 0 with -7 as described in Method 2 above and then press $\boxed{\text{ENTER}}$.

```
Y₁(0)
                           3
Y₁( -7)
                         108
```

Method 4: The TABLE feature can also be used to find function values. With $y_1 = 2x^2 - x + 3$ entered in the "Y =" screen and the table set in Ask mode, press $\boxed{\text{2nd}}$ $\boxed{\text{TABLE}}$ to display the TABLE screen. Then press 0 $\boxed{\text{ENTER}}$ to find $f(0)$ and $\boxed{(-)}$ 7 $\boxed{\text{ENTER}}$ to find $f(-7)$.

```
 X       Y₁
 0       3
-7       108


X=
```

GRAPHING FUNCTIONS DEFINED PIECEWISE

Operations from the TEST menu are used to enter functions that are defined piecewise. (TEST is the second operation associated with the $\boxed{\text{MATH}}$ key.) Select DOT mode from the MODE menu when graphing such functions. On the TI-83, DOT mode can also be selected by choosing the DOT style on the "Y =" screen. (See page 12 of this manual.) Any style selected on the TI-83 "Y =" screen overrides a MODE selection.

Example 4, page 102: Graph

$$f(x) = \begin{cases} 4, & \text{for } x \le 0, \\ 4 - x^2, & \text{for } 0 < x \le 2, \\ 2x - 6, & \text{for } x > 2. \end{cases}$$

Press $\boxed{\text{Y} =}$ and clear any functions that have previously been entered. With the cursor beside "Y1 =" enter the function as described in the middle of page 102 of the text by pressing $\boxed{(}$ $\boxed{4}$ $\boxed{)}$ $\boxed{(}$ $\boxed{\text{X, T, }\Theta}$ $\boxed{\text{2nd}}$ $\boxed{\text{TEST}}$ 6 0 $\boxed{)}$ $\boxed{+}$ $\boxed{(}$ $\boxed{4}$ $\boxed{-}$ $\boxed{\text{X, T, }\Theta}$ $\boxed{x^2}$ $\boxed{)}$ $\boxed{(}$ $\boxed{0}$ $\boxed{\text{2nd}}$ $\boxed{\text{TEST}}$ 5 $\boxed{\text{X, T, }\Theta}$ $\boxed{)}$ $\boxed{(}$ $\boxed{\text{X, T, }\Theta}$ $\boxed{\text{2nd}}$ $\boxed{\text{TEST}}$ 6 2 $\boxed{)}$ $\boxed{+}$ $\boxed{(}$ $\boxed{2}$ $\boxed{\text{X, T, }\Theta}$ $\boxed{-}$ $\boxed{6}$ $\boxed{)}$ $\boxed{(}$ $\boxed{\text{X, T, }\Theta}$ $\boxed{\text{2nd}}$ $\boxed{\text{TEST}}$ 3 2 $\boxed{)}$. Select a window and then press $\boxed{\text{GRAPH}}$.

   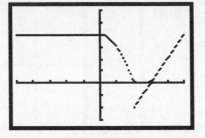

Example 6, page 103: Graph $f(x) = \text{INT}(x)$.

With the grapher set in DOT mode, press $\boxed{Y=}$ and clear any previously entered functions. Position the cursor beside "Y1 =" and select the greatest integer function from the MATH NUM menu as follows. On the TI-82 press $\boxed{\text{MATH}}$ $\boxed{\triangleright}$ 4 $\boxed{\text{X, T, }\Theta}$ and on the TI-83 press $\boxed{\text{MATH}}$ $\boxed{\triangleright}$ 5 $\boxed{\text{X, T, }\Theta,\ n}$ $\boxed{)}$. (The right parenthesis is optional.) Select a window and press $\boxed{\text{GRAPH}}$.

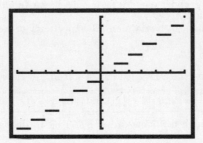

GRAPHING VERTICAL LINES

Although equations of vertical lines cannot be entered in the grapher in "Y =" form, vertical lines can be graphed using the DRAW feature. (DRAW is the second operation associated with the $\boxed{\text{PRGM}}$ key.)

Interactive Discovery, top of page 120: Graph $x = -5$ and $x = 2$.

To graph $x = -5$, first press $\boxed{Y=}$ and clear all previously entered equations. Then select a window. Now press $\boxed{\text{2nd}}$ $\boxed{\text{QUIT}}$ to go to the home screen. Press $\boxed{\text{2nd}}$ $\boxed{\text{DRAW}}$ 4 to select a vertical line. Then press $\boxed{(-)}$ 5 $\boxed{\text{ENTER}}$ to see the graph of $x = -5$. There are several ways to graph $x = -5$ and $x = 2$ on the same screen. For instance, after pressing $\boxed{\text{2nd}}$ $\boxed{\text{DRAW}}$ 4 $\boxed{(-)}$ 5 on the TI-82 press $\boxed{\text{2nd}}$ $\boxed{:}$ $\boxed{\text{2nd}}$ $\boxed{\text{DRAW}}$ 4 2 $\boxed{\text{ENTER}}$. On the TI-83 press $\boxed{\text{ALPHA}}$ $\boxed{:}$ rather than $\boxed{\text{2nd}}$ $\boxed{:}$. If you have pressed $\boxed{\text{2nd}}$ $\boxed{\text{DRAW}}$ 4 $\boxed{(-)}$ 5 followed by $\boxed{\text{ENTER}}$, press $\boxed{\text{2nd}}$ $\boxed{\text{QUIT}}$ to leave the graph screen and then press $\boxed{\text{2nd}}$ $\boxed{\text{DRAW}}$ 4 2 $\boxed{\text{ENTER}}$ to add the graph of $x = 2$.

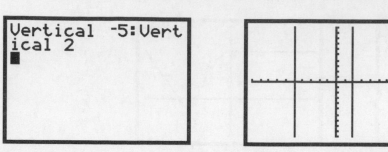

These drawings can be cleared from the graph screen by pressing $\boxed{\text{2nd}}$ $\boxed{\text{DRAW}}$ 1 to select the ClrDraw (clear drawing) operation. If ClrDraw was not accessed from the graph screen, it must be followed by $\boxed{\text{ENTER}}$. The drawings will also be cleared when another function is subsequently entered on the "Y =" screen and graphed.

LINEAR REGRESSION AND SCATTERPLOTS

The linear regression operation of the grapher enables us to fit a linear function to a set of data.

Example 1, page 129: Fit a regression line to the data on life expectancy of women on page 128 of the text. Then predict the life expectancy of women in 2000.

First we enter the data from the table on the STAT list editor screen. To clear any existing lists press $\boxed{\text{STAT}}$ 4 $\boxed{\text{2nd}}$ $\boxed{\text{L}_1}$ $\boxed{,}$ $\boxed{\text{2nd}}$ $\boxed{\text{L}_2}$ $\boxed{,}$ $\boxed{\text{2nd}}$ $\boxed{\text{L}_3}$ $\boxed{,}$ $\boxed{\text{2nd}}$ $\boxed{\text{L}_4}$ $\boxed{,}$ $\boxed{\text{2nd}}$ $\boxed{\text{L}_5}$ $\boxed{,}$ $\boxed{\text{2nd}}$ $\boxed{\text{L}_6}$ $\boxed{\text{ENTER}}$. (L_1 through L_6 are the second operations associated with the numeric keys 1 through 6.) Now press $\boxed{\text{STAT}}$ 1 to display the STAT list editor. We will enter the x-values in L_1 and the y-values in L_2. The cursor should be at the top of the L_1 column. To enter 0 press 0 $\boxed{\text{ENTER}}$. Continue typing the x-values 1 through 9, each followed by $\boxed{\text{ENTER}}$. Press $\boxed{\triangleright}$ to move to the top of the L_2 column. Type the y-values in succession, each followed by $\boxed{\text{ENTER}}$.

To see a scatterplot of the data first press $\boxed{\text{2nd}}$ $\boxed{\text{STAT PLOT}}$ 1. (STAT PLOT is the second operation associated with the $\boxed{\text{Y =}}$ key.) Position the cursor over On and press $\boxed{\text{ENTER}}$ to turn on the scatterplot of these data. The entries Type, Xlist, and Ylist should be as shown below on the left for the TI-82 and on the right for the TI-83. The last item, Mark, allows us to choose a box, a cross, or a dot for each point of the scatterplot. Here we have selected a box. All of these entries except for Xlist and Ylist on the TI-83 are chosen by positioning the cursor over each selection and pressing $\boxed{\text{ENTER}}$. Use the L_1 through L_6 keys to define Xlist and Ylist on the TI-83.

On the TI-83 the scatterplots can also be turned on from the "Y =" screen. In this case we would position the cursor over Plot 1 and press $\boxed{\text{ENTER}}$. Plot 1 will now be highlighted.

To see the scatterplot select a window and press $\boxed{\text{GRAPH}}$. Instead of entering the window dimensions directly, we can press $\boxed{\text{ZOOM}}$ 9. This activates the ZoomStat operation which automatically defines a viewing window that displays all the data points. The STAT lists and the scatterplot for these data are shown on page 129 of the text.

Press $\boxed{\text{STAT}}$ $\boxed{\triangleright}$ 5 $\boxed{\text{ENTER}}$ on the TI-82 or $\boxed{\text{STAT}}$ $\boxed{\triangleright}$ 4 $\boxed{\text{ENTER}}$ on the TI-83 to select LinReg(ax+b) from the STAT CALC menu and to display the coefficients a and b of the regression line $y = ax + b$ and the coefficient of linear correlation, r. Note that DiagnosticOn mode must have been selected from the CATALOG on the TI-83 in order for r to be displayed. In DiagnosticOn mode the TI-83 will, in fact, display both r^2 and r.

To select this mode, press $\boxed{\text{2nd}}$ $\boxed{\text{CATALOG}}$ and use $\boxed{\triangledown}$ to position the triangular selection cursor beside DiagnosticOn. To alleviate the tedium of scrolling through many items to reach DiagnosticOn, press $\boxed{\text{D}}$ after pressing $\boxed{\text{2nd}}$ $\boxed{\text{CATALOG}}$ to move quickly to the first catalog item that begins with the letter D. (D is the ALPHA operation associated with the $\boxed{x^{-1}}$ key.) Then use $\boxed{\triangledown}$ to scroll to DiagnosticOn. Note that it is not necessary to press $\boxed{\text{ALPHA}}$ before $\boxed{\text{D}}$ when the catalog is displayed. Press $\boxed{\text{ENTER}}$ to paste this instruction to the home screen and then press $\boxed{\text{ENTER}}$ a second time to set the mode.

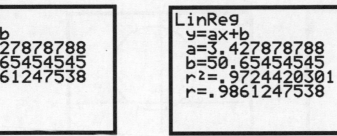

To enter the regression equation as y_1 in the "Y =" screen press $\boxed{\text{Y =}}$ and position the cursor beside "Y1 =". Then on the TI-82 press $\boxed{\text{VARS}}$ 5 $\boxed{\triangleright}$ $\boxed{\triangleright}$ 7 and on the TI-83 press $\boxed{\text{VARS}}$ 5 $\boxed{\triangleright}$ $\boxed{\triangleright}$ 1. The TI-83 also offers the option of specifying a y-variable to which the regression equation is stored before the equation is found. Store the equation as y_1, for example, by pressing $\boxed{\text{VARS}}$ $\boxed{\triangleright}$ 1 1 after $\boxed{\text{STAT}}$ $\boxed{\triangleright}$ 4 is pressed. The screen will display LinReg Y1. Then press $\boxed{\text{ENTER}}$ to see the regression equation and to store it as y_1.

To graph the regression line on the same screen as the scatterplot press $\boxed{\text{GRAPH}}$. (See page 129 of the text for this graph.) To turn off the scatterplot press $\boxed{\text{2nd}}$ $\boxed{\text{STAT PLOT}}$ 1, position the cursor over Off, and press $\boxed{\text{ENTER}}$. On the TI-83 we can also position the cursor over Plot 1 on the "Y =" screen and press $\boxed{\text{ENTER}}$. Now Plot 1 is no longer highlighted.

To predict the life expectancy of women in 2000 find the value of y_1 when $x = 10$ using one of the methods described in "Finding Function Values" on pages 29 and 30 of this manual.

GRAPHING CIRCLES

Although the standard form of the equation of a circle cannot be entered in the "Y =" screen of the TI-82 or the TI-83, circles can be graphed on these graphers. A square viewing window is required to give an accurate graph using either of the methods discussed below.

Method 1: We begin by solving the equation for y.

Example 5, page 138: Graph $x^2 + y^2 = 16$.

Solve the equation for y as shown on page 138 of the text, enter $y_1 = \sqrt{16 - x^2}$ and $y_2 = -\sqrt{16 - x^2}$, select a square window, and press $\boxed{\text{GRAPH}}$. Note that we can enter $y_2 = -y_1$ instead of $y_2 = -\sqrt{16 - x^2}$. The graph is shown on page 138 of the text.

Method 2: If the center and radius of a circle are known, the circle can be graphed using the DRAW feature.

Exercise 37, page 139: Graph $(x - 1)^2 + (y - 5)^2 = 36$.

The center of this circle is (1,5) and its radius is 6. To graph it using the DRAW feature first press $\boxed{\text{Y} =}$ and clear all previously entered equations. Then select a square window. We will use $[-12, 12, -4, 12]$, Xscl = 2, Yscl = 2. Press $\boxed{\text{2nd}}$ $\boxed{\text{QUIT}}$ to go to the home screen. Then press $\boxed{\text{2nd}}$ $\boxed{\text{DRAW}}$ 9 to display "Circle(." Enter the coordinates of the center and the radius, separating the entries by commas, and close the parentheses: 1 $\boxed{,}$ 5 $\boxed{,}$ 6 $\boxed{)}$ $\boxed{\text{ENTER}}$.

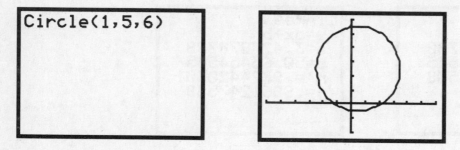

Note that the equation of a circle that is not centered at the origin, like the one in this example, is generally not easily solved for y, making Method 2 preferable for such equations. In fact, since there is no need to solve for y using this method, it provides a quick procedure for graphing the equation of any circle in standard form. This drawing can be cleared as described on page 32 of this manual.

THE ALGEBRA OF FUNCTIONS

The grapher can be used to evaluate and graph combinations of functions.

Example 1 (b), page 159: Given that $f(x) = x + 1$ and $g(x) = \sqrt{x + 3}$, find $(f + g)(6)$.

Press $\boxed{\text{Y} =}$ and enter $y_1 = x + 1$, $y_2 = \sqrt{x + 3}$, and $y_3 = y_1 + y_2$. To enter $y_3 = y_1 + y_2$ on the TI-82 press $\boxed{\text{2nd}}$ $\boxed{\text{Y-VARS}}$ 1 1 $\boxed{+}$ $\boxed{\text{2nd}}$ $\boxed{\text{Y-VARS}}$ 1 2. On the TI-83 press $\boxed{\text{VARS}}$ $\boxed{\triangleright}$ 1 1 $\boxed{+}$ $\boxed{\text{VARS}}$ $\boxed{\triangleright}$ 1 2. Note that $y_3 = f(x) + g(x)$, or $(f + g)(x)$. Use y_3 to find $(f + g)(6)$ employing one of the methods for finding function values described on pages 29 and 30 of this manual. We find that $(f + g)(6) = 10$.

To view the graphs of $f(x)$, $g(x)$, and $(f + g)(x)$ enter y_1, y_2, and y_3 as above, select a window, and press $\boxed{\text{GRAPH}}$. These graphs appear on page 159 of the text. It is possible to deselect one or two of these functions and display the graph(s) of the remaining function(s). For example, to display only the graph of y_3 without deleting the equations of y_1 and y_2, press $\boxed{Y=}$. Then move the cursor to y_1, position it over the equals sign, and press $\boxed{\text{ENTER}}$. This deselects or turns off y_1. Do the same for y_2. Now press $\boxed{\text{GRAPH}}$ and see only the graph of y_3.

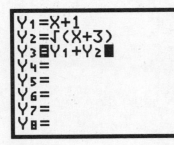

To select or turn on a function again, repeat this process. Note that the equals sign on a selected function is highlighted.

Example 3 (a), page 162: Given that $f(x) = 2x - 5$ and $g(x) = x^2 - 3x + 8$, find $(f \circ g)(7)$ and $(g \circ f)(7)$.

Press $\boxed{Y=}$ and enter $y_1 = 2x - 5$, $y_2 = x^2 - 3x + 8$, $y_3 = 2y_2 - 5$, and $y_4 = y_1^2 - 3y_1 + 8$. Use the $\boxed{\text{Y-VARS}}$ feature on a TI-82 or the $\boxed{\text{VARS}}$ feature on a TI-83 as described above to enter y_3 and y_4. Note that $y_3 = (f \circ g)(x)$ and $y_4 = (g \circ f)(x)$. Use y_3 and y_4 to find $(f \circ g)(7)$ and $(g \circ f)(7)$, respectively, employing one of the methods for finding function values described on pages 29 and 30 of this manual.

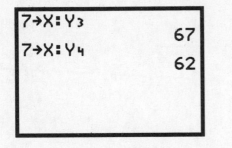

Chapter 2
Polynomial and Rational Functions

OPERATIONS WITH COMPLEX NUMBERS

Operations with complex numbers can be performed on the TI-83. First set the grapher in the complex $a + bi$ mode by pressing $\boxed{\text{MODE}}$, positioning the cursor over $a + bi$, and pressing $\boxed{\text{ENTER}}$.

Example 4, page 176:

(a) Add: $(8 + 6i) + (3 + 2i)$.

To find this sum press $8 \boxed{+} 6 \boxed{\text{2nd}} \boxed{i} \boxed{+} 3 \boxed{+} 2 \boxed{\text{2nd}} \boxed{i} \boxed{\text{ENTER}}$. (The number i is the second operation associated with the $\boxed{\cdot}$ key.) Note that it is not necessary to include parentheses when we are adding.

(b) Subtract: $(4 + 5i) - (6 - 3i)$.

Press $4 \boxed{+} 5 \boxed{\text{2nd}} \boxed{i} \boxed{-} \boxed{(} 6 \boxed{-} 3 \boxed{\text{2nd}} \boxed{i} \boxed{)} \boxed{\text{ENTER}}$. Note that, although the first set of parentheses is optional, the second set must be included so that the entire number $6 - 3i$ is subtracted.

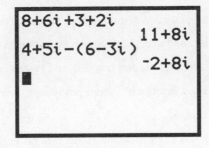

Example 5 (a), (b), (d), (e), page 177:

(a) Multiply: $\sqrt{-16} \cdot \sqrt{-25}$.

Press $\boxed{\text{2nd}} \boxed{\sqrt{}} \boxed{(-)} 1\,6 \boxed{)} \boxed{\text{2nd}} \boxed{\sqrt{}} \boxed{(-)} 2\,5 \boxed{)} \boxed{\text{ENTER}}$.

(b) Multiply: $\sqrt{-5} \cdot \sqrt{-7}$.

Press $\boxed{\text{2nd}} \boxed{\sqrt{}} \boxed{(-)} 5 \boxed{)} \boxed{\text{2nd}} \boxed{\sqrt{}} \boxed{(-)} 7 \boxed{)} \boxed{\text{ENTER}}$. Note that this operation produces a decimal approximation of the product. That is, $\sqrt{-5} \cdot \sqrt{-7} \approx -5.916079783$. The exact value of the product is $-\sqrt{35}$.

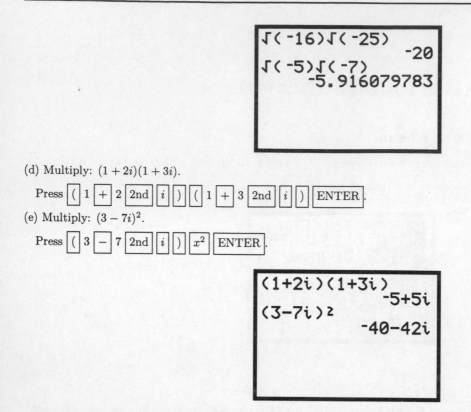

(d) Multiply: $(1 + 2i)(1 + 3i)$.

Press $\boxed{(}$ 1 $\boxed{+}$ 2 $\boxed{\text{2nd}}$ $\boxed{i}$ $\boxed{)}$ $\boxed{(}$ 1 $\boxed{+}$ 3 $\boxed{\text{2nd}}$ $\boxed{i}$ $\boxed{)}$ $\boxed{\text{ENTER}}$.

(e) Multiply: $(3 - 7i)^2$.

Press $\boxed{(}$ 3 $\boxed{-}$ 7 $\boxed{\text{2nd}}$ $\boxed{i}$ $\boxed{)}$ $\boxed{x^2}$ $\boxed{\text{ENTER}}$.

Complex numbers can also be divided in $a + bi$ mode. The real and imaginary parts of the quotient will be expressed in decimal form. For example, the quotient $(2 - 5i)/(1 - 6i)$ in Example 9, page 179 would be expressed as $.8648648649 + .1891891892i$.

QUADRATIC, CUBIC, AND QUARTIC REGRESSION

In addition to the linear regression discussed earlier, second degree, third degree, and fourth degree polynomial functions can be fit to data using the quadratic, cubic, and quartic regression operations, respectively, on the TI-82 and the TI-83.

The operations of entering data, making scatterplots, and graphing and evaluating quadratic, cubic, and quartic regression functions are the same as for linear regression functions. Before proceeding, reread the section on Linear Regression and Scatterplots beginning on page 32 of this manual.

Example 5, page 201: For the data on hours of sleep versus death rate on page 202 of the text, make a scatterplot for the data and determine which, if any, of the functions above fits the data. Then find the regression equation, graph the equation, and use it to make predictions.

Enter the data in L_1 and L_2 and make a scatterplot as described on page 32 of this manual. The scatterplot is shown in the text. It appears that a quadratic function fits the data. To find it press $\boxed{\text{STAT}}$ $\boxed{\triangleright}$ to view the STAT CALC menu. Then select QuadReg by pressing 6 on the TI-82 or 5 on the TI-83 followed by $\boxed{\text{ENTER}}$. The coefficients of the quadratic equation $y = ax^2 + bx + c$ are displayed. Note that at least three data points are required for quadratic regression.

The regression equation can be copied to the "Y =" screen using the $\boxed{\text{VARS}}$ operation as described on page 33 of this manual. The TI-83 also offers the usual option of selecting a y-variable name before the regression equation is found. Once the regression equation is entered in the "Y =" screen, it can be graphed and used to make predictions using one of the methods for finding function values described on pages 29 and 30 of this manual.

To fit a cubic or quartic function to a set of data, enter the data in L_1 and L_2 as described earlier. Then use $\boxed{\text{STAT}}$ $\boxed{\triangleright}$ to go to the STAT CALC menu. On the TI-82 we select cubic regression by pressing 7 and quartic regression by pressing 8. Press 6 for cubic regression on the TI-83 and 7 for quartic regression. At least four data points are required for cubic regression and at least five are required for quartic regression.

Chapter 3
Exponential and Logarithmic Functions

GRAPHING AN INVERSE FUNCTION

The DrawInv operation on the TI-82 and the TI-83 can be used to graph a function and its inverse on the same screen. A formula for the inverse function need not be found in order to do this. The grapher must be set in Func mode when this operation is used.

Example 7, page 255: Graph $f(x) = 2x - 3$ and $f^{-1}(x)$ using the same set of axes.

Enter $y_1 = 2x - 3$ and either clear or deselect all other functions on the "Y =" screen. Then press $\boxed{\text{2nd}}$ $\boxed{\text{DRAW}}$ 8 to select the DrawInv operation. (DRAW is the second operation associated with the $\boxed{\text{PRGM}}$ key.) On the TI-82 follow these keystrokes with $\boxed{\text{2nd}}$ $\boxed{\text{Y-VARS}}$ 1 1 to select function y_1. On the TI-83 y_1 is selected by pressing $\boxed{\text{VARS}}$ $\boxed{\triangleright}$ 1 1. Press $\boxed{\text{ENTER}}$ to see the graph of the function and its inverse.

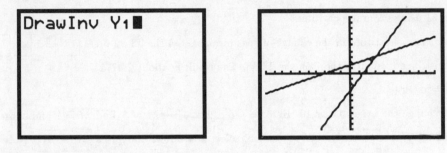

EVALUATING e^x, **Log** x, **and Ln** x

Use the grapher's scientific keys to evaluate e^x, $\log x$, and $\ln x$ for specific values of x.

Example 6 (a), (b), page 270: Find the value of e^3 and $e^{-0.23}$. Round to four decimal places.

To find e^3 press $\boxed{\text{2nd}}$ $\boxed{e^x}$ 3 $\boxed{\text{ENTER}}$. (e^x is the second operation associated with the $\boxed{\text{LN}}$ key.) The grapher returns 20.08553692. Thus, $e^3 \approx 20.0855$. To find $e^{-0.23}$ press $\boxed{\text{2nd}}$ $\boxed{e^x}$ $\boxed{(-)}$ $\boxed{\cdot}$ 2 3 $\boxed{\text{ENTER}}$. The grapher returns .7945336025, so $e^{-0.23} \approx 0.7945$.

Example 4 (a), (b), (c), page 279: Find the values of log 645,778, log 0.0000239, and log (−3). Round to four decimal places.

To find log 645,778 press $\boxed{\text{LOG}}$ 6 4 5 7 7 8 $\boxed{\text{ENTER}}$ and read 5.810083246. Thus, log 645,778 ≈ 5.8101. To find log 0.0000239 press $\boxed{\text{LOG}}$ $\boxed{\cdot}$ 0 0 0 0 2 3 9 $\boxed{\text{ENTER}}$. The grapher returns −4.621602099, so log 0.0000239 ≈ −4.6216. When we press $\boxed{\text{LOG}}$ $\boxed{(-)}$ 3 $\boxed{\text{ENTER}}$ on the TI-82 the message ERR: DOMAIN is returned. This indicates that −3 is not in the domain of the function log x. When the TI-83 is set in Real mode the keystrokes $\boxed{\text{LOG}}$ $\boxed{(-)}$ 3 $\boxed{\text{ENTER}}$ produce the message ERR: NONREAL ANS indicating that the result of this calculation is not a real number.

Example 5 (a), (b), (c), page 279: Find the values of ln 645,778, ln 0.0000239, and ln (−5). Round to four decimal places.

To find ln 645,778 and ln 0.0000239 repeat the keystrokes used above to find log 645,778 and log 0.0000239 but press $\boxed{\text{LN}}$ rather than $\boxed{\text{LOG}}$. We find that ln 645,778 ≈ 13.3782 and ln 0.0000239 ≈ −10.6416. When we press $\boxed{\text{LN}}$ $\boxed{(-)}$ 5 $\boxed{\text{ENTER}}$ on the TI-82 the message ERR: DOMAIN is returned indicating that −5 is not in the domain of the function ln x. When the TI-83 is set in Real mode these keystrokes produce the message ERR: NONREAL ANS indicating that the result of this calculation is not a real number.

USING THE CHANGE OF BASE FORMULA

To find a logarithm with a base other than 10 or e we use the change-of-base formula, $\log_b M = \dfrac{\log_a M}{\log_a b}$, where a and b are any logarithmic bases and M is any positive number.

Example 6, page 280: Find $\log_5 8$ using common logarithms.

We let a = 10, b = 5, and M = 8 and substitute in the change-of-base formula. Press $\boxed{\text{LOG}}$ 8 $\boxed{\div}$ $\boxed{\text{LOG}}$ 5 $\boxed{\text{ENTER}}$. On the TI-83 it is necessary to close the parentheses in the numerator to enter the expression correctly. Press $\boxed{\text{LOG}}$ 8 $\boxed{)}$ $\boxed{\div}$ $\boxed{\text{LOG}}$ 5 $\boxed{\text{ENTER}}$. In either case the result is about 1.2920.

Example 7, page 280: Find $\log_4 31$ using natural logarithms.

We let a = e, b = 4, and M = 31 and substitute in the change-of-base formula. On the TI-82 press $\boxed{\text{LN}}$ 3 1 $\boxed{\div}$ $\boxed{\text{LN}}$ 4 $\boxed{\text{ENTER}}$. A right parenthesis must be added after the 1 on the TI-83. The result is about 2.4771.

Example 9, page 281: Graph $y = \log_5 x$.

To use a grapher we must first change the base to e or 10. Here we use e. Let a = e, b = 5, and M = x and substitute in the change-of-base formula. Enter $y_1 = \dfrac{\ln x}{\ln 5}$ on the "Y =" screen, select a window, and press $\boxed{\text{GRAPH}}$. Note that since the TI-83 forces the use of parentheses with the ln function, the parentheses in the numerator must be closed on this grapher: $\ln(x)/\ln(5)$. The right parenthesis following the 5 is optional.

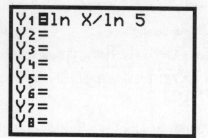
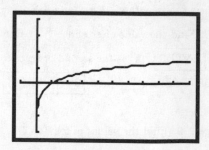

EXPONENTIAL, LOGARITHMIC, AND POWER REGRESSION

In addition to the types of polynomial regression discussed earlier, exponential, logarithmic, and power functions can be fit to data. The operations of entering data, making scatterplots, and graphing and evaluating these functions are the same as for linear regression functions. So are the procedures for copying a regression equation to the "Y =" screen, graphing it, and using it to find function values. Note that the coefficient of correlation, r, will be displayed on the TI-83 only if DiagnosticOn has been selected from the CATALOG. Before proceeding, reread the section on Linear Regression and Scatterplots beginning on page 32 of this manual.

Example 6 (a), page 310: Fit an exponential equation to the given data on cellular phones.

Enter the data in L_1 and L_2 as described on page 32 of this manual. Then press $\boxed{\text{STAT}}$ $\boxed{\triangleright}$ to view the STAT CALC menu. Select ExpReg by pressing $\boxed{\text{ALPHA}}$ A on the TI-82 or 0 on the TI-83 followed by $\boxed{\text{ENTER}}$. The values of a and b for the exponential function $y = ab^x$ are displayed along with the coefficient of correlation r. The TI-83 also displays r^2.

Exercise 26 (a), page 316: Fit a logarithmic function to the given data on forgetting.

After entering the data in L_1 and L_2 as described on page 32 of this manual, press $\boxed{\text{STAT}}$ $\boxed{\triangleright}$ to view the STAT CALC menu. Select LnReg by pressing 0 on the TI-82 or 9 on the TI-83 followed by $\boxed{\text{ENTER}}$. The values of a and b for the logarithmic function $y = a + b \ln x$ are displayed along with the coefficient of correlation r. The TI-83 also displays r^2.

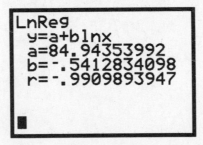

Example 7 (a), page 312: Fit a power function to the given data on cholesterol level and risk of heart attack.

Enter the data in L_1 and L_2 as described on page 32 of this manual. Then press $\boxed{\text{STAT}}$ $\boxed{\triangleright}$ to view the STAT CALC menu. Select PwrReg by pressing $\boxed{\text{ALPHA}}$ B on the TI-82 or $\boxed{\text{ALPHA}}$ A on the TI-83 followed by $\boxed{\text{ENTER}}$. The values of a and b for the power function $y = ax^b$ are displayed along with the coefficient of correlation r. The TI-83 also displays r^2.

LOGISTIC REGRESSION

A logistic function can be fit to data using the TI-83.

Exercise 28 (a), page 316: Fit a logistic function to the given data on the effect of advertising.

After entering the data in L_1 and L_2 as described on page 32 of this manual, press $\boxed{\text{STAT}}$ $\boxed{\triangleright}$ to view the STAT CALC menu. Select Logistic by pressing $\boxed{\text{ALPHA}}$ B $\boxed{\text{ENTER}}$. The values of a, b, and c for the logistic function $y = \dfrac{c}{1 + ae^{-bx}}$ are displayed.

```
Logistic
 y=c/(1+ae^( -bx))
 a=489.2438401
 b=.1299899024
 c=99.98884912
```

Chapter 4
The Trigonometric Functions

This chapter appears only in the text *ALGEBRA & TRIGONOMETRY: GRAPHS & MODELS* by Bittinger, Beecher, Ellenbogen, and Penna and should be disregarded by students using the text *COLLEGE ALGEBRA: GRAPHS & MODELS*.

CONVERTING BETWEEN D°M'S" AND DECIMAL DEGREE MEASURE

The ANGLE feature on the TI-82 and the TI-83 can be used to convert D°M'S" notation to decimal notation and vice versa.

Example 5, page 328: Convert 5°42'30" to decimal degree notation.

Enter 5°42'30" as 5'42'30' by pressing 5 | 2nd | | ANGLE | 2 4 2 | 2nd | | ANGLE | 2 3 0 | 2nd | | ANGLE | 2 | ENTER |. (ANGLE is the second operation associated with the | MATRIX | key.) On the TI-83 enter 5°42'30" by pressing 5 | 2nd | | ANGLE | 1 4 2 | 2nd | | ANGLE | 2 3 0 | ALPHA | | " | | ENTER |. (" is the ALPHA operation associated with the | + | key.) In either case the grapher returns 5.708333333, so 5°42'30" ≈ 5.71°.

Example 6, page 328: Convert 72.18° to D°M'S" notation.

Press 7 2 | · | 1 8 | 2nd | | ANGLE | 4 | ENTER |. The grapher returns 72°10'48".

The conversions in Examples 5 and 6 are shown for the TI-82 on the left below and for the TI-83 on the right.

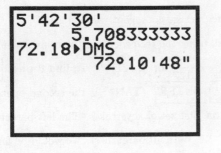

FINDING TRIGONOMETRIC FUNCTION VALUES

The grapher's SIN, COS, and TAN operations can be used to find the values of trigonometric functions. When angles are given in degree measure, the grapher must be set in Degree mode.

Example 7, page 328: Find the trigonometric function value, rounded to four decimal places, of each of the following.

a) tan 29.7°   b) sec 48°   c) sin 84°10'39"

a) Press | TAN | 2 9 | · | 7 | ENTER |. We find that tan 29.7° ≈ 0.5704.

b) The secant, cosecant, and cotangent functions can be found by taking the reciprocals of the cosine, sine, and tangent functions, respectively. This can be done either by entering the reciprocal or by using the | x^{-1} |. To find sec 48° we can enter the reciprocal of cos 48° by pressing 1 $\boxed{\div}$ $\boxed{\text{COS}}$ 4 8 $\boxed{\text{ENTER}}$. To find sec 48° using the $\boxed{x^{-1}}$ key on the TI-82 press $\boxed{(}$ $\boxed{\text{COS}}$ 4 8 $\boxed{)}$ $\boxed{x^{-1}}$ $\boxed{\text{ENTER}}$. On the TI-83 press $\boxed{\text{COS}}$ 4 8 $\boxed{)}$ $\boxed{x^{-1}}$ $\boxed{\text{ENTER}}$. The result is sec 48° ≈ 1.4945.

The output for the TI-82 is shown on the left below, and the TI-83 output is on the right.

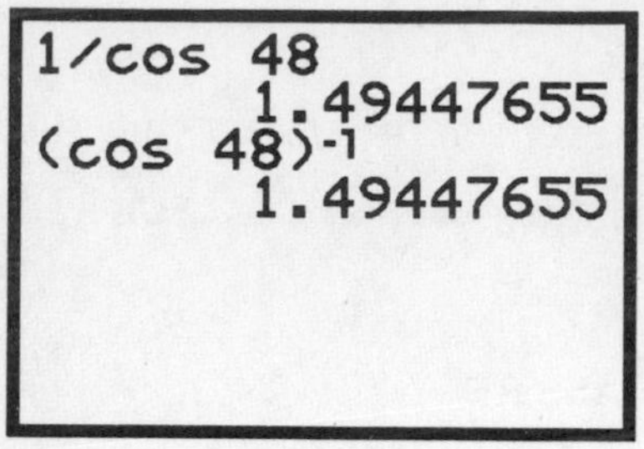

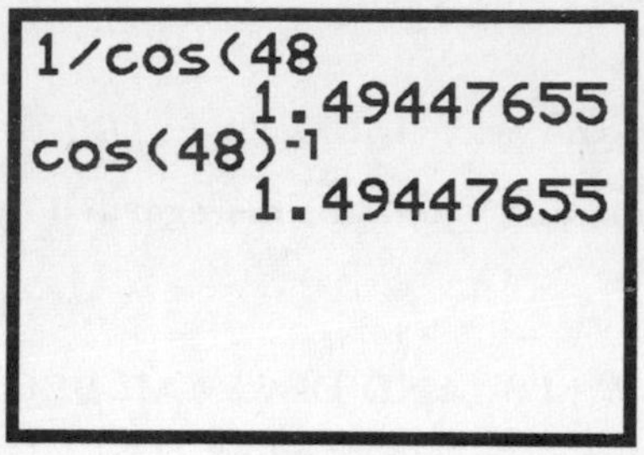

```
1/cos 48
         1.49447655
(cos 48)⁻¹
         1.49447655
```

```
1/cos(48
         1.49447655
cos(48)⁻¹
         1.49447655
```

c) Press $\boxed{\text{SIN}}$ followed by 84°10′39″ entered as described above in Converting Between D°M′S″ and Decimal Degree Measure for the grapher being used. Then press $\boxed{\text{ENTER}}$. We find that sin 84°10′39″ ≈ 0.9948.

FINDING ANGLES

The inverse trigonometric function keys provide a quick way to find an angle given a trigonometric function value for that angle.

Example 8, page 329: Find the acute angle, to the nearest tenth of a degree, whose sine value is approximately 0.20113.

Although the TABLE feature can be used to approximate this angle, it is faster to use the inverse sine key. With the grapher set in Degree mode press $\boxed{\text{2nd}}$ $\boxed{\text{SIN}^{-1}}$ $\boxed{\cdot}$ 2 0 1 1 3 $\boxed{\text{ENTER}}$. (SIN⁻¹ is the second operation associated with the $\boxed{\text{SIN}}$ key.) We find that the desired acute angle is approximately 11.6°.

Exercise 63, page 332: Find the acute angle, to the nearest tenth of a degree, whose cotangent value is 2.127.

Angles whose secant, cosecant, or cotangent values are known can be found using the reciprocals of the cosine, sine, and tangent functions, respectively. Since $\cot \theta = \dfrac{1}{\tan \theta} = 2.127$, we have $\tan \theta = \dfrac{1}{2.127}$, or $(2.127)^{-1}$. To find θ press $\boxed{\text{2nd}}$ $\boxed{\text{TAN}^{-1}}$ $\boxed{(}$ 1 $\boxed{\div}$ 2 $\boxed{\cdot}$ 1 2 7 $\boxed{)}$ $\boxed{\text{ENTER}}$ or $\boxed{\text{2nd}}$ $\boxed{\text{TAN}^{-1}}$ 2 $\boxed{\cdot}$ 1 2 7 $\boxed{x^{-1}}$ $\boxed{\text{ENTER}}$. (TAN⁻¹ is the second operation associated with the $\boxed{\text{TAN}}$ key.) Note that the parentheses are necessary in the first set of keystrokes. The left parenthesis must be keyed in on the TI-82 while it appears on the TI-83 along with "tan⁻¹." Without parentheses we would be finding the angle whose tangent is 1 and then dividing that angle by 2.127. We find that $\theta \approx 25.2°$.

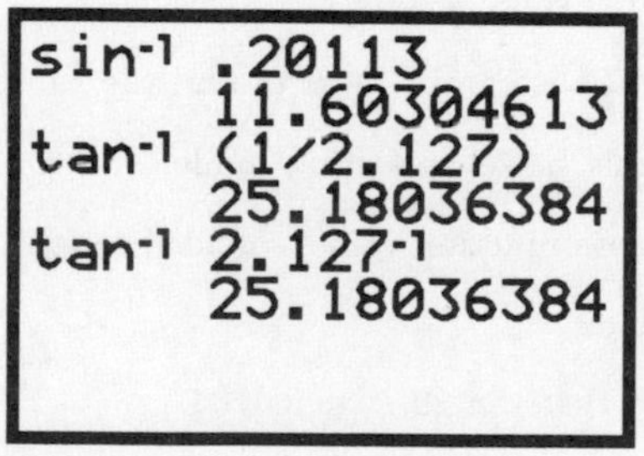

```
sin⁻¹ .20113
         11.60304613
tan⁻¹ (1/2.127)
         25.18036384
tan⁻¹ 2.127⁻¹
         25.18036384
```

CONVERTING BETWEEN DEGREE AND RADIAN MEASURE

We can use the grapher to convert from degree to radian measure and vice versa. The grapher should be set in Radian mode when converting from degree to radian measure and in Degree mode when converting from radian to degree measure.

Example 3, page 363: Convert each of the following to radians.

a) 120°   b) −297.25°

a) Set the grapher in Radian mode. Press 1 2 0 | 2nd | | ANGLE | 1 | ENTER | to enter 120°. The grapher returns a decimal approximation of the radian measure. We see that 120° ≈ 2.09 radians.

b) With the grapher set in Radian mode press | (−) | 2 9 7 | · | 2 5 | 2nd | | ANGLE | 1 | ENTER |. We see that −297.25° ≈ −5.19 radians.

Example 4, page 363: Convert each of the following to degrees.

a) $\frac{3\pi}{4}$ radians   b) 8.5 radians

a) Set the grapher in Degree mode. Then press | (| 3 | 2nd | | π | | ÷ | 4 |) | | 2nd | | ANGLE | 3 | ENTER | to enter $\frac{3\pi}{4}$ radians. (π is the second operation associated with the | ∧ | key). The grapher returns 135, so $3\pi/4$ radians = 135°. Note that the parentheses are necessary in order to enter the entire expression in radian measure. Without the parentheses, the grapher reads only the denominator, 4, in radian measure and an incorrect result occurs.

b) With the grapher set in Degree mode press 8 | · | 5 | 2nd | | ANGLE | 3 | ENTER |. The grapher returns 487.0141259, so 8.5 radians ≈ 487.01°.

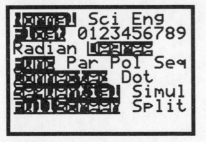

SINE REGRESSION

The SinReg operation on the TI-83 can be used to fit a sine curve $y = a\sin(bx + c) + d$ to a set of data. At least four data points are required and there must be at least two data points per period. The output of SinReg is always in radians, regardless of the Radian/Degree mode setting.

The operations of entering data, making scatterplots, and graphing and evaluating the regression function are the same as for linear regression functions. Reread the section on Linear Regression and Scatterplots beginning on page 32 of this manual to review these procedures.

Exercise 57 (a), page 402: Fit a sine function to the given data on ski sales.

Enter the data in L_1 and L_2 as described in Chapter 1 of this manual. Press $\boxed{\text{STAT}}$ $\boxed{\triangleright}$ to view the STAT CALC menu. Then select SinReg by pressing $\boxed{\text{ALPHA}}$ C. If the data is entered in a combination of lists other than L_1 and L_2 their names must be entered separated by a comma. Since we have used L_1 and L_2 this is not necessary in this case. We also have the usual TI-83 option of specifying a $y =$ variable to which the regression equation can be stored. To select y_1, for example, press $\boxed{\text{VARS}}$ $\boxed{\triangleright}$ 1 1. Now press $\boxed{\text{ENTER}}$ to see the coefficients a, b, c, and d of the sine regression function $y = a \sin(bx + c) + d$

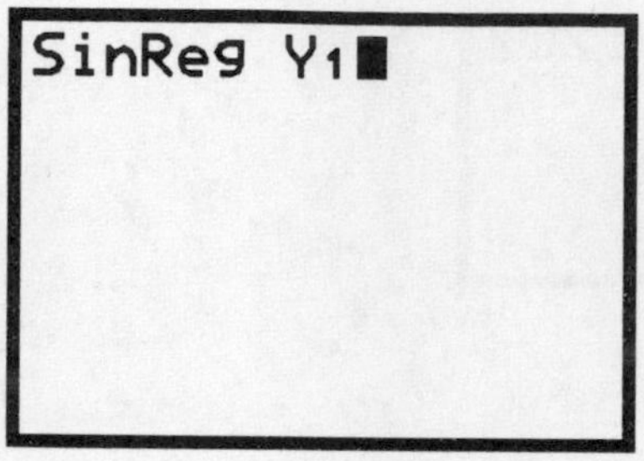

```
SinReg Y1■
```

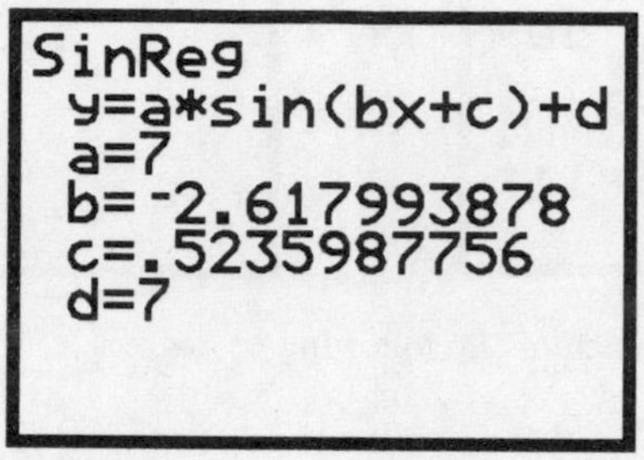

```
SinReg
y=a*sin(bx+c)+d
a=7
b=-2.617993878
c=.5235987756
d=7
```

Chapter 5
Trigonometric Identities, Inverse Functions, and Equations

This chapter appears only in the text *ALGEBRA & TRIGONOMETRY: GRAPHS & MODELS* by Bittinger, Beecher, Ellenbogen, and Penna and should be disregarded by students using the text *COLLEGE ALGEBRA: GRAPHS & MODELS*.

FINDING INVERSE FUNCTION VALUES

We can use a grapher to find inverse function values in both radians and degrees.

Example 2 (a), (e), page 441: Approximate $\cos^{-1}(-0.2689)$ and $\csc^{-1} 8.205$ in both radians and degrees.

To find inverse function values in radians, first set the grapher in Radian mode. Then, to approximate $\cos^{-1}(-0.2689)$, press 2nd COS⁻¹ (−) . 2 6 8 9 ENTER . The grapher returns 1.84304711, so $\cos^{-1}(-0.2689) \approx 1.8430$ radians.

To find $\csc^{-1} 8.205$, recall the identity $\csc\theta = \dfrac{1}{\sin\theta}$. Then $\csc^{-1} 8.205 = \sin^{-1}\left(\dfrac{1}{8.205}\right)$. On the TI-82 press 2nd SIN⁻¹ (1 ÷ 8 . 2 0 5) ENTER or 2nd SIN⁻¹ 8 . 2 0 5 x^{-1} ENTER . The readout is .1221806653, so $\csc^{-1} 8.205 \approx 0.1222$ radians. The TI-83 supplies the left parenthesis when 2nd SIN⁻¹ is pressed, so it is not necessary to enter this using a separate keystroke. The right parenthesis is optional on both the TI-82 and the TI-83.

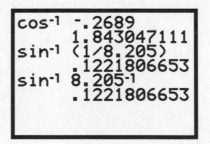

To find inverse function values in degrees, set the grapher in degree mode. Then use the keystrokes above to find that $\cos^{-1}(-0.2689) \approx 105.6°$ and $\csc^{-1} 8.205 \approx 7.0°$.

We also use reciprocal relationships to find function values for arcsecant and arccotangent.

Chapter 6
Applications of Trigonometry

This chapter appears only in the text *ALGEBRA & TRIGONOMETRY: GRAPHS & MODELS* by Bittinger, Beecher, Ellenbogen, and Penna and should be disregarded by students using the text *COLLEGE ALGEBRA: GRAPHS & MODELS*.

CONVERTING FROM RECTANGULAR TO POLAR COORDINATES

The grapher can be used to convert from rectangular to polar coordinates, expressing the result using either degrees or radians. The grapher will supply a positive value for r and an angle in the interval $(-180°, 180°]$, or $(-\pi, \pi]$.

Example 2 (a), page 498: Convert (3,3) to polar coordinates.

To find r, regardless of the type of angle measure, press 2nd ANGLE 5 3 , 3) ENTER . The readout is 4.242640687, so $r \approx 4.2426$. This is a decimal approximation for $3\sqrt{2}$. Now, to find θ in degrees, set the grapher in Degree mode and press 2nd ANGLE 6 3 , 3) ENTER . The readout is 45, so $\theta = 45°$. Thus polar notation for (3,3) is (4.2426, 45°).

 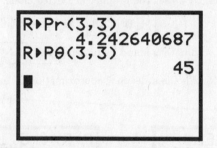

Set the grapher in Radian mode to find θ in radians. Repeat the keystrokes for finding θ above to find that $\theta \approx 0.7854$. This is a decimal approximation for $\pi/4$. Thus polar notation for (3,3) is (4.2426,0.7854).

 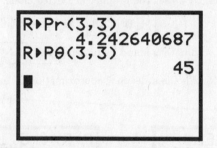

CONVERTING FROM POLAR TO RECTANGULAR COORDINATES

The grapher can also be used to convert from polar to rectangular coordinates.

Example 3, page 499: Convert each of the following to rectangular coordinates.

(a) $(10, \pi/3)$ (b) $(-5, 135°)$

(a) Since the angle is given in radians, set the grapher in Radian mode. To find the x-coordinate of rectangular notation, press 2nd ANGLE 7 1 0 , 2nd π ÷ 3) ENTER. The readout is 5, so $x = 5$. The y-coordinate is found by pressing 2nd ANGLE 8 1 0 , 2nd π ÷ 3) ENTER. The readout is 8.660254038, so $y \approx 8.6603$. This is a decimal approximation of $5\sqrt{3}$. Thus, rectangular notation for $(10, \pi/3)$ is (5,8.6603).

(b) The angle is given in degrees, so we set the grapher in Degree mode. To find the x-coordinate of rectangular notation, press 2nd ANGLE 7 (−) 5 , 1 3 5) ENTER. The readout is 3.535533906, so $x \approx 3.5355$. This is a decimal approximation of $\frac{5\sqrt{2}}{2}$. The y-coordinate is found by pressing 2nd ANGLE 8 (−) 5 , 1 3 5) ENTER. The readout is -3.535533906, so $y \approx -3.5355$. This is a decimal approximation of $-\frac{5\sqrt{2}}{2}$. Thus, rectangular notation for $(-5, 135°)$ is $(3.5355, -3.5355)$.

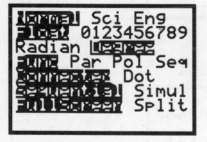

GRAPHING POLAR EQUATIONS

Polar equations can be graphed in either Radian mode or Degree mode. The equation must be written in the form $r = f(\theta)$ and the grapher must be set in Polar (Pol) mode. Typically we begin with a range of $[0, 2\pi]$ or $[0°, 360°]$, but it might be necessary to increase the range to ensure that sufficient points are plotted to display the entire graph.

Example 6, page 501: Graph: $r = 1 - \sin\theta$.

First set the grapher in Polar mode by pressing MODE ▽ ▽ ▽ ▷ ▷ ENTER. We will also select Radian mode.

The equation is given in $r = f(\theta)$ form. Press $\boxed{Y =}$ to enter it on the "Y =" screen. Clear any existing entries and, with the cursor beside "$r_1 =$," press $1 \boxed{-} \boxed{\text{SIN}} \boxed{\text{X,T,}\theta}$. Now press $\boxed{\text{WINDOW}}$ and enter the following settings:

$\theta\text{min} = 0$ (Smallest value of θ to be evaluated)
$\theta\text{max} = 2\pi$ (Largest value of θ to be evaluated)
$\theta\text{step} = \pi/24$ (Increment in θ values)
$\text{Xmin} = -3$
$\text{Xmax} = 3$
$\text{Xscl} = 1$
$\text{Ymin} = -3$
$\text{Ymax} = 1$
$\text{Yscl} = 1$

With these settings the grapher evaluates the function from $\theta = 0$ to $\theta = 2\pi$ in increments of $\pi/24$ and displays the graph in the square window $[-3, 3, -3, 1]$. Values entered in terms of π appear on the screen as decimal approximations. Press $\boxed{\text{GRAPH}}$ to display the graph.

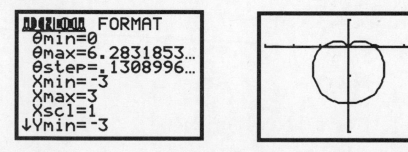

The curve can be traced with either rectángular or polar coordinates being displayed. The value of θ is also displayed when rectangular coordinates are selected. The choice of coordinates is made on the WINDOW FORMAT screen. Press $\boxed{\text{WINDOW}} \boxed{\triangleright}$ on the TI-82 or $\boxed{\text{2nd}} \boxed{\text{FORMAT}}$ on the TI-83 to display this screen. (FORMAT is the second operation associated with the $\boxed{\text{ZOOM}}$ key.) Then position the blinking cursor over RectGC to select rectangular coordinates or over PolarGC to select polar coordinates and press $\boxed{\text{ENTER}}$.

Chapter 7/4
Systems and Matrices

This chapter corresponds to Chapter 7 in *ALGEBRA & TRIGONOMETRY: GRAPHS & MODELS* by Bittinger, Beecher, Ellenbogen, and Penna and to Chapter 4 in *COLLEGE ALGEBRA: GRAPHS & MODELS*. The page number references show the *ALGEBRA & TRIGONOMETRY* page first followed by the *COLLEGE ALGEBRA* page.

MATRICES AND ROW-EQUIVALENT OPERATIONS

Matrices with up to 99 rows or columns can be entered on the grapher. As many as five matrices can be entered on the TI-82 while the TI-83 accepts as many as ten at one time. Row-equivalent operations can be performed on matrices on the grapher.

Example 1, page 542/342: Solve the following system:

$$2x - y + 4z = -3,$$
$$x - 2y - 10z = -6,$$
$$3x \qquad + 4z = 7.$$

First we enter the augmented matrix

$$\begin{bmatrix} 2 & -1 & 4 & -3 \\ 1 & -2 & -10 & -6 \\ 3 & 0 & 4 & 7 \end{bmatrix}$$

on the grapher. Begin by pressing $\boxed{\text{MATRX}}$ $\boxed{\triangleright}$ $\boxed{\triangleright}$ to display the MATRIX EDIT menu. Then select the matrix to be defined. We will select matrix [**A**] by pressing 1. Now the MATRIX EDIT screen appears. The dimensions of the matrix are displayed on the top line of this screen, with the cursor on the row dimension. Enter the dimensions of the augmented matrix, 3 x 4, by pressing 3 $\boxed{\text{ENTER}}$ 4 $\boxed{\text{ENTER}}$. Now the cursor moves to the element in the first row and first column of the matrix. Enter the elements of the first row by pressing 2 $\boxed{\text{ENTER}}$ $\boxed{(-)}$ 1 $\boxed{\text{ENTER}}$ 4 $\boxed{\text{ENTER}}$ $\boxed{(-)}$ 3 $\boxed{\text{ENTER}}$. The cursor moves to the element in the second row and first column of the matrix. Enter the elements of the second and third rows of the augmented matrix by typing each in turn followed by $\boxed{\text{ENTER}}$ as above. Note that the screen only displays three columns of the matrix. The arrow keys can be used to move the cursor to any element at any time.

Row-equivalent operations are performed by making selections from the MATRIX MATH menu. To view this menu press $\boxed{\text{2nd}}$ $\boxed{\text{QUIT}}$ to leave the MATRIX EDIT screen. Then press $\boxed{\text{MATRX}}$ $\boxed{\triangleright}$. Now on the TI-82 press the $\boxed{\triangledown}$ key ten times to see the four row-equivalent operations, 8: rowSwap(, 9: row+(, 0: *row(, and A: *row+(. On the TI-83 press $\boxed{\triangledown}$ fifteen times or $\boxed{\triangle}$ one time to see these operations. They are items C, D, E, and F on the TI-83 MATRIX MATH menu. These operations interchange two rows of a matrix, add two rows, multiply a row by a number, and multiply a row by a number and add it to a second row, respectively.

We will use the grapher to perform the row-equivalent operations that were done algebraically in the text. First, to interchange row 1 and row 2 of matrix [**A**], with the MATRIX MATH menu displayed on the TI-82, press 8 to select rowSwap. On the TI-83 press $\boxed{\text{ALPHA}}$ C to select this operation. Then press $\boxed{\text{MATRX}}$ 1 to select [**A**]. Follow this with a comma and the rows to be interchanged, $\boxed{,}$ 1 $\boxed{,}$ 2 $\boxed{)}$ $\boxed{\text{ENTER}}$.

```
rowSwap([A],1,2)
 [[1  -2  -10  -6]
  [2  -1   4   -3]
  [3   0   4    7 ]]
■
```

The grapher will not store the matrix produced using a row-equivalent operation, so when several operations are to be performed in succession it is helpful to store the result of each operation as it is produced. For example, to store the matrix resulting from interchanging the first and second rows of [**A**] as matrix [**B**] press $\boxed{\text{STO}\triangleright}$ $\boxed{\text{MATRX}}$ 2 $\boxed{\text{ENTER}}$ immediately after interchanging the rows. This can also be done before $\boxed{\text{ENTER}}$ is pressed at the end of the rowSwap.

Next we multiply the first row of [**B**] by -2, add it to the second row and store the result as [**B**] again on the TI-82 by pressing $\boxed{\text{MATRX}}$ $\boxed{\triangleright}$ $\boxed{\text{ALPHA}}$ A $\boxed{(-)}$ 2 $\boxed{,}$ $\boxed{\text{MATRX}}$ 2 $\boxed{,}$ 1 $\boxed{,}$ 2 $\boxed{)}$ $\boxed{\text{STO}\triangleright}$ $\boxed{\text{MATRX}}$ 2 $\boxed{\text{ENTER}}$. On the TI-83 press F rather than A. These keystrokes select *row+(from the MATRIX MATH menu; then they specify that the value of the multiplier is -2, the matrix being operated on is [**B**], and that a multiple of row 1 is being added to row 2; finally they store the result as [**B**].

To multiply row 1 by -3, add it to row 3, and store the result as [**B**] on the TI-82 press $\boxed{\text{MATRX}}$ $\boxed{\triangleright}$ $\boxed{\text{ALPHA}}$ A $\boxed{(-)}$ 3 $\boxed{,}$ $\boxed{\text{MATRX}}$ 2 $\boxed{,}$ 1 $\boxed{,}$ 3 $\boxed{)}$ $\boxed{\text{STO}\triangleright}$ $\boxed{\text{MATRX}}$ 2 $\boxed{\text{ENTER}}$. Press F rather than A on the TI-83.

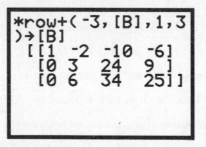

Now multiply the second row by $1/3$ and store the result as [**B**] again. On the TI-82 press $\boxed{\text{MATRX}}$ $\boxed{\triangleright}$ 0 1 $\boxed{(\div)}$ 3 $\boxed{,}$ $\boxed{\text{MATRX}}$ 2 $\boxed{,}$ 2 $\boxed{)}$ $\boxed{\text{STO}\triangleright}$ $\boxed{\text{MATRX}}$ 2 $\boxed{\text{ENTER}}$. On the TI-83 press $\boxed{\text{ALPHA}}$ E rather than 0. These keystrokes select *row(from the MATRIX MATH menu; then they specify that the value of the multiplier is $1/3$, the matrix being operated on is [**B**], and row 2 is being multiplied; finally they store the result as [**B**]. The keystrokes 1 $\boxed{(\div)}$ 3 could be replaced with 3 $\boxed{x^{-1}}$.

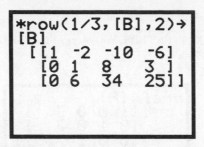

```
*row(1/3,[B],2)→
[B]
 [[1 -2 -10 -6]
  [0  1   8   3]
  [0  6  34  25]]
```

Multiply the second row by −6 and add it to the third row using *row+(. On the TI-82 press [MATRX] [▷] [ALPHA] A [(−)] 6 [,] [MATRX] 2 [,] 2 [,] 3 [)] [STO▷] [MATRX] 2 [ENTER]. Press F rather than A on the TI-83.

On the TI-82 the entry in the third row, second column is 1E−13. This is an approximation of 0 that occurs because of the manner in which the grapher performs calculations and should be treated as 0. In fact, it would be a good idea to return to the MATRIX EDIT screen at this point to replace this entry of [B] with 0. Press [MATRX] [▷] [▷] 2 to display [B]. Then move the cursor to the third row, second column and press 0 [ENTER]. Now press [2nd] [QUIT] to leave this screen.

```
*row+( -6,[B],2,3
)→[B]
 [[1 -2 -10 -6]
  [0  1   8   3]
  [0  0 -14  7 ]]
```

Finally, multiply the third row by −1/14 on the TI-82 by pressing [MATRX] [▷] 0 [(−)] 1 [(÷)] 1 4 [,] [MATRX] 2 [,] 3 [)] [ENTER]. On the TI-83 press [ALPHA] E rather than 0. The keystrokes [(−)] 1 [(÷)] 1 4 could be replaced with [(−)] 1 4 [x^{-1}].

```
*row( -1/14,[B],3
)
 [[1 -2 -10 -6 ]
  [0  1   8   3 ]
  [0  0   1  -.5]]
```

Write the system of equations that corresponds to the final matrix. Then use back-substitution to solve for x, y, and z as illustrated in the text.

Instead of stopping with row-echelon form as we did above, we can continue to apply row-equivalent operations until the matrix is in reduced row-echelon form as in Example 3 on page 544/344 of the text. Reduced row-echelon form of a matrix can be found directly on the TI-83 by using the rref(operation from the MATRIX MATH menu. For example, to find reduced row-echelon form for matrix **A** in Example 1 above, after entering [**A**] and leaving the MATRIX EDIT screen press MATRX ▷ ALPHA B MATRX 1 ENTER . We can read the solution of the system of equations, $(3, 7, -0.5)$ directly from the resulting matrix.

```
rref([A]
    [[1 0 0 3   ]
     [0 1 0 7   ]
     [0 0 1 -.5]]
```

MATRIX OPERATIONS

We can use the grapher to add and subtract matrices, to multiply a matrix by a scalar, and to multiply matrices.

Example 1 (a), page 549/349: Find **A** + **B** for

a) $\mathbf{A} = \begin{bmatrix} -5 & 0 \\ 4 & \frac{1}{2} \end{bmatrix}$, $\mathbf{B} = \begin{bmatrix} 6 & -3 \\ 2 & 3 \end{bmatrix}$.

Enter **A** and **B** on the MATRIX EDIT screen as [**A**] and [**B**] as described earlier in this chapter. Press 2nd QUIT to leave this screen. Then press MATRX 1 + MATRX 2 ENTER to display the sum.

```
[A]+[B]
    [[1  -3 ]
     [6 3.5]]
```

Example 2, page 550/350: Find **C** − **D** for each of the following.

a) $\mathbf{C} = \begin{bmatrix} 1 & 2 \\ -2 & 0 \\ -3 & -1 \end{bmatrix}$, $\mathbf{D} = \begin{bmatrix} 1 & -1 \\ 1 & 3 \\ 2 & 3 \end{bmatrix}$ b) $\mathbf{C} = \begin{bmatrix} 5 & -6 \\ -3 & 4 \end{bmatrix}$, $\mathbf{D} = \begin{bmatrix} -4 \\ 1 \end{bmatrix}$

a) Enter **C** and **D** on the MATRIX EDIT screen as [**C**] and [**D**]. Press 2nd QUIT to leave this screen. Then press MATRX 3 − MATRX 4 ENTER to display the difference.

```
[C]-[D]
            [[0   3 ]
             [-3  -3]
             [-5  -4]]
```

b) Enter **C** and **D** on the MATRIX EDIT screen as [**C**] and [**D**]. Press 2nd QUIT to leave this screen. Then press MATRX 3 − MATRX 4 ENTER . The grapher returns the message ERR:DIM MISMATCH, indicating that this subtraction is not possible. This is the case because the matrices have different orders.

```
ERR:DIM MISMATCH
1 Goto
2:Quit
```

Example 4, page 551/351: Find 3**A** and (-1)**A**, for $\mathbf{A} = \begin{bmatrix} -3 & 0 \\ 4 & 5 \end{bmatrix}$

Enter **A** on the MATRIX EDIT screen as [**A**]. Press 2nd QUIT to leave this screen. Then to find 3**A** press 3 MATRX 1 ENTER and to find (-1)**A** press (−) 1 MATRX 1 ENTER . Note that (-1)**A** is the opposite, or additive inverse, of **A** and can also be found by pressing (−) MATRX 1 ENTER .

```
3[A]
            [[-9  0 ]
             [12  15]]
-1[A]
            [[3   0 ]
             [-4  -5]]
■
```

Example 6 (a), (d), page 553/353: For

$$\mathbf{A} = \begin{bmatrix} 3 & 1 & -1 \\ 2 & 0 & 3 \end{bmatrix}, \mathbf{B} = \begin{bmatrix} 1 & 6 \\ 3 & -5 \\ -2 & 4 \end{bmatrix}, \text{ and } \mathbf{C} = \begin{bmatrix} 4 & -6 \\ 1 & 2 \end{bmatrix}$$

find each of the following.

a) **AB**   d) **AC**

First enter **A**, **B**, and **C** as [**A**], [**B**], and [**C**] on the MATRIX EDIT screen. Press 2nd QUIT to leave this screen.

a) To find **AB** press MATRX 1 MATRX 2 ENTER .

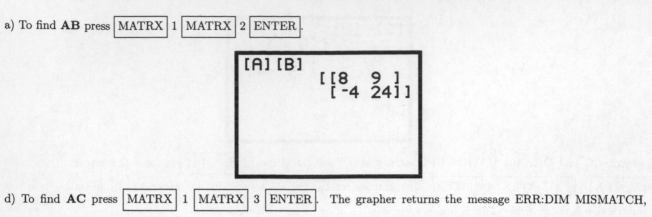

d) To find **AC** press MATRX 1 MATRX 3 ENTER . The grapher returns the message ERR:DIM MISMATCH, indicating that this multiplication is not possible. This is the case because the number of columns in **A** is not the same as the number of rows in **C**. Thus, the matrices cannot be multiplied in this order.

FINDING THE INVERSE OF A MATRIX

The inverse of a matrix can be found quickly on the grapher.

Example 3, page 562/362: Find $\mathbf{A}^{-1}$, where

$$\mathbf{A} = \begin{bmatrix} -2 & 3 \\ -3 & 4 \end{bmatrix}.$$

Enter **A** as [**A**] on the MATRIX EDIT screen. Then press 2nd QUIT to leave this screen. Now press MATRX 1 x^{-1} ENTER .

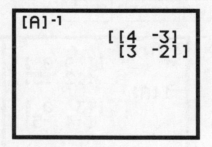

Exercise 9, page 564/364: Find $\mathbf{A}^{-1}$, where

$$\mathbf{A} = \begin{bmatrix} 6 & 9 \\ 4 & 6 \end{bmatrix}.$$

Enter **A** as [**A**] on the MATRIX EDIT screen and then press 2nd QUIT to leave this screen. Now press MATRX 1 x^{-1} ENTER . The grapher returns the message ERR:SINGULAR MAT, indicating that $\mathbf{A}^{-1}$ does not exist.

MATRIX SOLUTIONS OF SYSTEMS OF EQUATIONS

We can write a system of n linear equations in n variables as a matrix equation $\mathbf{AX} = \mathbf{B}$. If **A** has an inverse the solution of the system of equations is given by $\mathbf{X} = \mathbf{A}^{-1}\mathbf{B}$.

Example 4, page 563/363: Use an inverse matrix to solve the following system of equations:

$$x + 2y - z = -2,$$
$$3x + 5y + 3z = 3,$$
$$2x + 4y + 3z = 1.$$

Enter $\mathbf{A} = \begin{bmatrix} 1 & 2 & -1 \\ 3 & 5 & 3 \\ 2 & 4 & 3 \end{bmatrix}$ and $\mathbf{B} = \begin{bmatrix} -2 \\ 3 \\ 1 \end{bmatrix}$ on the MATRIX EDIT screen as [**A**] and [**B**]. Press $\boxed{\text{2nd}}$ $\boxed{\text{QUIT}}$ to leave

this screen. Then press $\boxed{\text{MATRX}}$ 1 $\boxed{x^{-1}}$ $\boxed{\text{MATRX}}$ 2 $\boxed{\text{ENTER}}$. The result is the 3 x 1 matrix $\begin{bmatrix} 5 \\ -3 \\ 1 \end{bmatrix}$, so the solution is

$(5, -3, 1)$.

```
[A]⁻¹[B]
              [ [5  ]
               [ -3]
               [1  ] ]
■
```

GRAPHS OF INEQUALITIES

We can graph linear inequalities on the grapher, shading the region of the solution set. The grapher should be set in Func mode at this point.

Example 1, page 567/367: Graph: $y < x + 3$.

First we graph the related equation $y = x + 3$. We use the standard window $[-10, 10, -10, 10]$. Since the inequality symbol is $<$ we know that the line $y = x + 3$ is not part of the solution set. In a hand-drawn graph we would use a dashed line to indicate this. This can also be done on the TI-83 by selecting the dotted GraphStyle as described on page 12 of this manual. On the TI-82, however, the only option is to use a solid line, keeping in mind that it is not part of the solution set. After determining that the solution set of the inequality consists of all points below the line, we use the grapher's SHADE operation to shade this region. SHADE is item 7 on the DRAW DRAW menu. To access it press $\boxed{\text{2nd}}$ $\boxed{\text{DRAW}}$ 7.

Now enter a lower function and an upper function. The region between them will be shaded. We want to shade the area between the bottom of the window, $y = -10$, and the line $y = x + 3$ so we enter $\boxed{(-)}$ 1 0 $\boxed{,}$ $\boxed{\text{X,T,}\Theta}$ $\boxed{+}$ 3 $\boxed{)}$ $\boxed{\text{ENTER}}$. We can also enter $x + 3$ as y_1 using the YVARS feature. The result is shown below.

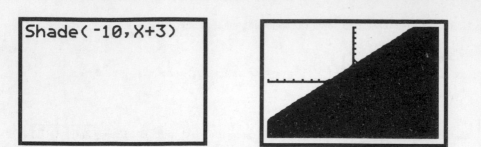

The "shade below" GraphStyle on the TI-83 can also be used to shade this region. After entering the related equation, cycle through the Graph Style options on the "Y =" screen as described on page 12 of this manual until the "shade below" option appears. Then press $\boxed{\text{GRAPH}}$ to display the graph of the inequality. Note that when the "shade below" GraphStyle is selected it is not also possible to select the dotted Graphstyle so we must keep in mind the fact that the line $y = x + 3$ is not included in the solution set.

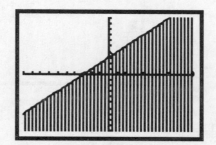

We can also use the SHADE operation to graph a system of inequalities when the solution set lies between the graphs of two functions.

Exercise 37, page 574/374: Graph:
$$y \leq x,$$
$$y \geq 3 - x.$$

First graph the related equations $y = x$ and $y = 3 - x$ and determine that the solution set consists of all the points on or above the graph of $y = 3 - x$ and on or below the graph of $y = x$. We will shade this region by pressing $\boxed{\text{2nd}}$ $\boxed{\text{DRAW}}$ 7 3 $\boxed{-}$ $\boxed{\text{X,T,}\Theta}$ $\boxed{)}$ $\boxed{,}$ $\boxed{\text{X,T,}\Theta}$ $\boxed{\text{ENTER}}$. These keystrokes select the SHADE operation from the DRAW DRAW menu and then enter $y = 3 - x$ as the lower function and $y = x$ as the upper function. We could also enter these functions as y_2 and y_1, respectively, using the YVARS operation.

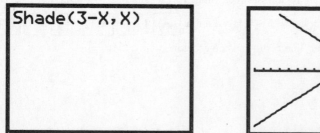

On the TI-83 we can also graph systems of inequalities by shading the solution set of each inequality in the system with a different pattern. When the "shade above" or "shade below" Graph Style options are selected the TI-83 rotates through four shading patterns. Vertical lines shade the first function, horizontal lines the second, negatively sloping diagonal lines the third, and positively sloping diagonal lines the fourth. These patterns repeat if more than four functions are graphed.

Example 5, page 570/370: Graph the solution set of the system
$$x + y \leq 4,$$
$$x - y \geq 2.$$

First graph the equation $x + y = 4$, entering it in the form $y = -x + 4$. We determine that the solution set of $x + y \leq 4$ consists of all points below the line $x + y = 4$, or $y = -x + 4$, so we select the "shade below" GraphStyle for this function. Next graph $x - y = 2$, entering it in the form $y = x - 2$. The solution set of $x - y \geq 2$ is all points below the line $x - y = 2$, or $y = x - 2$, so we also choose the "shade below" GraphStyle for this function. Now press $\boxed{\text{GRAPH}}$ to display the solution sets of each inequality in the system and the region where they overlap. The region of overlap is the solution set of the system of inequalities.

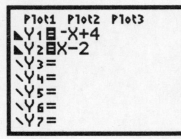
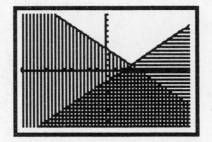

Chapter 8/5
Conic Sections

This chapter corresponds to Chapter 8 in *ALGEBRA & TRIGONOMETRY: GRAPHS & MODELS* **by Bittinger, Beecher, Ellenbogen, and Penna and to Chapter 5 in** *COLLEGE ALGEBRA: GRAPHS & MODELS*. **The page number references show the** *ALGEBRA & TRIGONOMETRY* **page first followed by the** *COLLEGE ALGEBRA* **page.**

Many conic sections are represented by equations that are not functions. Consequently, these equations must be entered on the TI-82 and the TI-83 as two equations, each of which is a function. We have already done this for circles in Chapter G of this manual. Now we turn our attention to parabolas, ellipses, and hyperbolas.

GRAPHING PARABOLAS

To graph a parabola of the form $y^2 = 4px$ or $(y - k)^2 = 4p(x - h)$, we must first solve the equation for y.

Example 4, page 594/394: Graph the parabola $y^2 - 2y - 8x - 31 = 0$.

In the text we used the quadratic formula to solve the equation for y:
$$y = \frac{2 \pm \sqrt{32x + 128}}{2}.$$

One way to produce the graph of the parabola is to enter $y_1 = \dfrac{2 + \sqrt{32x + 128}}{2}$ and $y_2 = \dfrac{2 - \sqrt{32x + 128}}{2}$, select a window, and press $\boxed{\text{GRAPH}}$ to see the graph. Here we use $[-12, 12, -8, 8]$. The first equation produces the top half of the parabola and the second equation produces the lower half.

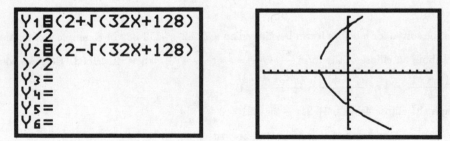

We can also enter $y_1 = \sqrt{32x + 128}$. Then use the Y-VARS operation to enter $y_2 = \dfrac{2 + y_1}{2}$ and $y_3 = \dfrac{2 - y_1}{2}$. For example, to enter $y_2 = \dfrac{2 + y_1}{2}$ on the TI-82 position the cursor beside "Y2 =" and press $\boxed{(}$ $\boxed{2}$ $\boxed{+}$ $\boxed{\text{2nd}}$ $\boxed{\text{Y-VARS}}$ $\boxed{1}$ $\boxed{1}$ $\boxed{)}$ $\boxed{\div}$ 2. On the TI-83 press $\boxed{(}$ $\boxed{2}$ $\boxed{+}$ $\boxed{\text{VARS}}$ $\boxed{\triangleright}$ $\boxed{1}$ $\boxed{1}$ $\boxed{)}$ $\boxed{\div}$ 2. Enter $y_3 = \dfrac{2 - y_1}{2}$ in a similar manner. Finally, deselect y_1 by moving the cursor to the equals sign following Y1 and pressing $\boxed{\text{ENTER}}$. The top half of the graph is produced by y_2 and the lower half by y_3. The expression for y_1 was entered to avoid entering the square root more than once. By deselecting y_1 we prevent its graph from appearing on the screen with the graph of the parabola.

```
Y₁=√(32X+128)
Y₂₌(2+Y₁)/2
Y₃₌(2-Y₁)/2
Y₄=
Y₅=
Y₆=
Y₇=
Y₈=
```

We could also use the standard equation of the parabola found in the text:

$$(y-1)^2 = 8(x+4).$$

Solve this equation for y.

$$y - 1 = \pm\sqrt{8(x+4)}$$
$$y = 1 \pm \sqrt{8(x+4)}$$

Then enter $y_1 = 1 + \sqrt{8(x+4)}$ and $y_2 = 1 - \sqrt{8(x+4)}$, or enter $y_1 = \sqrt{8(x+4)}$, $y_2 = 1 + y_1$, and $y_3 = 1 - y_1$, and deselect y_1 as described above.

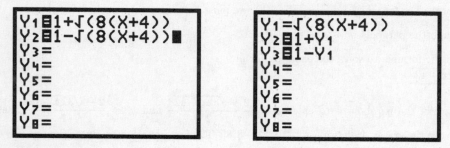

```
Y₁₌1+√(8(X+4))
Y₂₌1-√(8(X+4))■
Y₃=
Y₄=
Y₅=
Y₆=
Y₇=
Y₈=
```

```
Y₁=√(8(X+4))
Y₂₌1+Y₁
Y₃₌1-Y₁
Y₄=
Y₅=
Y₆=
Y₇=
Y₈=
```

GRAPHING ELLIPSES

The equation of an ellipse must be solved for y before it can be entered on a TI-82 or a TI-83. In Example 2 of Section 8.2 of the text the procedure for graphing an ellipse of the form $\dfrac{x^2}{a^2} + \dfrac{y^2}{b^2} = 1$ or $\dfrac{x^2}{b^2} + \dfrac{y^2}{a^2} = 1$ is described. Here we consider ellipses of the form $\dfrac{(x-h)^2}{a^2} + \dfrac{(y-k)^2}{b^2} = 1$ or $\dfrac{(x-h)^2}{b^2} + \dfrac{(y-k)^2}{a^2} = 1$

Example 4, page 604/404: Graph the ellipse $4x^2 + y^2 + 24x - 2y + 21 = 0$.

Completing the square in the text, we found that the equation can be written as

$$\frac{(x+3)^2}{4} + \frac{(y-1)^2}{16} = 1.$$

Solve this equation for y.

$$\frac{(x+3)^2}{4} + \frac{(y-1)^2}{16} = 1$$

$$\frac{(y-1)^2}{16} = 1 - \frac{(x+3)^2}{4}$$

$$(y-1)^2 = 16 - 4(x+3)^2 \qquad \text{Multiplying by 16}$$

$$y - 1 = \pm\sqrt{16 - 4(x+3)^2}$$

$$y = 1 \pm \sqrt{16 - 4(x+3)^2}$$

Now we can produce the graph in either of two ways. One is to enter $y_1 = 1 + \sqrt{16 - 4(x+3)^2}$ and $y_2 =$

$1 - \sqrt{16 - 4(x+3)^2}$, select a square window, and press $\boxed{\text{GRAPH}}$. Here we use $[-9, 9, -6, 6]$. The first equation produces the top half of the ellipse and the second equation produces the lower half.

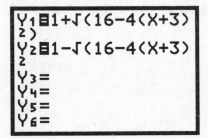 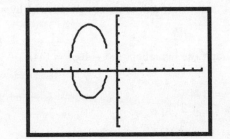

We can also enter $y_1 = \sqrt{16 - 4(x+3)^2}$ and use the Y-VARS operation as described above in Graphing Parabolas to enter $y_2 = 1 + y_1$ and $y_3 = 1 - y_1$. Then deselect y_1, select a square window, and press $\boxed{\text{GRAPH}}$. We use y_1 to eliminate the need to enter the square root more than once. Deselecting it prevents the graph of y_1 from appearing on the screen with the graph of the ellipse. The top half of the graph is produced by y_2 and the lower half by y_3.

```
Y₁=√(16-4(X+3)²)

Y₂⊟1+Y₁
Y₃⊟1-Y₁
Y₄=
Y₅=
Y₆=
Y₇=
```

We could also begin by using the quadratic formula to solve the original equation for y.

$$4x^2 + y^2 + 24x - 2y + 21 = 0$$

$$y^2 - 2y + (4x^2 + 24x + 21) = 0$$

$$y = \frac{-(-2) \pm \sqrt{(-2)^2 - 4 \cdot 1 \cdot (4x^2 + 24x + 21)}}{2 \cdot 1}$$

$$y = \frac{2 \pm \sqrt{4 - 16x^2 - 96x - 84}}{2}$$

$$y = \frac{2 \pm \sqrt{-16x^2 - 96x - 80}}{2}$$

Then enter $y_1 = \dfrac{2 + \sqrt{-16x^2 - 96x - 80}}{2}$ and $y_2 = \dfrac{2 - \sqrt{-16x^2 - 96x - 80}}{2}$, or enter $y_1 = \sqrt{-16x^2 - 96x - 80}$, $y_2 = \dfrac{2 + y_1}{2}$, and $y_3 = \dfrac{2 - y_1}{2}$, and deselect y_1.

```
Y₁⊟(2+√(-16X²-96
X-80))/2
Y₂⊟(2-√(-16X²-96
X-80))/2
Y₃=
Y₄=
Y₅=
Y₆=
```

```
Y₁=√(-16X²-96X-8
0)
Y₂⊟(2+Y₁)/2
Y₃⊟(2-Y₁)/2
Y₄=
Y₅=
Y₆=
Y₇=
```

Select a square window and press $\boxed{\text{GRAPH}}$ to display the graph.

GRAPHING HYPERBOLAS

As with equations of circles, parabolas, and ellipses, equations of hyperbolas must be solved for y before they can be entered on a TI-82 or a TI-83.

Example 2, page 610/410: Graph the hyperbola $9x^2 - 16y^2 = 144$.

First solve the equation for y.
$$9x^2 - 16y^2 = 144$$
$$-16y^2 = -9x^2 + 144$$
$$y^2 = \frac{-9x^2 + 144}{-16}$$
$$y = \pm\sqrt{\frac{-9x^2 + 144}{-16}}, \text{ or } \pm\sqrt{\frac{9x^2 - 144}{16}}$$
It is not necessary to simplify further.

Now enter $y_1 = \sqrt{\frac{9x^2 - 144}{16}}$ and either $y_2 = -\sqrt{\frac{9x^2 - 144}{16}}$ or $y_2 = -y_1$, select a square window, and press $\boxed{\text{GRAPH}}$. Here we use $[-9, 9, -6, 6]$. The top half of the graph is produced by y_1 and the lower half by y_2.

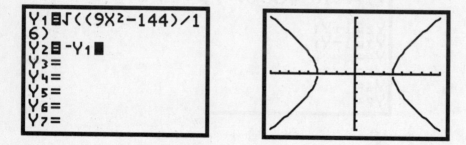

Example 3, page 613/413: Graph the hyperbola $4y^2 - x^2 + 24y + 4x + 28 = 0$.

In the text we completed the square to get the standard form of the equation. Now solve the equation for y.
$$\frac{(y+3)^2}{1} - \frac{(x-2)^2}{4} = 1$$
$$(y+3)^2 = \frac{(x-2)^2}{4} + 1$$
$$y + 3 = \pm\sqrt{\frac{(x-2)^2}{4} + 1}$$
$$y = -3 \pm \sqrt{\frac{(x-2)^2}{4} + 1}$$

The graph can be produced in either of two ways. One is to enter $y_1 = -3 + \sqrt{\frac{(x-2)^2}{4} + 1}$ and $y_2 = -3 - \sqrt{\frac{(x-2)^2}{4} + 1}$, select a square window, and press $\boxed{\text{GRAPH}}$. Here we use $[-12, 12, -9, 9]$. The first equation produces the top half of the hyperbola and the second the lower half.

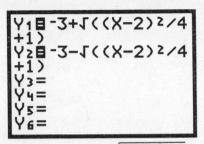 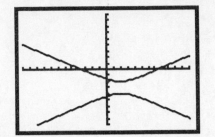

We can also enter $y_1 = \sqrt{\dfrac{(x-2)^2}{4} + 1}$, $y_2 = -3 + y_1$, and $y_3 = -3 - y_1$. Then deselect y_1, select a square window, and press $\boxed{\text{GRAPH}}$. Again, y_1 is used to eliminate the need to enter the square root more than once. Deselecting it prevents the graph of y_1 from appearing on the screen with the graph of the hyperbola. The top half of the graph is produced by y_2 and the lower half by y_3.

Chapter 9/6
Sequences, Series, and Combinatorics

This chapter corresponds to Chapter 9 in *ALGEBRA & TRIGONOMETRY: GRAPHS & MODELS* by Bittinger, Beecher, Ellenbogen, and Penna and to Chapter 6 in *COLLEGE ALGEBRA: GRAPHS & MODELS*. **The page number references show the** *ALGEBRA & TRIGONOMETRY* **page first followed by the** *COLLEGE ALGEBRA* **page.**

Both the graphing capabilities and the computational capabilities of the grapher can be used when working with sequences, series, and combinatorics.

EVALUATING AND GRAPHING SEQUENCES

The grapher can be used to construct a table showing the terms of a sequence and to graph a sequence.

Example 3, page 633/433: Construct a table of values and a graph for the first 10 terms of the sequence whose general term is given by

$$a_n = \frac{n}{n+1}.$$

First we use the TI-82 to construct the table and graph the sequence. Begin by setting the grapher in SEQUENCE and DOT modes. Press $\boxed{\text{MODE}}$ $\boxed{\triangledown}$ $\boxed{\triangledown}$ $\boxed{\triangledown}$ $\boxed{\triangleright}$ $\boxed{\triangleright}$ $\boxed{\triangleright}$ $\boxed{\text{ENTER}}$ to select SEQUENCE mode, followed immediately by $\boxed{\triangledown}$ $\boxed{\triangleright}$ $\boxed{\text{ENTER}}$ to select DOT mode. Now press $\boxed{\text{Y}=}$. Position the cursor beside "$U_n =$" and enter $n/(n+1)$ by pressing $\boxed{\text{2nd}}$ $\boxed{n}$ $\boxed{\div}$ $\boxed{(}$ $\boxed{\text{2nd}}$ $\boxed{n}$ $\boxed{+}$ $\boxed{1}$ $\boxed{)}$. (n is the second operation associated with the 9 key.) Then press $\boxed{\text{WINDOW}}$ to display the WINDOW screen. Press $\boxed{\triangledown}$ to position the cursor beside "U_nStart =" and enter the first term of the sequence: when $n = 1$, $n/(n+1) = 1/(1+1) = 1/2$, or 0.5, so we press $\boxed{\cdot}$ $\boxed{5}$ $\boxed{\text{ENTER}}$.

To construct the table of values for this sequence, press $\boxed{\text{2nd}}$ $\boxed{\text{TblSet}}$ and set TblMin = 1, ΔTbl = 1, and Indpnt: Auto. Now press $\boxed{\text{2nd}}$ $\boxed{\text{TABLE}}$ to display the table.

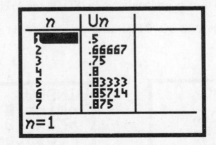

We see that when $n = 1$, a_n, or $U_1 = 0.5$; when $n = 2$, a_n, or $U_2 = 0.66667$; and so on. We can scroll through the table to find additional sequence values. To find a specific term of the sequence, set the table in Ask mode and then enter the desired value of n on the TABLE screen as described on page 10 of this manual.

To graph the sequence first press $\boxed{\text{WINDOW}}$. We have already entered U_nStart $= .5$. Now set nStart $= 1$ to define the initial value of n in the calculation of sequence values; set nMin $= 1$ and nMax $= 10$ to set the values of n at which plotting begins and ends at 1 and 10, respectively. Now set Xmin $= 0$, Xmax $= 10$, Xscl $= 1$, Ymin $= 0$, Ymax $= 1$, and Yscl $= 1$ to define the window dimensions and the spacing between tick marks. It will be necessary to use the $\boxed{\bigtriangledown}$ key to display and enter Xscl, Ymin, Ymax, and Yscl. The window format should be set on Time. While the WINDOW screen is displayed, press $\boxed{\triangleright}$ to display the WINDOW FORMAT screen. If Time is not selected, position the cursor over it and press $\boxed{\text{ENTER}}$. Now press $\boxed{\text{GRAPH}}$ to display the graph of the first 10 terms of the sequence.

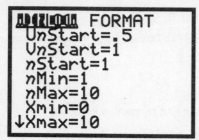
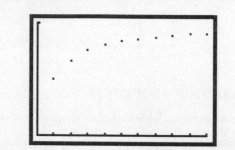

Now we do Example 3 on the TI-83. Begin by setting the grapher in SEQUENCE mode. Press $\boxed{\text{MODE}}$ $\boxed{\bigtriangledown}$ $\boxed{\bigtriangledown}$ $\boxed{\bigtriangledown}$ $\boxed{\triangleright}$ $\boxed{\triangleright}$ $\boxed{\triangleright}$ $\boxed{\text{ENTER}}$. Then press $\boxed{Y=}$. Set the graph-style to "dot" beside "u(n) =" by positioning the cursor on the graph-style icon and pressing $\boxed{\text{ENTER}}$ until the dot icon appears. Now press $\boxed{\triangleright}$ $\boxed{\triangleright}$ and enter $n/(n+1)$ beside "u(n) =" by pressing $\boxed{\text{X,T,}\theta\text{,}n}$ $\boxed{\div}$ $\boxed{(}$ $\boxed{\text{X,T,}\theta\text{,}n}$ $\boxed{+}$ 1 $\boxed{)}$. Press $\boxed{\bigtriangledown}$ $\boxed{\cdot}$ 5 to enter the first term of the sequence, $1/(1+1)$, or .5, beside "u(nMin) =." Construct the table of values as described above, keeping in mind that TblMin on the TI-82 corresponds to TblStart on the TI-83.

To graph the sequence first press $\boxed{\text{WINDOW}}$ to display the WINDOW screen. Set nMin $= 1$ and nMax $= 10$ to define the smallest and largest values of n for which terms of the sequence are calculated. Also set PlotStart $= 1$ and PlotStep $= 1$ to define the first term of the sequence to be plotted and the incremental n value. Set Xmin $= 0$, Xmax $= 10$, Xscl $= 1$, Ymin $= 0$, Ymax $= 1$, and Yscl $= 1$ to define the window dimensions and the spacing between tick marks. It will be necessary to use the $\boxed{\bigtriangledown}$ key to display and enter Ymin, Ymax, and Yscl. The window format should be set on Time. Press $\boxed{\text{2nd}}$ $\boxed{\text{FORMAT}}$ to display the WINDOW FORMAT screen. If Time is not selected, position the cursor over it and press $\boxed{\text{ENTER}}$.

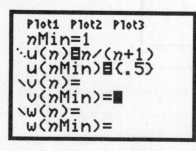

Press $\boxed{\text{GRAPH}}$ to display the graph.

Recursively defined sequences can also be entered on the grapher.

Example 7, page 636/436: Find the first 5 terms of the sequence defined by

$$a_1 = 5, \ a_{k+1} = 2a_k - 3, \ \text{for } k \geq 1.$$

On the TI-82, press $\boxed{\text{Y}=}$ and enter the recursive function beside "U_n =" by pressing 2 $\boxed{\text{2nd}}$ $\boxed{\text{U}_{n-1}}$ $\boxed{-}$ 3. (U_{n-1} is the second operation associated with the $\boxed{7}$ key.) Now press $\boxed{\text{WINDOW}}$ to display the window screen. Beside "U_nStart =" enter the first term of the sequence, 5. Press $\boxed{\text{2nd}}$ $\boxed{\text{TblSet}}$ to display the TABLE SETUP screen and set TblMin = 1, ΔTbl = 1, and Indpnt: Auto. Now press $\boxed{\text{2nd}}$ $\boxed{\text{TABLE}}$ to display the table of values.

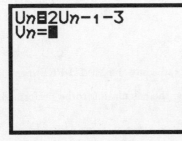
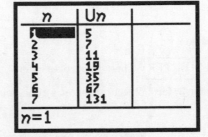

We see that $a_1 = 5$, $a_2 = 7$, $a_3 = 11$, $a_4 = 19$, and $a_5 = 35$.

On the TI-83, press $\boxed{\text{Y}=}$ and enter the recursive function beside "u(n) =" by pressing 2 $\boxed{\text{2nd}}$ $\boxed{\text{u}}$ $\boxed{(}$ $\boxed{\text{X,T,}\theta,n}$ $\boxed{-}$ 1 $\boxed{)}$ $\boxed{-}$ 3. (u is the second operation associated with the $\boxed{7}$ key.) Also set u(nMin) = 5, the first term of the sequence. Set up and display the table of values as described above, again keeping in mind that TblMin on the TI-82 corresponds to TblStart on the TI-83.

As with the TI-82, we see that $a_1 = 5$; $a_2 = 7$, $a_3 = 11$, $a_4 = 19$, and $a_5 = 35$.

EVALUATING FACTORIALS, PERMUTATIONS, AND COMBINATIONS

Operations from the MATH PRB (probability) menu can be used to evaluate factorials, permutations, and combinations.

Exercise 6, page 677/477: Evaluate 7!.

Press 7 $\boxed{\text{MATH}}$ $\boxed{\triangleright}$ $\boxed{\triangleright}$ $\boxed{\triangleright}$ 4 $\boxed{\text{ENTER}}$. These keystrokes enter 7, display the MATH PRB menu, select item 4, !, from that menu, and then cause 7! to be evaluated. The result is 5040.

Exercise 9, page 677/477: Evaluate $\dfrac{9!}{5!}$.

Press 9 $\boxed{\text{MATH}}$ $\boxed{\triangleright}$ $\boxed{\triangleright}$ $\boxed{\triangleright}$ 4 $\boxed{\div}$ 5 $\boxed{\text{MATH}}$ $\boxed{\triangleright}$ $\boxed{\triangleright}$ $\boxed{\triangleright}$ 4 $\boxed{\text{ENTER}}$. The result is 3024.

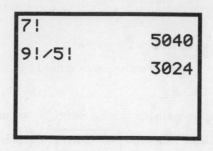

Example 6, page 674/474: Compute $_8P_4$.

Press 8 $\boxed{\text{MATH}}$ $\boxed{\triangleright}$ $\boxed{\triangleright}$ $\boxed{\triangleright}$ 2 4 $\boxed{\text{ENTER}}$. These keystrokes enter 8, for 8 objects, display the MATH PRB menu, select item 2, $_nP_r$, from that menu, enter 4, for 4 objects taken at a time, and then cause the calculation to be performed. The result is 1680.

Example 3, page 682/482: Evaluate $\binom{7}{5}$.

Press 7 $\boxed{\text{MATH}}$ $\boxed{\triangleright}$ $\boxed{\triangleright}$ $\boxed{\triangleright}$ 3 5 $\boxed{\text{ENTER}}$. These keystrokes enter 7, for 7 objects, display the MATH PRB menu, select item 3, $_nC_r$, from that menu, enter 5, for 5 objects taken at a time, and then cause the calculation to be performed. The result is 21.

```
8 nPr 4
                    1680
7 nCr 5
                      21
■
```

Programs For The TI-82
Graphics Calculator

PROGRAMS FOR THE TI-82 GRAPHICS CALCULATOR
(Created by Dave Slomer, Winton Woods High School, Cincinnati, OH.)

QUADFORM

This program solves a quadratic equation of form $Ax^2 + Bx + C = 0$.

INPUT: A, B, C
OUTPUT: Real or complex solutions

```
:Prompt A,B,C
:B^2-4*A*C→D
:Disp "ROOTS:"
:If D≥∅:Then
:Disp (-B+√(D))/(2*A)
:Disp (-B-√(D))/(2*A)
:Else
:Disp -B/(2*A),"+/-",√(-D)/(2*A),"I"
:End
```

SYNDIV

This program does synthetic division to divide a polynomial by a linear factor with leading coefficient 1.

INPUT: List of coefficients of the dividend, enclosed in braces, in order of descending powers and the constant term of the linear divisor.

OUTPUT: The coefficients of the quotient, in order of descending powers, and remainder.

```
:Disp "ENTER {LIST} OF
:Disp "DIVIDEND COEFFS:"
:Input L1
:Input "DIVISOR CONSTANT TERM:",C
:dim (L1)→L
:L1(1)→S
:Disp "QUOTIENT COEFFS="
:For(I,1,L-1)
:Pause S
:C*S+L1(I+1)→S
:End
:Disp "REMAINDER=",S
```

LOGBASE

This program computes logarithms of any base.

INPUT: Number (X) and base (B)
OUTPUT: $\log_B(X)$

```
:Prompt X
:Input "NEW BASE:",B
:log (X)/log (B)
```

TRISOL9∅

This program solves right triangles ABC in which legs L and M are opposite angles A and B, respectively.

INPUT: One side and any other part (except the right angle, C)

OUTPUT: First, the sides; then, the acute angles

```
:Degree
:Menu("TRISOL9∅","HA",P,"HL",Q,"LA",R,"LL",S)
:Lbl P
:Prompt H,A
:9∅-A→B
:H*sin (A)→L
:H*sin (B)→M
:Goto X
:Lbl Q
:Prompt H,L
:√(H^2-L^2)→M
:sin⁻¹ (L/H)→A
:9∅-A→B
:Goto X
:Lbl R
:Prompt L,A
:9∅-A→B
:L/tan (A)→M
:√(L^2+M^2)→H
:Goto X
:Lbl S
:Prompt L,M
:√(L^2+M^2)→H
:tan⁻¹ (L/M)→A
:9∅-A→B
:Lbl X
:Disp L,M,H,A,B
```

TRISOL

This program solves triangle ABC, in which sides L, M, and N are opposite angles A, B, and C, respectively. It covers the "no solution" case as well as the "two solutions" case.

INPUT: Three parts of a triangle, including at least one side

OUTPUT: First the sides, then the angles. The AAS case is not included, so in this case it is necessary to find the third angle by hand and then use ASA.

```
:Degree
:Disp "ANGLES A,B,C"
:Disp "SIDES L,M,N"
:Menu("TRISOL","SSS",P,"SAS",Q,"(A)ASA",R,"SSA",S)
:Lbl P
:Prompt L,M,N
:cos⁻¹ ((M^2+N^2-L^2)/(2*M*N))→A
:cos⁻¹ ((L^2+N^2-M^2)/(2*L*N))→B
:18Ø-A-B→C
:Goto X
:Lbl Q
:Prompt L,C,M
:√(L^2+M^2-2*L*M*cos (C))→N
:cos⁻¹ ((M^2+N^2-L^2)/(2*M*N))→A
:18Ø-A-C→B
:Goto X
:Lbl R
:Prompt A,N,B
:18Ø-A-B→C
:sin (A)*N/(sin (C))→L
:sin (B)*N/(sin (C))→M
:Goto X
:Lbl S
:Prompt L,M,B
:L*sin (B)/M→Z
:If Z>1:Then:Disp "NO SOL":Stop:End
:sin⁻¹ (Z)→A
:18Ø-A-B→C
:sin (C)*M/(sin (B))→N
:Disp L,M,N,A,B,C
:If B≥A:Stop
:Disp "2ND SOL...":Pause
:18Ø-A→A
:18Ø-A-B→C
:sin (C)*M/(sin (B))→N
:Lbl X
:Disp L,M,N,A,B,C
```

DEMOIVRE

This program helps visualize Nth roots of a complex number $A + Bi$.

INPUT: A, B, N

OUPUT: Traceable graph of the N points (A, B) corresponding to the roots

```
:Param
:Degree
:Input "REAL PART:",A
:Input "IMAG PART:",B
:Input "INDEX:",N
:√(A²+B²)^(1/N)→R
:If A=Ø:Then
:18Ø-abs (B)/B*9Ø
:Else
:tan⁻¹ (B/A)+18Ø*(A<Ø)
:End
:Ans/N→H
:"R*cos (T)"→X1T
:"R*sin (T)"→Y1T
:H→Tmin
:H+36Ø→Tmax
:36Ø/N→Tstep
:1.5R→Ymax
:-Ymax→Ymin
:1.5Ymax→Xmax
:-Xmax→Xmin
:Trace
```

SYSLINEQ

This program solves systems of N linear equations in N variables, considered to be of the form $AX = B$, where A is the $N \times N$ matrix of coefficients of the variables, B is the $N \times 1$ matrix of coefficients of the right-hand side, and X is the $N \times 1$ matrix of unique solutions (if any).

INPUT: MATRIX A and MATRIX B

OUTPUT: MATRIX X or message "NO SOLUTION" or message "INFINITELY MANY SOLUTIONS"

```
:Pause augment([A],[B])
:If det ([A])≠Ø:Then
:Pause ([A]⁻¹[B])ᵀ
:Else
:Ø→K
:[A]→[E]
:dim [A]:Ans(1)→R
:For(J,1,R)
:For(I,1,R)
:[B](I,1)→[E](I,J)
:End
:If det ([E])≠Ø:1→K
:End
:If K=1
:Then:Disp "NO SOL"
:Else:Disp "INF MANY SOL"
:End
:End
```

AP

This program finds the Nth term of an arithmetic sequence $a_N = A + (N-1)*D$

INPUT: A, N, D
OUTPUT: a_N

```
:Prompt A,D,N
:A+D*(N-1)
```

GP

This program finds the Nth term of a geometric sequence $a_N = A * R^{N-1}$.

INPUT: A, R, N
OUTPUT: a_N

```
:Prompt A,R,N
:A*R^(N-1)
```

LOAN

This program computes various parts of mortgage payments via the "present value" formula.
$L = PM(1 - (1 + R/M)^{-MY})/R$, whose parameters are defined as follows:

L = the loan amount (wanted now, in the present),
P = the periodic loan payment,
R = the nominal (stated) interest rate,
M = the number of annual conversions, and
Y = the number of years of the loan.

INPUT: Menu choices about which parameter to change and which to find
OUTPUT: Values of all parameters

```
:"L-P*M*(1-(1+R/M)^-(M*Y))/R"→Y∅
:Func:FnOff ∅
:Lbl ∅
:ClrHome
:Disp "L,P,R,Y,M:"
:Disp L,P,R,Y,M:Pause
:Menu("CHANGE:","(L)OAN AMT",1,"(P)AYMENT AMT",2,"(R)ATE OF INT",3,"(Y)EARS",4,"ANN.
CONV. (M)",5,"<<COMPUTE>>",7,"<<REVIEW>>",∅)
:Lbl 1:Prompt L:Goto ∅
:Lbl 2:Prompt P:Goto ∅
:Lbl 3:Prompt R:Goto ∅
:Lbl 4:Prompt Y:Goto ∅
:Lbl 5:Prompt M:Goto ∅
:Lbl 7
:Menu("FIND:","LOAN AMT",A,"PAYMENT AMT",B,"RATE OF INT",C,"YEARS",D,"<<RETURN>>",∅)
:Lbl A:solve(Y∅,L,1)→L:Goto 8
:Lbl B:solve(Y∅,P,1)→P:Goto 8
:Lbl C:solve(Y∅,R,1)→R:Goto 8
:Lbl D:solve(Y∅,Y,1)→Y
:Lbl 8:Pause Ans:Goto ∅
```

The TI-85
Graphics Calculator

Preliminaries

Press $\boxed{\text{ON}}$ to turn on the TI-85 graphing calculator. ($\boxed{\text{ON}}$ is the key at the bottom left-hand corner of the keypad.) The display contrast can be adjusted by first pressing $\boxed{\text{2nd}}$. ($\boxed{\text{2nd}}$ is the yellow key in the left column of the keypad.) Then press and hold $\boxed{\triangle}$ to increase the contrast or $\boxed{\triangledown}$ to decrease the contrast. To turn the grapher off, press $\boxed{\text{2nd}}$ $\boxed{\text{OFF}}$. (OFF is the second operation associated with the $\boxed{\text{ON}}$ key.) The grapher will turn itself off automatically after about five minutes without any activity.

It will be helpful to read the Getting Started section (pages 1 - 22) of the TI-85 Guidebook before proceeding.

Press $\boxed{\text{2nd}}$ $\boxed{\text{MODE}}$ to display the MODE settings. (MODE is the second operation associated with the $\boxed{\text{MORE}}$ key.) Initially you should select the settings on the left side of the display.

To change a setting use $\boxed{\triangledown}$ or $\boxed{\triangle}$ to move the blinking cursor to the line of that setting. Then use $\boxed{\triangleright}$ or $\boxed{\triangleleft}$ to move the cursor to the desired setting and press $\boxed{\text{ENTER}}$. Press $\boxed{\text{CLEAR}}$ or $\boxed{\text{2nd}}$ $\boxed{\text{QUIT}}$ to leave the MODE screen. (QUIT is the second operation associated with the $\boxed{\text{EXIT}}$ key.)

Chapter G
Introduction to Graphs and Graphers

SETTING THE VIEWING WINDOW

The viewing window is the portion of the coordinate plane that appears on the grapher's screen. It is defined by the minimum and maximum values of x and y: xMin, xMax, yMin, and yMax. The notation [Xmin, Xmax, Ymin, Ymax] is used in the text to represent these window settings or dimensions. For example, $[-12, 12, -8, 8]$ denotes a window that displays the portion of the x-axis from -12 to 12 and the portion of the y-axis from -8 to 8. In addition, the distance between tick marks on the axes is defined by the settings xScl and yScl. The window corresponding to the settings $[-20, 30, -12, 20]$, xScl $= 5$, yScl $= 2$, is shown below.

Press the GRAPH key in the left column of the keypad to display one level of GRAPH menus. Press F2 to select the RANGE menu which displays the current window settings on your grapher. The standard settings are shown below.

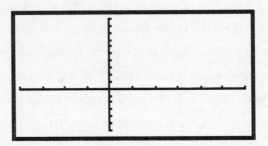

To change a setting press $\triangledown$ to move the cursor to the setting you wish to change and enter the new value. For example, to change from the standard settings to $[-20, 30, -12, 20]$, xScl $= 5$, yScl $= 2$, press (−) 2 0 ENTER 3 0 ENTER 5 ENTER (−) 1 2 ENTER 2 0 ENTER 2 ENTER. You must use the gray (−) key on the bottom row of the keypad rather than the black − key in the right-hand column to enter a negative number. (−) represents "the opposite of" or "the additive inverse of" whereas − is the subtraction key. The $\triangledown$ key may be used instead of ENTER after typing each window setting.

To return quickly to the standard window setting $[-10, 10, -10, 10]$, xScl $= 1$, yScl $= 1$, select the operations ZOOM and ZSTD from the GRAPH menu by pressing F3 followed by F4. If the GRAPH menu is not displayed, it will be necessary to press $\boxed{\text{GRAPH}}$ first.

GRAPHING EQUATIONS

An equation must be solved for y before it can be graphed on the TI-85.

Example 8 (a), page 8 (Page numbers refer to pages in the textbook.): To graph $2x + 3y = 18$, first solve for y, obtaining $y = \dfrac{18 - 2x}{3}$. Then press $\boxed{\text{GRAPH}}$ and select the menu y(x) = by pressing $\boxed{\text{F1}}$. If there is currently an expression displayed for $y1$, press $\boxed{\text{CLEAR}}$ to delete it. Do the same for expressions that appear on all other lines by using $\boxed{\triangledown}$ to move the cursor to a line and then pressing $\boxed{\text{CLEAR}}$. Then use $\boxed{\triangle}$ to move the cursor to the top line beside "$y1 =$." Now press $\boxed{(}$ 18 $\boxed{-}$ 2 $\boxed{x\text{-VAR}}$ $\boxed{)}$ $\boxed{\div}$ 3 to enter the right-hand side of the equation. Note that without the parentheses the expression $18 - \dfrac{2x}{3}$ would have been entered.

You can edit your entry if necessary. If, for instance, you pressed 5 instead of 8, use the $\boxed{\triangleleft}$ key to move the cursor to 5 and then press 8 to overwrite it. If you forgot to type the right parenthesis, move the cursor to the division symbol /; then press $\boxed{\text{2nd}}$ $\boxed{\text{INS}}$ $\boxed{)}$ to insert the parenthesis before the division symbol. (INS is the second operation associated with the $\boxed{\text{DEL}}$ key.) You can continue to insert symbols immediately after the first insertion without pressing $\boxed{\text{2nd}}$ $\boxed{\text{INS}}$ again. If you typed 25 instead of 2, move the cursor to 5 and press $\boxed{\text{DEL}}$. This will delete the 5.

Once the equation is entered correctly, press $\boxed{\text{2nd}}$ $\boxed{\text{M2}}$ to select the RANGE menu and then select a viewing window. (M2 is the second operation associated with the $\boxed{\text{F2}}$ key.) Then press $\boxed{\text{F5}}$ to display the graph. You may change the viewing window as desired to reveal more or less of the graph. The standard window is shown here. The menus at the bottom of the window can be removed from the graph by pressing $\boxed{\text{CLEAR}}$. They will reappear when either $\boxed{\text{EXIT}}$ or $\boxed{\text{GRAPH}}$ is pressed.

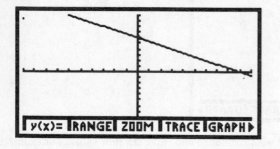
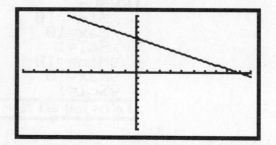

Example 8(c), page 8: To graph $x = y^2 + 1$, first solve the equation for y: $y = \pm\sqrt{x - 1}$. To obtain the entire graph of $x = y^2 + 1$, you must graph $y_1 = \sqrt{x - 1}$ and $y_2 = -\sqrt{x - 1}$ on the same screen. Press $\boxed{\text{GRAPH}}$ $\boxed{\text{F1}}$ to select the y(x) = menu and clear any expressions that currently appear. With the cursor beside "$y1 =$" press $\boxed{\text{2nd}}$ $\boxed{\sqrt{}}$ $\boxed{(}$ $\boxed{x\text{-VAR}}$ $\boxed{-}$ 1 $\boxed{)}$. ($\sqrt{}$ is the second operation associated with the $\boxed{x^2}$ key.) Note that if the parentheses had not been used, the equation entered would have been $y_1 = \sqrt{x} - 1$.

Now use $\boxed{\triangledown}$ to move the cursor beside "$y2 =$." If "$y2 =$" is not visible, press $\boxed{\triangledown}$ and it will appear. There are two ways to enter $y_2 = -\sqrt{x - 1}$. One way is to enter the expression $-\sqrt{x - 1}$ directly by pressing $\boxed{(-)}$ $\boxed{\text{2nd}}$ $\boxed{\sqrt{}}$ $\boxed{(}$ $\boxed{x\text{-VAR}}$ $\boxed{-}$

1 $\boxed{)}$.

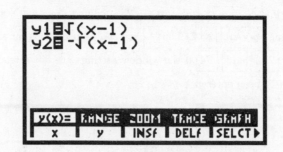

The other method of entering y_2 is based on the observation that $-\sqrt{x-1}$ is the opposite of the expression for y_1. That is, $y_2 = -y_1$. To enter this, place the cursor beside "$y2 =$" and press $\boxed{(-)}$ $\boxed{F2}$ 1. This enters the opposite of y_1 as the expression for y_2.

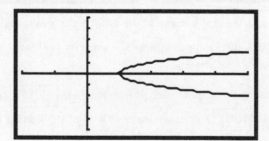

Press $\boxed{2nd}$ $\boxed{M2}$ to select the RANGE menu. Enter a viewing window and press $\boxed{F5}$ to display the graph. The window shown here is $[-2, 5, -5, 5]$, xScl $= 1$, yScl $= 1$.

The top half is the graph of y_1, the bottom half is the graph of y_2, and together they yield the graph of $x = y^2 + 1$.

SQUARING THE VIEWING WINDOW

In the standard window, the distance between tick marks on the y-axis is about $7/12$ the distance between tick marks on the x-axis. It is often desirable to choose window dimensions for which these distances are the same, creating a "square" window. Any window in which the ratio of the length of the y-axis to the length of the x-axis is $7/12$ will produce this effect. (The actual ratio of the distances is $73/124$ which is a little closer to $10/17$ than to $7/12$, but the last ratio is easier to work with than either of the other two and still gives a good representation.)

The desired ratio can be produced by selecting dimensions for which yMax $-$ yMin $= \dfrac{7}{12}$(xMax $-$ xMin). For example, the windows $[-12, 12, -7, 7]$ and $[-24, 24, -14, 14]$ are square. To illustrate this, graph the circle $x^2 + y^2 = 25$ in the standard window by first entering $y_1 = \sqrt{25 - x^2}$ and $y_2 = -\sqrt{25 - x^2}$ or $y_2 = -y_1$. Note that x^2 can be entered either by pressing $\boxed{x\text{-VAR}}$ $\boxed{x^2}$ or by pressing $\boxed{x\text{-VAR}}$ $\boxed{\wedge}$ 2. The $\boxed{\wedge}$ key can be used to enter any exponent, but for the exponent 2 the $\boxed{x^2}$ is more efficient. Press $\boxed{\text{2nd}}$ $\boxed{\text{M3}}$ $\boxed{\text{F4}}$ if the window settings are not already standard or press $\boxed{\text{2nd}}$ $\boxed{\text{M5}}$ if the standard settings have previously been entered.

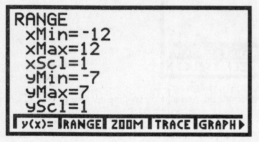
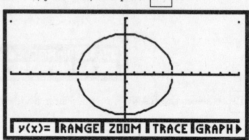

Note that the graph does not appear to be a circle.

Now change the window dimensions to $[-12, 12, -7, 7]$, xScl = 1, yScl = 1, and press $\boxed{\text{F5}}$.

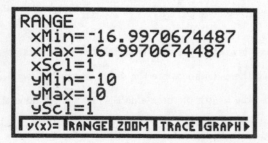
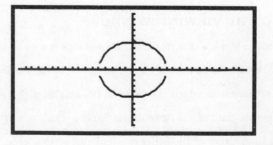

Although the software used to produce the graph shown above distorts the graph slightly, on your grapher screen you can observe that the distance between tick marks appears to be the same on both axes and that the graph appears to be a circle.

The window can also be squared using the grapher's ZSQR feature. Press $\boxed{\text{F3}}$ $\boxed{\text{F4}}$ to return to the graph of $x^2 + y^2 = 25$ in the standard window. Now press $\boxed{\text{MORE}}$ to display the next level of the ZOOM menus and then press $\boxed{\text{F2}}$ to select ZSQR. The resulting window dimensions and graph are shown below. Again, the software used to produce the graph introduces some distortion, but your grapher screen will show a graph that appears to be a circle.

IDENTITIES

An equation that is true for every possible real-number substitution for the variable is an identity. The grapher can be used to provide a partial check whether an equation is an identity.

Example 9 (a), page 11: Determine whether $(x^2)^3 = x^6$ appears to be an identity.

To determine whether this equation appears to be an identity, graph $y_1 = (x^2)^3$ and $y_2 = x^6$. Examine the graphs in several viewing windows. The graphs appear to coincide no matter what the window. Thus, although there is a possibility that the graphs fail to coincide outside the windows that were examined, the equation appears to be an identity.

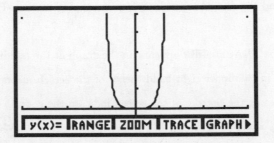

Example 9 (b), page 11: Determine whether $\sqrt{x+4} = \sqrt{x} + 2$ appears to be an identity.

To determine whether this equation appears to be an identity, graph $y_1 = \sqrt{x+4}$ and $y_2 = \sqrt{x} + 2$. Note that parentheses must be used when entering $\sqrt{x+4}$: $\boxed{\text{2nd}}$ $\boxed{\sqrt{}}$ $\boxed{(}$ $\boxed{x\text{-VAR}}$ $\boxed{+}$ $\boxed{4}$ $\boxed{)}$. Without parentheses the expression entered would be $\sqrt{x} + 4$.

Any window that includes a portion of the first quadrant will show that the graphs differ. Thus, the equation is not an identity.

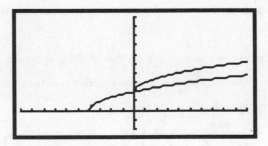

SOLVING EQUATIONS USING TRACE AND ZOOM

There are several techniques that can be used to solve equations with a grapher. One such technique uses the grapher's TRACE and ZOOM features.

Example 10, page 13: Solve $x^3 - 3x + 1 = 0$. Approximate the solutions to three decimal places.

The solutions of this equation are the first coordinates of the x-intercepts of the graph of $y = x^3 - 3x + 1$. To find these coordinates we first graph $y = x^3 - 3x + 1$ in a viewing window that shows all of the x-intercepts. Here we use the standard window, $[-10, 10, -10, 10]$.

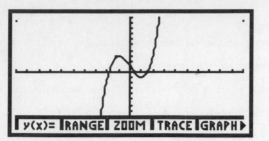

We see that x-intercepts occur near $x = -2$, $x = 0$, and $x = 2$. A portion of the viewing window can be enlarged near each of these values in order to find the desired three decimal place approximation. For example, let's examine the graph near $x = 0$.

Press $\boxed{\text{F4}}$ to select TRACE. The TRACE cursor appears on the graph at the middle x-value of the window, in this case at $x = 0$. The number 1 appears in the upper right-hand corner of the screen indicating that the cursor is on the graph of equation y_1. The x-and y-values at the bottom of the screen indicate the coordinates of the point where the cursor is positioned, in this case at $x = 0$, $y = 1$.

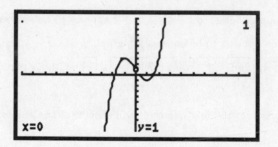

Pressing $\boxed{\triangleleft}$ or $\boxed{\triangleright}$ moves the cursor to the left or right along the curve. Note that the TRACE cursor always remains on the curve.

In order to find the middle x-intercept, we enlarge the portion of the graph near $x = 0$ by first positioning the cursor as close to this intercept as possible. That is, near $x = 0$, position the cursor as close as possible to $y = 0$. Press $\boxed{\text{EXIT}}$. Then press $\boxed{\text{F3}}$ $\boxed{\text{F2}}$ $\boxed{\text{ENTER}}$ to zoom in on the graph near $x = 0$.

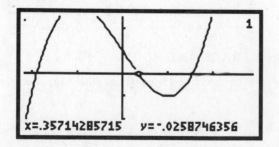

Press $\boxed{\text{GRAPH}}$ $\boxed{\text{F4}}$ to select TRACE again and move the cursor as close as possible to $y = 0$ near $x = 0$. Now press $\boxed{\text{EXIT}}$ $\boxed{\text{F3}}$ $\boxed{\text{F2}}$ $\boxed{\text{ENTER}}$ again to enlarge this portion of the graph further.

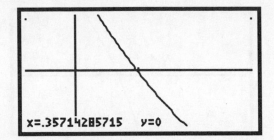

x=.3571428571S   y=0

Continue tracing and zooming in until the x-values determined by positioning the cursor just to the left and just to the right of the x-intercept are the same when rounded to three decimal places. We find that $x \approx 0.347$ at the middle x-intercept. This is one solution of the equation $x^3 - 3x + 1 = 0$.

To find a second solution of the equation press $\boxed{\text{GRAPH}}$ $\boxed{\text{F3}}$ $\boxed{\text{F4}}$ to return to the standard window; then trace to a position on the curve near another x-intercept and zoom in as described above. Continue to trace and zoom in until the desired accuracy is obtained. Repeat this process to find the third solution. The other two solutions are about -1.879 and 1.532.

At any point in this process, we can zoom out to the previous window by pressing $\boxed{\text{GRAPH}}$ $\boxed{\text{F3}}$ $\boxed{\text{F3}}$ $\boxed{\text{ENTER}}$. This can be repeated as many times as desired.

The ZOOM BOX operation can also be used to enlarge a portion of the viewing window. We select diagonally opposed corners of a box that defines the new window. For example, graph $y = x^3 - 3x + 1$ in the standard window. Either one or two rows of menus will appear at the bottom of the screen, depending on the order in which the graph and the window were chosen. If one row appears, press $\boxed{\text{F3}}$ $\boxed{\text{F1}}$ to access the BOX operation. If there are two rows, press $\boxed{\text{F1}}$ to select Box. Then move the cursor from the center of the screen to any corner of the box to be defined. Note that the cursor used in this operation is a free-moving cursor. That is, it can be positioned at any point on the screen as opposed to the trace cursor whose position is restricted to points on the graph.

Press $\boxed{\text{ENTER}}$ and a small square dot appears, indicating that the first corner has been selected. Now use $\boxed{\triangleleft}$, $\boxed{\triangleright}$, $\boxed{\triangle}$, and/or $\boxed{\triangledown}$ to move the cursor to the corner of the box diagonally opposite this one. As you move the cursor away from the first corner the boundaries of the box appear on the screen and change as the position of the cursor changes.

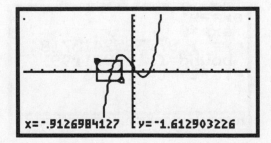

x=⁻.9126984127   y=⁻1.612903226

When the box is defined as you want it, press $\boxed{\text{ENTER}}$ to show only the portion of the graph in the box.

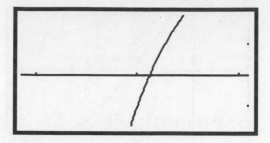

Now we can zoom in or use ZOOM BOX again to further enlarge a portion of the graph.

SOLVING EQUATIONS USING SOLVER

The SOLVER operation can be used to solve equations. An equation need not be written with 0 on one side of the equals sign when this operation is used.

Example 10, page 13: Solve $x^3 - 3x + 1 = 0$. Approximate the solutions to three decimal places.

Begin as in the procedure described above for using TRACE and ZOOM by graphing $y = x^3 - 3x + 1$ in a window that shows all of the x-intercepts. Note again that the x-intercepts occur near $x = -2$, $x = 0$, and $x = 2$. We will first find the solution near $x = -2$.

Access the SOLVER operation by pressing $\boxed{\text{2nd}}$ $\boxed{\text{SOLVER}}$. (SOLVER is the second operation associated with the $\boxed{\text{GRAPH}}$ key.) The notation "eqn:" appears on the screen with the blinking cursor positioned to the right of the colon. If an expression appears on this line, delete it by pressing $\boxed{\text{CLEAR}}$. Then since the equation has already been entered on the "y(x) =" screen as $y1$, we can enter it here by pressing $\boxed{\text{F4}}$ $\boxed{\text{ENTER}}$. It can also be entered by pressing $\boxed{x\text{-VAR}}$ $\boxed{\wedge}$ 3 $\boxed{-}$ 3 $\boxed{x\text{-VAR}}$ $\boxed{+}$ 1 $\boxed{\text{ENTER}}$. Note that we have entered the expression $x^3 - 3x + 1$ rather than the equation $x^3 - 3x + 1 = 0$. The SOLVER edit screen now appears with the blinking cursor positioned to the right of the notation "exp =." Since we are seeking the values of x for which the expression $x^3 - 3x + 1$ is equal to 0, type 0 $\boxed{\text{ENTER}}$ here. The cursor now appears beside "$x =$," where a guess for the solution should be entered. Since we are seeking the solution near $x = -2$, type $\boxed{(-)}$ 2 here. Press $\boxed{\text{F5}}$ to select the SOLVE operation. The grapher returns the value -1.8793852415718. Thus one solution is about -1.879. Note that the cursor must be positioned on the "$x =$" line when SOLVE is selected.

To find the solution near $x = 0$ clear the solution that was just found. This is the entry beside "$x =$." Now enter 0 on this line and press $\boxed{\text{F5}}$ to solve again. The grapher returns the value $.34729635533385$. To find the solution near $x = 2$, repeat the previous process, entering 2 on the "$x =$" line. The value 1.5320888862379 is returned. Thus, as we saw before, the other two solutions are about 0.347 and 1.532.

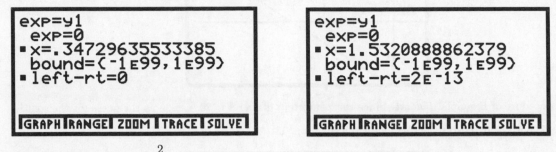

Example 12, page 15: Solve: $\frac{2}{3}x - 7 = 5$.

The most direct option is to graph is to graph $y_1 = \frac{2}{3}x - 7$ and $y_2 = 5$ in a window that shows the point of intersection of the graphs. Here we use $[-5, 30, -10, 10]$, xScl $= 5$, yScl $= 1$.

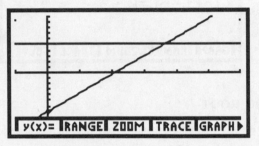

Now press $\boxed{\text{2nd}}$ $\boxed{\text{SOLVER}}$ to access the SOLVER operation. Since $\frac{2}{3}x - 7$ and 5 have already been entered in the "y(x) =" screen as $y1$ and $y2$, respectively, enter $y1 = y2$ beside "eqn:" by pressing $\boxed{\text{F4}}$ $\boxed{\text{ALPHA}}$ $\boxed{=}$ $\boxed{\text{F5}}$. (= is the ALPHA operation associated with the $\boxed{\text{STO}\triangleright}$ key.) We could also enter $\frac{2}{3}x - 7 = 5$ directly by pressing $\boxed{(}$ $\boxed{2}$ $\boxed{\div}$ $\boxed{3}$ $\boxed{)}$ $\boxed{x\text{-VAR}}$ $\boxed{-}$ 7 $\boxed{\text{ALPHA}}$ $\boxed{=}$ 5. Now press enter and the cursor appears beside "$x =$," where a guess for the solution should be entered. The graph shows that the point of intersection is near $x = 20$, so we enter 20 for the guess. Then, with the cursor on the "$x =$" line, press $\boxed{\text{F5}}$ to select SOLVE. The grapher returns the solution, 18.

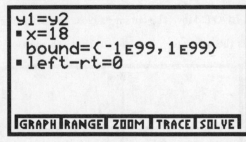

Another option is to write the equation with 0 on one side of the equals sign: $\frac{2}{3}x - 7 - 5 = 0$, or $\frac{2}{3}x - 12 = 0$. Then graph $y = \frac{2}{3}x - 12$ in a window that shows the x-intercept. Here we use $[-5, 35, -10, 10]$, xScl $= 5$, yScl $= 2$.

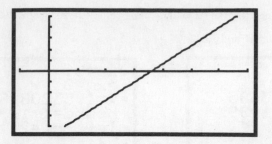

Repeat the procedure of Example 10 above. Since the x-intercept is near $x = 20$, use 20 as the guess for the solution on the "$x =$" line. The grapher returns the solution of the equation, 18.

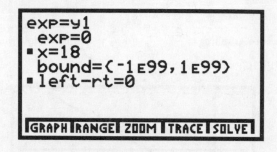

SOLVING EQUATIONS USING ROOT

A solution of an equation with zero on one side is usually called a zero, but is sometimes called a root. The ROOT operation can also be used to solve an equation.

Example 10, page 13: Solve $x^3 - 3x + 1 = 0$. Approximate the solutions to three decimal places.

Graph $y = x^3 - 3x + 1$ in the standard window as before. We will use ROOT to find the solution of $x^3 - 3x + 1 = 0$ near $x = 0$. Access the ROOT operation by pressing $\boxed{\text{MORE}}$ $\boxed{\text{F1}}$ to select the MATH menu. Now the choices LOWER, UPPER, and ROOT appear on the screen below the graph. Press $\boxed{\text{F1}}$ to select LOWER. Position the cursor just to the left of the x-intercept near 0 and press $\boxed{\text{ENTER}}$. Then press $\boxed{\text{F2}}$ to select UPPER. Position the cursor just to the right of the intercept and press $\boxed{\text{ENTER}}$ again. The upper and lower bounds are indicated by two delineators shown near the top of the screen. Now press $\boxed{\text{F3}}$ to select ROOT. Move the cursor as close to the x-intercept as possible and press $\boxed{\text{ENTER}}$. The x-value that the grapher returns is the solution. We see again that the solution is about 0.347.

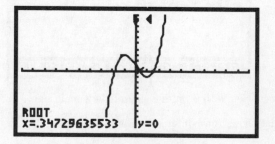

The other two solutions of the equation can be found by using the ROOT operation two more times.

FINDING POINTS OF INTERSECTION

There are several ways in which the grapher can be used to determine the point(s) of intersection of two graphs.

Example 11, page 14: Find the point of intersection of the graphs of the equations $y_1 = 3x^5 - 20x^3$ and $y_2 = 34.7 - 1.28x^2$. Approximate the coordinates to three decimal places.

First graph the equations in a window that shows all of the points of intersection. We use $[-4, 4, -80, 80]$, $xScl = 1$, $yScl = 20$ here.

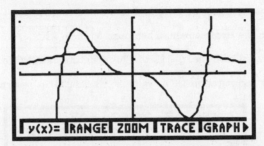

There are three points of intersection. One way to find their coordinates is to use TRACE and ZOOM. (See "Solving Equations Using Trace and Zoom" on page 91 of this manual.) Another method is to use the ISECT operation. We will illustrate its use by finding the point of intersection at the far left. After graphing y_1 and y_2 as above, access ISECT by pressing $\boxed{\text{MORE}}$ $\boxed{\text{F1}}$ to select MATH. Set the lower and upper bounds as described in the previous example. Then press $\boxed{\text{MORE}}$ $\boxed{\text{F5}}$ to select ISECT. The cursor appears on the graph of y_1. Press $\boxed{\text{ENTER}}$. The cursor moves to the next function, y_2. Move the cursor as close as possible to the point of intersection and press $\boxed{\text{ENTER}}$ again. The grapher returns the coordinates of the point of intersection. We see that they are about $(-2.463, 26.936)$.

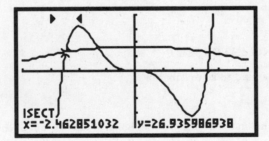

The coordinates of the other two points of intersection can be found by using the ISECT operation two more times.

The SOLVER feature can also be used to find the x-coordinates of the points of intersection by finding solutions of $y_1 = y_2$. Again it is necessary to graph y_1 and y_2 in order to find guesses for the solutions.

To find the point of intersection on the far left, first note that its x-coordinate is about -2.5. This is the value we will use for the guess. Press $\boxed{\text{2nd}}$ $\boxed{\text{SOLVER}}$ then $\boxed{\text{F4}}$ $\boxed{\text{ALPHA}}$ $\boxed{=}$ $\boxed{\text{F5}}$ $\boxed{\text{ENTER}}$ to enter $y_1 = y_2$ beside "eqn:." Now type -2.5 following "$x =$." Press $\boxed{\text{F5}}$ to select SOLVE. The grapher returns the value -2.4628510317595. This is the first coordinate of the point of intersection.

This value must be substituted into either y_1 or y_2 to find the second coordinate. To substitute in y_1 after using SOLVE first press 2nd QUIT to return to the Home screen. Then press 3 2nd ANS ∧ 5 − 20 2nd ANS ∧ 3 ENTER. (ANS is the second operation associated with the (−) key. This operation recalls the answer to the previous computation, thus allowing it to be used in a new computation.) The value 26.9359869381 is returned.

```
3 Ans^5-20 Ans^3
            26.9359869381
■
```

Thus, we see that the coordinates of the point of intersection are about $(-2.463, 26.936)$. If we had used the rounded x-value of -2.463 in y_1 to compute the corresponding y-value, the result would have been 26.908. If we had used the rounded x-value in y_2, the resulting y-value would have been 26.935. To achieve the greatest accuracy, then, it is important to use the unrounded x-value in this computation.

SOLVING EQUATIONS USING INTERSECT

The ISECT operation can also be used to solve equations.

Example 12, page 15: Solve: $\frac{2}{3}x - 7 = 5$.

The solution of this equation is the first coordinate of the point of intersection of the graphs of $y_1 = \frac{2}{3}x - 7$ and $y_2 = 5$. Thus, we graph these equations in a window that shows the point of intersection and use ISECT as described in "Finding Points of Intersection" on page 97 of this manual. The x-coordinate of the point of intersection is 18. This is the solution of the equation.

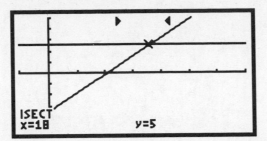

SELECTING DOT MODE

When graphing an equation in which a variable appears in a denominator, DrawDot mode should be used. To select this mode press GRAPH MORE F3 to select FORMT (format) and use ▽ and ▷ to position the blinking cursor over "DrawDot." Then press ENTER.

```
RectGC  PolarGC
CoordOn CoordOff
DrawLine DrawDot
SeqG    SimulG
GridOff GridOn
AxesOn  AxesOff
LabelOff LabelOn
y(x)= RANGE ZOOM TRACE GRAPH▶
```

See page 16 in the text for further explanation of why DrawDot mode is used in certain cases and for an illustration of an equation graphed in both DrawLine (or CONNECTED) and DrawDot (or DOT) modes.

Chapter R
Basic Concepts of Algebra

SCIENTIFIC NOTATION

To enter a number in scientific notation, first type the decimal portion of the number; then press $\boxed{\text{EE}}$. Finally type the exponent, which can be at most three digits. For example, to enter 1.789×10^{-11} in scientific notation, press 1 $\boxed{\cdot}$ 7 9 $\boxed{\text{EE}}$ $\boxed{(-)}$ 1 1. To enter 6.084×10^{23} in scientific notation, press 6 $\boxed{\cdot}$ 0 8 4 $\boxed{\text{EE}}$ 2 3. The decimal portion of each number appears before a small E while the exponent follows the E.

```
6.084E23
```

To use the grapher to convert from decimal notation to scientific notation, first select Scientific mode by pressing $\boxed{\text{2nd}}$ $\boxed{\text{MODE}}$ $\boxed{\triangleright}$ $\boxed{\text{ENTER}}$.

Example 3, page 28 (Page numbers refer to pages in the textbook.): Convert 38,500,000,000 to scientific notation.

With the grapher in Scientific mode, type 38500000000 followed by $\boxed{\text{ENTER}}$. The grapher returns 3.85E10, indicating that the scientific notation is 3.85×10^{10}.

Example 4, page 28: Convert 0.00000000000000000000000000167 to scientific notation.

With the grapher in Scientific mode, type .00000000000000000000000000167 $\boxed{\text{ENTER}}$. The grapher returns 1.67E−27, indicating that the scientific notation is 1.67×10^{-27}.

```
Normal Sci Eng
Float 012345678901
Radian Degree
RectC PolarC
Func Pol Param DifEq
Dec Bin Oct Hex
RectV CylV SphereV
dxDer1 dxNDer
```

```
38500000000
                3.85E10
.00000000000000000000
000000167
                1.67E-27
```

Even if Normal mode is selected for a computation, the TI-85 will display results less than 0.001 or greater than or equal to 999,999,999,999.5 in scientific notation. Thus, the only numbers that can be converted to decimal notation using this grapher are those within this range.

To use the grapher to convert from scientific notation to decimal notation, first set the grapher in Normal mode. Then type a number using scientific notation as described above, followed by ENTER .

Example 5 (a), page 28: Convert 7.632×10^{-4} to decimal notation.

Since $7.632 \times 10^{-4} < 0.001$, the grapher cannot be used for this conversion. To confirm this, with the grapher set in Normal mode, press 7 $\cdot$ 6 3 2 EE (−) 4 ENTER . The grapher returns scientific notation rather than decimal notation.

Example 5 (b), page 28: Convert 9.4×10^5 to decimal notation.

Since $0.001 \le 9.4 \times 10^5 \le 999,999,999,999.5$, the grapher can be used to make this conversion. With the grapher set in Normal mode, press 9 $\cdot$ 4 EE 5 ENTER . The grapher returns decimal notation, 940000.

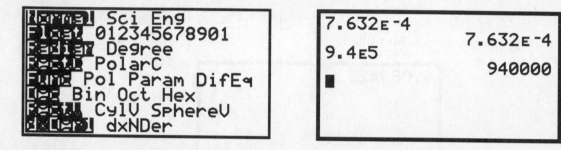

To express the result of a computation in scientific notation, set the grapher in Scientific mode before performing the computation.

EXPRESSIONS WITH RATIONAL EXPONENTS

When using the TI-85 to find real-number roots of the form $a^{m/n}$, where $a < 0$, m and n are natural numbers with no common factors other than 1, and $m > 1$, we must enter the expression as $((a)^m)^{1/n}$ or $((a)^{1/n})^m$. Similarly, to graph $y = x^{m/n}$, enter $y = ((x)^m)^{1/n}$ or $y = ((x)^{1/n})^m$. To illustrate this, first enter $(-8)^{4/3}$. The grapher returns a representation for a non-real complex number rather than the real-number value 16. (Complex numbers will be introduced in Chapter 2 of the text.) Now enter $((-8)^4)^{1/3}$ and $((-8)^{1/3})^4$. In each case the result is 16.

```
((-8)^4)^(1/3)
                          16
((-8)^(1/3))^4
                          16
■
```

Now graph $y_1 = x^{4/3}$. Notice that the graph contains no points corresponding to negative x-values.

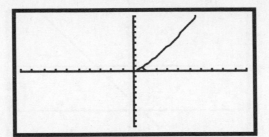

Then graph $y_1 = (x^4)^{1/3}$. This graph includes negative as well as nonnegative x-values. The same result is obtained for $y_1 = (x^{1/3})^4$.

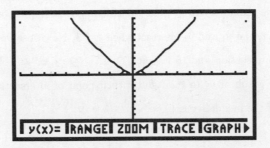

CHECKING SOLUTIONS OF INEQUALITIES

Solutions of inequalities can be checked graphically.

Example 1 (b), page 67: The possible solution set of $13 - 7y \geq 10y - 4$ is $\{y|y \leq 1\}$. Check with a grapher.

Replace y with x and graph $y_1 = 13 - 7x$ and $y_2 = 10x - 4$ in a window that shows the point of intersection of the graphs. The standard window is shown here.

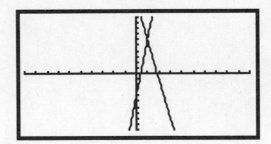

Now use ISECT or TRACE and ZOOM to find the first coordinate of the point of intersection, 1. Then observe that the graph of y_1 lies on or above the graph of y_2 at the point of intersection and to its left. That is, $y_1 \geq y_2$, or $13 - 7x \geq 10x - 4$, for $\{x|x \leq 1\}$. Thus, the solution set of the original inequality, $13 - 7y \geq 10y - 4$, is $\{y|y \leq 1\}$.

Example 4, page 70: The possible solution set of $2x - 5 \leq -7$ *or* $2x - 5 > 1$ is $(-\infty, -1] \cup (3, \infty)$. Check with a grapher.

Graph $y_1 = 2x - 5$, $y_2 = -7$, and $y_3 = 1$ in a window that shows the points of intersection of the graphs. The standard window is shown here.

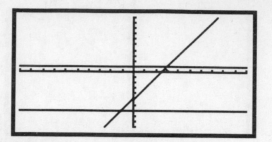

Now use ISECT or TRACE and ZOOM to find the first coordinates of the points of intersection. Since the graphs of more than two functions appear on the screen, when using ISECT to find the point of intersection of y_1 and y_3 it might be necessary to use ▽ or △ to move the cursor to y_3 before positioning it near the point of intersection.

When $x = -1$, y_1 and y_2 intersect, and y_1 and y_3 intersect when $x = 3$. Now observe that the graph of y_1 lies on or below the graph of y_2 at their point of intersection and to its left. Thus, $y_1 \leq y_2$, or $2x - 5 \leq -7$, on $(-\infty, -1]$. Also observe that the graph of y_1 lies above the graph of y_3 to the right of their point of intersection. That is, $y_1 > y_3$, or $2x - 5 > 1$, on $(3, \infty)$. Then the solution set of the inequality is $(-\infty, -1] \cup (3, \infty)$.

Chapter 1
Graphs, Functions, and Models

FINDING FUNCTION VALUES

When a formula for a function is given, function values for real-numbered inputs can be found in several ways on a grapher.

Example 4 (a), (b), page 87 (Page numbers refer to pages in the textbook.): For $f(x) = 2x^2 - x + 3$, find $f(0)$ and $f(-7)$.

Method 1: Substitute the inputs directly in the formula. For example, to find $f(0)$ press 2 $\boxed{\times}$ 0 $\boxed{x^2}$ $\boxed{-}$ 0 $\boxed{+}$ 3 $\boxed{\text{ENTER}}$.
To find $f(-7)$ press 2 $\boxed{(}$ $\boxed{(-)}$ 7 $\boxed{)}$ $\boxed{x^2}$ $\boxed{-}$ $\boxed{(}$ $\boxed{(-)}$ 7 $\boxed{)}$ $\boxed{+}$ 3 $\boxed{\text{ENTER}}$.

```
2*0²-0+3
                        3
2(-7)²-(-7)+3
                     108
■
```

Method 2: Enter $y_1 = 2x^2 - x + 3$ in the "y(x) =" screen. Then press $\boxed{\text{2nd}}$ $\boxed{\text{QUIT}}$ to go to the home screen. (QUIT is the second operation associated with the $\boxed{\text{EXIT}}$ key.) Now to find $f(0)$, the value of y_1 when $x = 0$, press 0 $\boxed{\text{STO} \triangleright}$ $\boxed{x\text{-VAR}}$ $\boxed{\text{2nd}}$ $\boxed{:}$ $\boxed{\text{2nd}}$ $\boxed{\text{VARS}}$ $\boxed{\text{MORE}}$ $\boxed{\text{F3}}$ to select EQU. Then use $\boxed{\triangledown}$ to move the triangular selection indicator beside $y1$ and press $\boxed{\text{ENTER}}$ $\boxed{\text{ENTER}}$. (: is the second operation associated with the $\boxed{\cdot}$ key. $\boxed{\text{VARS}}$ is the second operation associated with the $\boxed{3}$ key.) This series of keystrokes stores 0 as the value of x and then substitutes it in the function y_1. To find the function value at $x = -7$, repeat this process, using -7 in place of 0 or press $\boxed{\text{2nd}}$ $\boxed{\text{ENTRY}}$ to recall the previous entry, move the cursor to 0, and replace 0 with -7. Note that since two keystrokes are required to enter -7, it is necessary to use $\boxed{\text{2nd}}$ $\boxed{\text{INS}}$ to change 0 to -7. That is, with the cursor on 0 press $\boxed{(-)}$ $\boxed{\text{2nd}}$ $\boxed{\text{INS}}$ 7 $\boxed{\text{ENTER}}$ to make this change.

```
0→x:y1
                        3
-7→x:y1
                     108
```

Method 3: Enter $y_1 = 2x^2 - x + 3$ in the "y(x) =" screen and press $\boxed{\text{2nd}}$ $\boxed{\text{QUIT}}$ to go to the home screen. Then, to find

$f(0)$ press [2nd] [MATH] [F5] to select MISC. (MATH is the second operation associated with the [×] key.) Then press [MORE] [F5] to select "eval" followed by 0 [ENTER]. To find $f(-7)$ either repeat this process entering -7 in place of 0 or recall the first entry and replace 0 with -7 and press [ENTER].

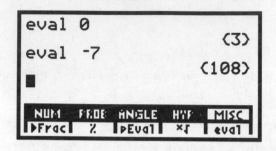

GRAPHING FUNCTIONS DEFINED PIECEWISE

Operations from the TEST menu are used to enter functions that are defined piecewise. (TEST is the second operation associated with the [2] key.) Select DrawDot mode from the FORMT menu after pressing [GRAPH] [MORE] when graphing such functions.

Example 4, page 102: Graph

$$f(x) = \begin{cases} 4, & \text{for } x \le 0, \\ 4 - x^2, & \text{for } 0 < x \le 2, \\ 2x - 6, & \text{for } x > 2, \end{cases}$$

Press [GRAPH] [F1] to select y(x) = and clear any functions that have previously been entered. With the cursor beside "$y1 =$" enter the function as described in the middle of page 102 of the text by pressing [(] [4] [)] [(] [x-VAR] [2nd] [TEST] [F4] [0] [)] [+] [(] [4] [−] [x-VAR] [x^2] [)] [(] [0] [F2] [x-VAR] [)] [(] [x-VAR] [F4] [2] [)] [+] [(] [2] [x-VAR] [−] [6] [)] [(] [x-VAR] [F3] [2] [)]. Select a window and then press [GRAPH].

Example 6, page 103: Graph $f(x) = \text{INT}(x)$.

With the grapher set in DrawDot mode, press [GRAPH] [F1] to select y(x) = and clear any previously entered functions. Position the cursor beside "$y1 =$" and select the greatest integer function from the MATH NUM menu as follows. Press [2nd] [MATH] [F1] to select NUM. Then press [F4] to select int followed by [x-VAR]. Now press [EXIT] to return to the menu that allows you to select a window and graph the function.

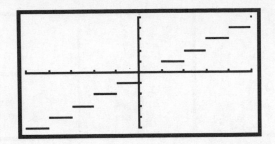

GRAPHING VERTICAL LINES

Although equations of vertical lines cannot be entered in the grapher in "y(x) =" form, vertical lines can be graphed using the DRAW feature or by typing an instruction on the home screen. DRAW is accessed by pressing $\boxed{\text{GRAPH}}$ $\boxed{\text{MORE}}$.

Interactive Discovery, top of page 120: Graph $x = -5$ and $x = 2$.

To graph $x = -5$ using the DRAW feature, first press $\boxed{\text{GRAPH}}$ $\boxed{\text{F1}}$ to select y(x) = and clear all previously entered equations. Then select a window. On the RANGE screen press $\boxed{\text{MORE}}$ $\boxed{\text{F2}}$ to select DRAW. Then press $\boxed{\text{F3}}$ to select VERT. Use $\boxed{\triangleleft}$ and $\boxed{\triangleright}$ to position the cursor where the line should be located and press $\boxed{\text{ENTER}}$. To graph $x = 2$ on the same screen use $\boxed{\triangleright}$ and $\boxed{\triangleleft}$ to reposition the cursor and press $\boxed{\text{ENTER}}$.

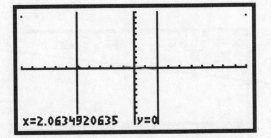

As the coordinates at the bottom of the window indicate, this method does not allow precise placement of vertical lines. Vertical lines can be placed precisely by drawing them from the home screen as described below. First clear the drawings shown above from the screen by pressing $\boxed{\text{GRAPH}}$ $\boxed{\text{MORE}}$ $\boxed{\text{F2}}$ or $\boxed{\text{EXIT}}$ $\boxed{\text{2nd}}$ $\boxed{\text{M2}}$ to access the DRAW menu. Then press $\boxed{\text{MORE}}$ $\boxed{\text{F5}}$ to select the CLDRW (clear drawing) operation.

To graph $x = -5$ from the home screen, first press $\boxed{\text{GRAPH}}$ $\boxed{\text{F1}}$ to select y(x) = and clear all previously entered equations. Then select a window. Now press $\boxed{\text{2nd}}$ $\boxed{\text{QUIT}}$ to go to the home screen. Press $\boxed{\text{ALPHA}}$ $\boxed{\text{ALPHA}}$ to lock in the uppercase ALPHA keys and type VERT; press $\boxed{(-)}$ to provide a space, then $\boxed{\text{ALPHA}}$ to unlock the uppercase ALPHA keys. Press $\boxed{(-)}$ 5 $\boxed{\text{ENTER}}$ to see the graph of $x = -5$. To graph $x = -5$ and $x = 2$ on the same screen, after pressing $\boxed{\text{ENTER}}$ press $\boxed{\text{2nd}}$ $\boxed{\text{QUIT}}$ $\boxed{\text{2nd}}$ $\boxed{\text{ENTRY}}$. Then edit this entry to change -5 to 2 and press $\boxed{\text{ENTER}}$.

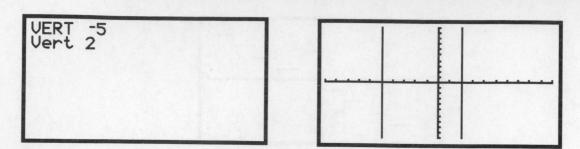

These lines can be cleared from the graph screen using the DRAW menu as described above. Whether graphed using DRAW or from the home screen, graphs of vertical lines will also be cleared when another function is subsequently entered on the "y(x) =" screen and graphed.

LINEAR REGRESSION AND SCATTERPLOTS

The linear regression operation of the grapher enables us to fit a linear function to a set of data.

Example 1, page 129: Fit a regression line to the data on life expectancy of women on page 128 of the text. Then predict the life expectancy of women in 2000.

First we enter the data from the table on the STAT list editor screen. To clear any existing lists press $\boxed{\text{STAT}}$ $\boxed{\text{F2}}$ $\boxed{\text{ENTER}}$ $\boxed{\text{ENTER}}$ $\boxed{\text{F5}}$ to select CLRxy.

```
x=xStat        y=yStat
 X1=█
 y1=1



  CALC   EDIT  DRAW  FCST
 INSi  DELi  SORTX SORTY CLRxy
```

To enter the first x-value press 0 $\boxed{\text{ENTER}}$; type the first y value to the right of "$y_1 =$" and press $\boxed{\text{ENTER}}$. Press 1 $\boxed{\text{ENTER}}$ to enter the second x-value and then type the second y value to the right of "$y_2 =$." Press $\boxed{\text{ENTER}}$ and continue in this manner until all pairs of data are entered. However, do not press $\boxed{\text{ENTER}}$ after the last y-value.

Press $\boxed{\text{2nd}}$ $\boxed{\text{M1}}$ to select CALC. Then press $\boxed{\text{ENTER}}$ $\boxed{\text{ENTER}}$ $\boxed{\text{F2}}$ to select LINR and display the coefficients a and b of the regression line $y = a + bx$, the coefficient of linear correlation (denoted "corr"), and the number of data points, n.

```
LinR
 a=50.6545454545
 b=3.42787878788
 corr=.986124753829
 n=10

  CALC  EDIT  DRAW  FCST
 1-VAR  LINR  LNR  EXPR  PWRR ▶
```

To see a scatterplot of the data press $\boxed{\text{2nd}}$ $\boxed{\text{M3}}$ to select DRAW and then $\boxed{\text{F2}}$ to select SCAT. To draw the regression line on the same screen as the scatterplot press $\boxed{\text{F4}}$ to select DRREG.

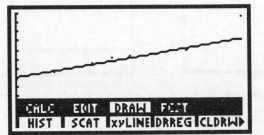

To enter the regression equation as y_1 in the "y(x) =" screen, with the CALC menu and the LinR screen still displayed, press $\boxed{\text{MORE}}$ $\boxed{\text{F4}}$ to select STREG (store regression). Then type $y1$ to the right of the blinking cursor beside "Name =" by pressing $\boxed{\text{2nd}}$ $\boxed{\text{alpha}}$ $\boxed{y}$ $\boxed{\text{2nd}}$ $\boxed{\text{alpha}}$ $\boxed{1}$ $\boxed{\text{ENTER}}$. (alpha is the second operation associated with the ALPHA key. It is used when we want to type lowercase letters.)

To predict the life expectancy of women in 2000 find the value of y_1 when $x = 10$ using one of the methods described in "Finding Function Values" on page 105 of this manual.

GRAPHING CIRCLES

Although the standard form of the equation of a circle cannot be entered in the "y(x) =" screen, the TI-85 can be used to graph circles. A square viewing window is required to give an accurate graph using either of the methods discussed below.

Method 1: We begin by solving the equation for y.

Example 5, page 138: Graph $x^2 + y^2 = 16$.

Solve the equation for y as shown on page 138 of the text, enter $y_1 = \sqrt{16 - x^2}$ and $y_2 = -\sqrt{16 - x^2}$, select a square window, and press $\boxed{\text{GRAPH}}$. Note that we can enter $y_2 = -y_1$ instead of $y_2 = -\sqrt{16 - x^2}$. The graph is shown on page 138 of the text.

Method 2: If the center and radius of a circle are known, the circle can be graphed by typing an instruction on the home screen.

Exercise 37, page 139: Graph $(x - 1)^2 + (y - 5)^2 = 36$.

The center of this circle is (1,5) and its radius is 6. To graph it using the DRAW feature first press $\boxed{\text{GRAPH}}$ $\boxed{\text{F1}}$ to select y(x) = and clear all previously entered equations. Then select a square window. We will use $[-12, 12, -2, 12]$. Press $\boxed{\text{2nd}}$ $\boxed{\text{QUIT}}$ to go to the home screen. Now press $\boxed{\text{ALPHA}}$ $\boxed{\text{ALPHA}}$ and type CIRCL. Press $\boxed{\text{ALPHA}}$ $\boxed{(}$. Enter the coordinates of the center and the radius, separating the entries by commas, and close the parentheses: $\boxed{1}$ $\boxed{,}$ $\boxed{5}$ $\boxed{,}$ $\boxed{6}$ $\boxed{)}$ $\boxed{\text{ENTER}}$.

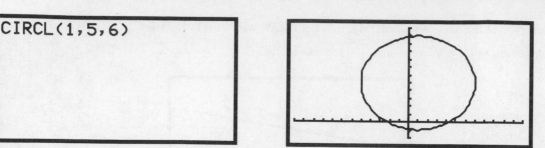

As before, the software used to produce the the graph above causes distortion. Nevertheless, when the circle is graphed on a grapher in a square window, there is no distortion.

A circle graphed from the home screen can be cleared from the graph screen by pressing $\boxed{\text{MORE}}$ $\boxed{\text{F2}}$ to access the DRAW menu. Then press $\boxed{\text{MORE}}$ $\boxed{\text{F5}}$ to select the CLDRW (clear drawing) operation. The graph will also be cleared when another function is subsequently entered on the "y(x) =" screen and graphed.

A circle can also graphed using the DRAW feature, but this method does not yield as accurate a graph as the other two methods.

Note that the equation of a circle that is not centered at the origin, like the one in Example 37 above, is generally not easily solved for y, making Method 2 preferable for such equations. In fact, since there is no need to solve for y using this method, it provides a quick procedure for graphing the equation of any circle in standard form.

THE ALGEBRA OF FUNCTIONS

The grapher can be used to evaluate and graph combinations of functions.

Example 1 (b), page 159: Given that $f(x) = x + 1$ and $g(x) = \sqrt{x+3}$, find $(f+g)(6)$.

Press $\boxed{\text{GRAPH}}$ $\boxed{\text{F1}}$ to select y(x) = and enter $y_1 = x + 1$, $y_2 = \sqrt{x+3}$, and $y_3 = y_1 + y_2$. To enter $y_3 = y_1 + y_2$ press $\boxed{\text{F2}}$ 1 $\boxed{+}$ $\boxed{\text{F2}}$ 2. Note that $y_3 = f(x) + g(x)$, or $(f+g)(x)$. Use y_3 to find $(f+g)(6)$ using one of the methods for finding function values described on page 105 of this manual. We find that $(f+g)(6) = 10$.

To view the graphs of $f(x)$, $g(x)$, and $(f+g)(x)$ enter y_1, y_2, and y_3 as above, select a window, and press $\boxed{\text{F5}}$ to select GRAPH. These graphs appear on page 159 of the text. It is possible to deselect one or two of these functions and display the graph(s) of the remaining function(s). For example, to display only the graph of y_3 without deleting the equations of y_1 and y_2, press $\boxed{\text{F1}}$ to select y(x) =. Then move the cursor to y_1 and press $\boxed{\text{F5}}$ to select SELCT. This deselects or turns off y_1. Do the same for y_2. Now press $\boxed{\text{2nd}}$ $\boxed{\text{M5}}$ to select GRAPH and see only the graph of y_3.

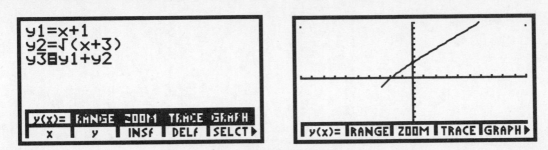

To select or turn on a function again, repeat this process. The SELECT operation reverses the selection status of a function. That is, it deselects a selected function and selects a deselected function. Note that the equals sign on a selected function is highlighted.

Example 3 (a), page 162: Given that $f(x) = 2x - 5$ and $g(x) = x^2 - 3x + 8$, find $(f \circ g)(7)$ and $(g \circ f)(7)$.

Press $\boxed{\text{GRAPH}}$ $\boxed{\text{F1}}$ to select y(x) = and enter $y_1 = 2x - 5$, $y_2 = x^2 - 3x + 8$, $y_3 = 2y_2 - 5$, and $y_4 = y_1^2 - 3y_1 + 8$. Use the y menu operation as described in Example 1(b) above to enter y_3 and y_4. Note that $y_3 = (f \circ g)(x)$ and $y_4 = (g \circ f)(x)$. Use y_3 and y_4 to find $(f \circ g)(7)$ and $(g \circ f)(7)$, respectively, employing one of the methods for finding function values described on page 105 of this manual. Note that when we use the "eval" operation from the MATH menu with all four of the functions y_1, y_2, y_3, and y_4 selected, then the last two values displayed correspond to $y_3(7)$ and $y_4(7)$, respectively, or to $(f \circ g)(7)$ and $(g \circ f)(7)$. This situation is shown in the figure on the right below.

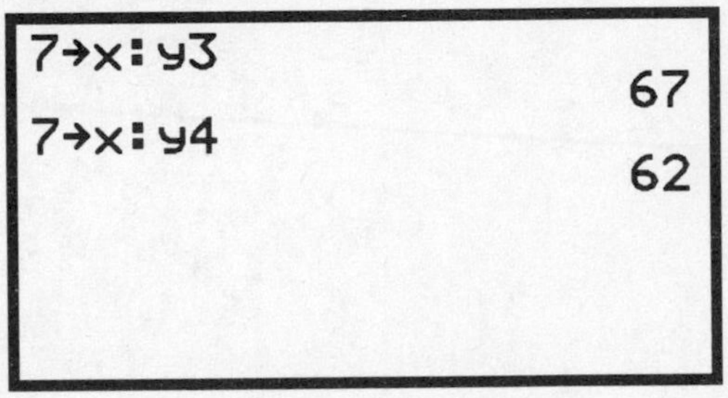

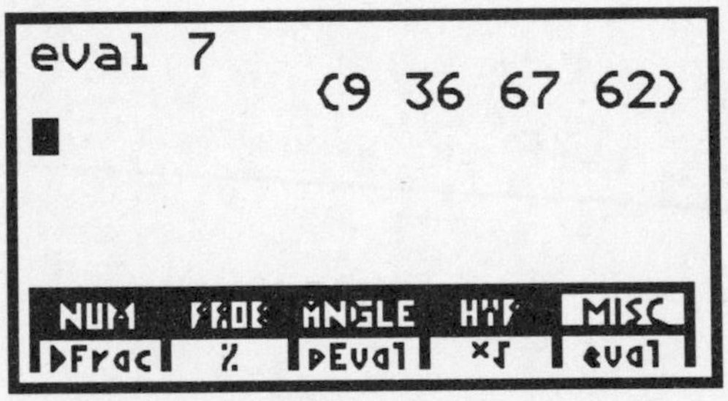

Chapter 2
Polynomial and Rational Functions

OPERATIONS WITH COMPLEX NUMBERS

Operations with complex numbers can be performed on the TI-85. First check to see that the grapher is set in rectangular complex mode. If it is not, press $\boxed{\text{2nd}}$ $\boxed{\text{MODE}}$, position the cursor over RectC, and press $\boxed{\text{ENTER}}$.

Example 4, page 176:

(a) Add: $(8 + 6i) + (3 + 2i)$.

A complex number $a + bi$ is entered on the TI-85 as the ordered pair (a, b). Thus, to find this sum press $\boxed{(}\,8\,\boxed{,}\,6\,\boxed{)}$ $\boxed{+}\,\boxed{(}\,3\,\boxed{,}\,2\,\boxed{)}\,\boxed{\text{ENTER}}$. The grapher returns (11,8) which corresponds to the number $11 + 8i$.

(b) Subtract: $(4 + 5i) - (6 - 3i)$.

Press $\boxed{(}\,4\,\boxed{,}\,5\,\boxed{)}\,\boxed{-}\,\boxed{(}\,6\,\boxed{,}\,\boxed{(-)}\,3\,\boxed{)}\,\boxed{\text{ENTER}}$. The grapher returns $(-2, 8)$ which corresponds to the number $-2 + 8i$.

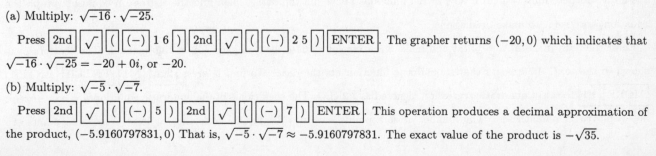

Example 5 (a), (b), (d), (e), page 177:

(a) Multiply: $\sqrt{-16} \cdot \sqrt{-25}$.

Press $\boxed{\text{2nd}}\,\boxed{\sqrt{}}\,\boxed{(}\,\boxed{(-)}\,1\,6\,\boxed{)}\,\boxed{\text{2nd}}\,\boxed{\sqrt{}}\,\boxed{(}\,\boxed{(-)}\,2\,5\,\boxed{)}\,\boxed{\text{ENTER}}$. The grapher returns $(-20, 0)$ which indicates that $\sqrt{-16} \cdot \sqrt{-25} = -20 + 0i$, or -20.

(b) Multiply: $\sqrt{-5} \cdot \sqrt{-7}$.

Press $\boxed{\text{2nd}}\,\boxed{\sqrt{}}\,\boxed{(}\,\boxed{(-)}\,5\,\boxed{)}\,\boxed{\text{2nd}}\,\boxed{\sqrt{}}\,\boxed{(}\,\boxed{(-)}\,7\,\boxed{)}\,\boxed{\text{ENTER}}$. This operation produces a decimal approximation of the product, $(-5.9160797831, 0)$ That is, $\sqrt{-5} \cdot \sqrt{-7} \approx -5.9160797831$. The exact value of the product is $-\sqrt{35}$.

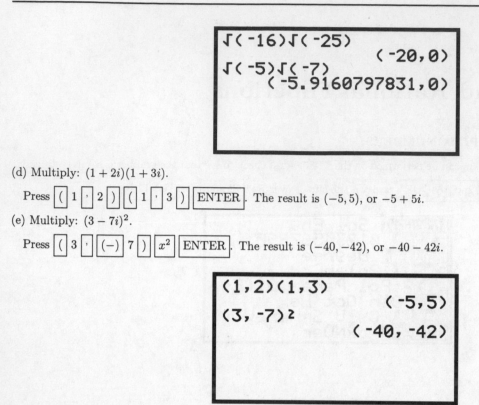

(d) Multiply: $(1 + 2i)(1 + 3i)$.

Press $\boxed{(}$ $\boxed{1}$ $\boxed{,}$ $\boxed{2}$ $\boxed{)}$ $\boxed{(}$ $\boxed{1}$ $\boxed{,}$ $\boxed{3}$ $\boxed{)}$ $\boxed{\text{ENTER}}$. The result is $(-5, 5)$, or $-5 + 5i$.

(e) Multiply: $(3 - 7i)^2$.

Press $\boxed{(}$ $\boxed{3}$ $\boxed{,}$ $\boxed{(-)}$ $\boxed{7}$ $\boxed{)}$ $\boxed{x^2}$ $\boxed{\text{ENTER}}$. The result is $(-40, -42)$, or $-40 - 42i$.

Complex numbers can also be divided in RectC mode. The real and imaginary parts of the quotient will be expressed in decimal form. For example, the quotient $(2 - 5i)/(1 - 6i)$ in Example 9 on page 179 of the textbook would be expressed as $(.864864864865, .189189189189)$.

QUADRATIC, CUBIC, AND QUARTIC REGRESSION

In addition to the linear regression discussed earlier, second degree, third degree, and fourth degree polynomial functions can be fit to data using the quadratic, cubic, and quartic regression operations, respectively.

The operations of entering data, making scatterplots, and graphing and evaluating quadratic, cubic, and quartic regression functions are the same as for linear regression functions. Before proceeding, reread the section on Linear Regression and Scatterplots beginning on page 108 of this manual.

Example 5, page 201: For the data on hours of sleep versus death rate on page 202 of the text, make a scatterplot for the data and determine which, if any, of the functions above fits the data. Then find the regression equation, graph the equation, and use it to make predictions.

Enter the data in xStat and yStat and make a scatterplot as described on page 108 of this manual. The scatterplot is shown in the text. It appears that a quadratic function fits the data. To find it press $\boxed{\text{2nd}}$ $\boxed{\text{M1}}$ $\boxed{\text{ENTER}}$ $\boxed{\text{ENTER}}$ $\boxed{\text{MORE}}$ $\boxed{\text{F1}}$ to select quadratic regression, denoted as P2REG. The coefficients of the quadratic equation $y = ax^2 + bx + c$ are displayed in parentheses. The number of data points n is also displayed. Note that at least three data points are required for quadratic regression.

The regression equation can be copied to the "y(x) =" screen as described in the discussion of linear regression on page 109 of this manual. Then it can be graphed and used to make predictions using one of the methods for finding function values described on page 105.

To fit a cubic or quartic function to a set of data, enter the data in xStat and yStat as described earlier. Then press [2nd] [M1] [ENTER] [ENTER] [MORE]. Select cubic regression by pressing [F2] to select P3REG and quartic regression by pressing [F4] to select P4REG. At least four data points are required for cubic regression and at least five are required for quartic regression.

Chapter 3
Exponential and Logarithmic Functions

GRAPHING AN INVERSE FUNCTION

The DrawInv operation on the TI-85 can be used to graph a function and its inverse on the same screen. A formula for the inverse function need not be found in order to do this. The grapher must be set in Func mode when this operation is used.

Example 7, page 255: Graph $f(x) = 2x - 3$ and $f^{-1}(x)$ using the same set of axes.

Be sure the GRAPH FORMT is set to DrawLine and then enter $y_1 = 2x - 3$ and either clear or deselect all other functions on the "y(x) =" screen. Press $\boxed{\text{2nd}}$ $\boxed{\text{M5}}$ to select GRAPH. Then press $\boxed{\text{MORE}}$ $\boxed{\text{F2}}$ to select DRAW and $\boxed{\text{MORE}}$ $\boxed{\text{MORE}}$ $\boxed{\text{F2}}$ to select the DrInv operation. Press $\boxed{\text{2nd}}$ $\boxed{\text{alpha}}$ and then type $y1$. Press $\boxed{\text{ENTER}}$ to see the graph of the function and its inverse.

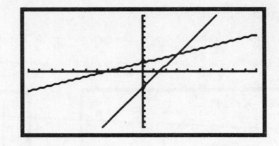

EVALUATING e^x, Log x, and Ln x

Use the grapher's scientific keys to evaluate e^x, $\log x$, and $\ln x$ for specific values of x.

Example 6 (a), (b), page 270: Find the value of e^3 and $e^{-0.23}$. Round to four decimal places.

To find e^3 press $\boxed{\text{2nd}}$ $\boxed{e^x}$ 3 $\boxed{\text{ENTER}}$. (e^x is the second operation associated with the $\boxed{\text{LN}}$ key.) The grapher returns 20.0855369232. Thus, $e^3 \approx 20.0855$. To find $e^{-0.23}$ press $\boxed{\text{2nd}}$ $\boxed{e^x}$ $\boxed{(-)}$ $\boxed{\cdot}$ 2 3 $\boxed{\text{ENTER}}$. The grapher returns .794533602503, so $e^{-0.23} \approx 0.7945$.

Example 4 (a), (b), (c), page 279: Find the values of log 645,778, log 0.0000239, and log (−3). Round to four decimal places.

To find log 645,778 press $\boxed{\text{LOG}}$ 6 4 5 7 7 8 $\boxed{\text{ENTER}}$ and read 5.81008324563. Thus, log $645,778 \approx 5.8101$. To find log 0.0000239 press $\boxed{\text{LOG}}$ $\boxed{\cdot}$ 0 0 0 0 2 3 9 $\boxed{\text{ENTER}}$. The grapher returns −4.62160209905, so log $0.0000239 \approx -4.6216$. When we press $\boxed{\text{LOG}}$ $\boxed{(-)}$ 3 $\boxed{\text{ENTER}}$ the result is a non-real complex number. This indicates that −3 is not in the domain of the function $\log x$.

Example 5 (a), (b), (c), page 279: Find the values of ln 645,778, ln 0.0000239, and ln (−5). Round to four decimal places.

To find ln 645,778 and ln 0.0000239 repeat the keystrokes used above to find log 645,778 and log 0.0000239 but press $\boxed{\text{LN}}$ rather than $\boxed{\text{LOG}}$. We find that ln 645,778 $\approx$ 13.3782 and ln 0.0000239 $\approx$ −10.6416. When we press $\boxed{\text{LN}}$ $\boxed{(-)}$ 5 $\boxed{\text{ENTER}}$ the result is a non-real complex number, indicating that −5 is not in the domain of the function ln x.

USING THE CHANGE OF BASE FORMULA

To find a logarithm with a base other than 10 or e we use the change-of-base formula, $\log_b M = \dfrac{\log_a M}{\log_a b}$, where a and b are any logarithmic bases and M is any positive number.

Example 6, page 280: Find $\log_5 8$ using common logarithms.

We let $a = 10$, $b = 5$, and $M = 8$ and substitute in the change-of-base formula. Press $\boxed{\text{LOG}}$ 8 $\boxed{\div}$ $\boxed{\text{LOG}}$ 5 $\boxed{\text{ENTER}}$. The result is about 1.2920.

Example 7, page 280: Find $\log_4 31$ using natural logarithms.

We let $a = e$, $b = 4$, and $M = 31$ and substitute in the change-of-base formula. Press $\boxed{\text{LN}}$ 3 1 $\boxed{\div}$ $\boxed{\text{LN}}$ 4 $\boxed{\text{ENTER}}$. The result is about 2.4771.

Example 9, page 281: Graph $y = \log_5 x$.

To use a grapher we must first change the base to e or 10. Here we use e. Let $a = e$, $b = 5$, and $M = x$ and substitute in the change-of-base formula. Enter $y_1 = \dfrac{\ln x}{\ln 5}$ on the "y(x) =" screen, select a window, and select GRAPH from the menus.

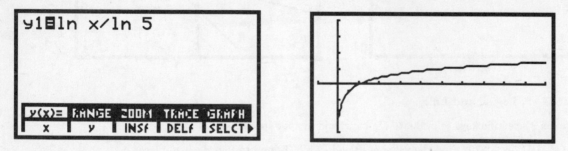

EXPONENTIAL, LOGARITHMIC, AND POWER REGRESSION

In addition to the types of polynomial regression discussed earlier, exponential, logarithmic, and power functions can be fit to data. The operations of entering data, making scatterplots, and graphing and evaluating these functions are the same as for linear regression functions. So are the procedures for copying a regression equation to the "y(x) =" screen, graphing it, and using it to find function values. Before proceeding, reread the section on Linear Regression and Scatterplots beginning on page 108 of this manual.

Example 6 (a), page 310: Fit an exponential equation to the given data on cellular phones.

Enter the data in xStat and yStat as described on page 108 of this manual. Then press $\boxed{\text{2nd}}$ $\boxed{\text{M1}}$ $\boxed{\text{ENTER}}$ $\boxed{\text{ENTER}}$ $\boxed{\text{F4}}$ to select EXPR. The values of a and b for the exponential function $y = ab^x$ are displayed along with the coefficient of correlation and the number of data points n.

```
ExpR
 a=.303970333897
 b=1.62732831731
 corr=.986060679135
 n=10

 CALC  EDIT  DRAW  FCST
1-VAR LINR  LNR  EXPR PWRR ▶
```

Exercise 26 (a), page 316: Fit a logarithmic function to the given data on forgetting.

After entering the data in xStat and yStat as described on page 108 of this manual, press 2nd M1 ENTER ENTER F3 to select LNR. The values of a and b for the logarithmic function $y = a + b \ln x$ are displayed along with the coefficient of correlation and the number of data points n.

```
LnR
 a=84.9435399216
 b=-.541283409758
 corr=-.990989394703
 n=6

 CALC  EDIT  DRAW  FCST
1-VAR LINR  LNR  EXPR PWRR ▶
```

Example 7 (a), page 312: Fit a power function to the given data on cholesterol level and risk of heart attack.

Enter the data in xStat and yStat as described on page 108 of this manual. Then press 2nd M1 ENTER ENTER F5 to select PWRR. The values of a and b for the power function $y = ax^b$ are displayed along with the coefficient of correlation and the number of data points n.

```
PwrR
 a=.024178957415
 b=1.52745717151
 corr=.973936133593
 n=5

 CALC  EDIT  DRAW  FCST
1-VAR LINR  LNR  EXPR PWRR ▶
```

Chapter 4
The Trigonometric Functions

This chapter appears only in the text *ALGEBRA & TRIGONOMETRY: GRAPHS & MODELS* by Bittinger, Beecher, Ellenbogen, and Penna and should be disregarded by students using the text *COLLEGE ALGEBRA: GRAPHS & MODELS*.

CONVERTING BETWEEN D°M′S″ AND DECIMAL DEGREE MEASURE

The ANGLE feature can be used to convert D°M′S″ notation to decimal notation and vice versa. ANGLE is accessed by pressing $\boxed{\text{2nd}}$ $\boxed{\text{MATH}}$ $\boxed{\text{F3}}$.

Example 5, page 328: Convert 5°42′30″ to decimal degree notation.

Enter 5°42′30″ as 5′42′30′ by pressing 5 $\boxed{\text{2nd}}$ $\boxed{\text{MATH}}$ $\boxed{\text{F3}}$ 5 $\boxed{\text{F3}}$ 4 2 $\boxed{\text{F3}}$ 3 0 $\boxed{\text{F3}}$ $\boxed{\text{ENTER}}$. The grapher returns 5.70833333333, so 5°42′30″ ≈ 5.71°.

Example 6, page 328: Convert 72.18° to D°M′S″ notation.

Press 7 2 $\boxed{\cdot}$ 1 8 $\boxed{\text{2nd}}$ $\boxed{\text{MATH}}$ $\boxed{\text{F3}}$ to select ANGLE. Then press $\boxed{\text{F4}}$ to select DMS followed by $\boxed{\text{ENTER}}$. The grapher returns 72°10′48″.

```
5'42'30'
              5.70833333333
72.18▶DMS
                  72°10'48"



 NUM   PROB  ANGLE  HYP   MISC
  °     r           '    ▶DMS
```

FINDING TRIGONOMETRIC FUNCTION VALUES

The grapher's SIN, COS, and TAN operations can be used to find the values of trigonometric functions. When angles are given in degree measure, the grapher must be set in Degree mode.

Example 7, page 328: Find the trigonometric function value, rounded to four decimal places, of each of the following.

a) tan 29.7°   b) sec 48°   c) sin 84°10′39″

a) Press $\boxed{\text{TAN}}$ 2 9 $\boxed{\cdot}$ 7 $\boxed{\text{ENTER}}$. We find that tan 29.7° ≈ 0.5704.

b) The secant, cosecant, and cotangent functions can be found by taking the reciprocals of the cosine, sine, and tangent functions, respectively. This can be done either by entering the reciprocal or by using the $\boxed{x^{-1}}$ key. To find sec 48° we can enter the reciprocal of cos 48° by pressing 1 $\boxed{\div}$ $\boxed{\text{COS}}$ 4 8 $\boxed{\text{ENTER}}$. To find sec 48° using the $\boxed{x^{-1}}$ key press $\boxed{(}$ $\boxed{\text{COS}}$ 4 8 $\boxed{)}$ $\boxed{\text{2nd}}$ $\boxed{x^{-1}}$ $\boxed{\text{ENTER}}$. (x^{-1} is the second operation associated with the $\boxed{\text{EE}}$ key.) The result is sec 48° ≈ 1.4945.

```
1/cos 48
            1.49447654986
(cos 48)⁻¹
            1.49447654986
■
```

c) Press SIN followed by 84°10′39″ entered as described above in Converting Between D°M′S″ and Decimal Degree Measure. Then press ENTER . We find that sin 84°10′39″ ≈ 0.9948.

FINDING ANGLES

The inverse trigonometric function keys provide a quick way to find an angle given a trigonometric function value for that angle.

Example 8, page 329: Find the acute angle, to the nearest tenth of a degree, whose sine value is approximately 0.20113.

With the grapher set in Degree mode press 2nd   SIN⁻¹   . 2 0 1 1 3 ENTER . (SIN⁻¹ is the second operation associated with the SIN key.) We find that the desired acute angle is approximately 11.6°.

Exercise 63, page 332: Find the acute angle, to the nearest tenth of a degree, whose cotangent value is 2.127.

Angles whose secant, cosecant, or cotangent values are known can be found using the reciprocals of the cosine, sine, and tangent functions, respectively. Since $\cot \theta = \dfrac{1}{\tan \theta} = 2.127$, we have $\tan \theta = \dfrac{1}{2.127}$, or $(2.127)^{-1}$. To find θ press 2nd   TAN⁻¹   (1 ÷ 2 . 1 2 7)   ENTER or 2nd   TAN⁻¹ 2 . 1 2 7 2nd x^{-1} ENTER . (TAN⁻¹ is the second operation associated with the TAN key.) Note that the parentheses are necessary in the first set of keystrokes. Without parentheses we would be finding the angle whose tangent is 1 and then dividing that angle by 2.127. We find that $\theta \approx$ 25.2°.

```
sin⁻¹ .20113
            11.6030461313
tan⁻¹ (1/2.127)
            25.1803638359
tan⁻¹ 2.127⁻¹
            25.1803638359
■
```

CONVERTING BETWEEN DEGREE AND RADIAN MEASURE

We can use the grapher to convert from degree to radian measure and vice versa. The grapher should be set in Radian mode when converting from degree to radian measure and in Degree mode when converting from radian to degree measure.

Example 3, page 363: Convert each of the following to radians.

a) 120°   b) −297.25°

a) Set the grapher in Radian mode. Press 1 2 0 [2nd] [MATH] [F3] [F1] [ENTER] to enter 120°. The grapher returns a decimal approximation of the radian measure. We see that 120° ≈ 2.09 radians.

b) With the grapher set in Radian mode and with the ANGLE menu displayed, press [(−)] 2 9 7 [·] 2 5 [F1] [ENTER]. We see that −297.25° ≈ −5.19 radians.

```
120°
              2.09439510239
-297.25°
              -5.18799120155
■

NUM  PROB  ANGLE  HYP  MISC
  °    r     '   ▸DMS
```

Example 4, page 363: Convert each of the following to degrees.

a) $\frac{3\pi}{4}$ radians   b) 8.5 radians

a) Set the grapher in Degree mode. Then press [(] 3 [2nd] [π] [÷] 4 [)] [2nd] [MATH] [F3] [F2] [ENTER] to enter $\frac{3\pi}{4}$ radians. (π is the second operation associated with the [∧] key). The grapher returns 135, so $\frac{3\pi}{4}$ radians = 135°. Note that the parentheses are necessary in order to enter the entire expression in radian measure. Without the parentheses, the grapher reads only the denominator, 4, in radian measure and an incorrect result occurs.

b) With the grapher set in Degree mode and with the ANGLE menu displayed, press 8 [·] 5 [F2] [ENTER]. The grapher returns 487.014125861, so 8.5 radians ≈ 487.01°.

```
(3π/4)ʳ
                        135
8.5ʳ
              487.014125861


NUM  PROB  ANGLE  HYP  MISC
  °    r     '   ▸DMS
```

Chapter 5
Trigonometric Identities, Inverse Functions, and Equations

This chapter appears only in the text *ALGEBRA & TRIGONOMETRY: GRAPHS & MODELS* by Bittinger, Beecher, Ellenbogen, and Penna and should be disregarded by students using the text *COLLEGE ALGEBRA: GRAPHS & MODELS*.

FINDING INVERSE FUNCTION VALUES

We can use a grapher to find inverse function values in both radians and degrees.

Example 2 (a), (e), page 441: Approximate $\cos^{-1}(-0.2689)$ and $\csc^{-1} 8.205$ in both radians and degrees.

To find inverse function values in radians, first set the grapher in Radian mode. Then, to approximate $\cos^{-1}(-0.2689)$, press $\boxed{\text{2nd}}$ $\boxed{\text{COS}^{-1}}$ $\boxed{(-)}$. 2 6 8 9 $\boxed{\text{ENTER}}$. The grapher returns 1.84304711148, so $\cos^{-1}(-0.2689) \approx 1.8430$ radians.

To find $\csc^{-1} 8.205$, recall the identity $\csc\theta = \dfrac{1}{\sin\theta}$. Then $\csc^{-1} 8.205 = \sin^{-1}\left(\dfrac{1}{8.205}\right)$. Press $\boxed{\text{2nd}}$ $\boxed{\text{SIN}^{-1}}$ $\boxed{(}$ 1 $\boxed{\div}$ 8 . 2 0 5 $\boxed{)}$ $\boxed{\text{ENTER}}$ or $\boxed{\text{2nd}}$ $\boxed{\text{SIN}^{-1}}$ 8 . 2 0 5 $\boxed{\text{2nd}}$ $\boxed{x^{-1}}$ $\boxed{\text{ENTER}}$. The readout is .122180665346, so $\csc^{-1} 8.205 \approx 0.1222$ radians.

```
cos-1 -.2689
            1.84304711148
sin-1 (1/8.205)
             .122180665346
sin-1 8.205-1
             .122180665346
```

To find inverse function values in degrees, set the grapher in degree mode. Then use the keystrokes above to find that $\cos^{-1}(-0.2689) \approx 105.6°$ and $\csc^{-1} 8.205 \approx 7.0°$.

```
cos-1 -.2689
            105.598820932
sin-1 (1/8.205)
            7.00043646242
sin-1 8.205-1
            7.00043646242
```

We also use reciprocal relationships to find function values for arcsecant and arccotangent.

Chapter 6
Applications of Trigonometry

CONVERTING FROM RECTANGULAR TO POLAR COORDINATES

This chapter appears only in the text *ALGEBRA & TRIGONOMETRY: GRAPHS & MODELS* by Bittinger, Beecher, Ellenbogen, and Penna and should be disregarded by students using the text *COLLEGE ALGEBRA: GRAPHS & MODELS*.

The grapher can be used to convert from rectangular to polar coordinates, expressing the result using either degrees or radians. The grapher will supply a positive value for r and an angle in the interval $(-180°, 180°]$, or $(-\pi, \pi]$.

Example 2 (a), page 498: Convert (3,3) to polar coordinates.

Set the grapher in Degree mode and PolarC mode. Then press ⎡(⎤⎡3⎤⎡,⎤⎡3⎤⎡)⎤ ⎡ENTER⎤. The readout is $(4.24264068712∠45)$, so $r \approx 4.2426$ (a decimal approximation for $3\sqrt{2}$) and $\theta = 45°$. Thus, polar notation for (3,3) is $(4.2426, 45°)$.

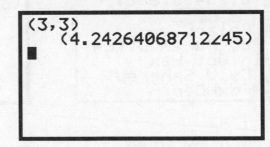

Set the grapher in Radian mode and PolarC mode to find θ in radians. Repeat the keystrokes for finding (3,3) above to find that r is the same and $\theta \approx 0.7854$ (a decimal approximation for $\pi/4$). Thus polar notation for (3,3) is $(4.2426, 0.7854)$.

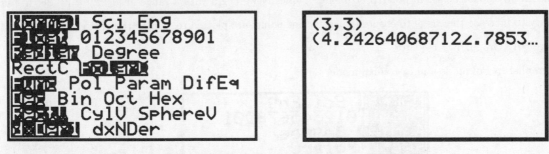

CONVERTING FROM POLAR TO RECTANGULAR COORDINATES

The grapher can also be used to convert from polar to rectangular coordinates.

Example 3, page 499: Convert each of the following to rectangular coordinates.

(a) $(10, \pi/3)$ (b) $(-5, 135°)$

(a) Set the grapher in RectC mode and, since the angle is given in radians, set it in Radian mode also. Press ⎡(⎤⎡1⎤⎡0⎤⎡2nd⎤

$\boxed{\angle}$ $\boxed{\text{2nd}}$ $\boxed{\pi}$ $\boxed{\div}$ 3 $\boxed{)}$ $\boxed{\text{ENTER}}$. ($\angle$ is the second operation associated with the $\boxed{\cdot}$ key.) The readout is (5,8.66025403784), where 8.66025403784 is a decimal approximation of $5\sqrt{3}$. Thus, rectangular notation for $(10, \pi/3)$ is (5,8.6603).

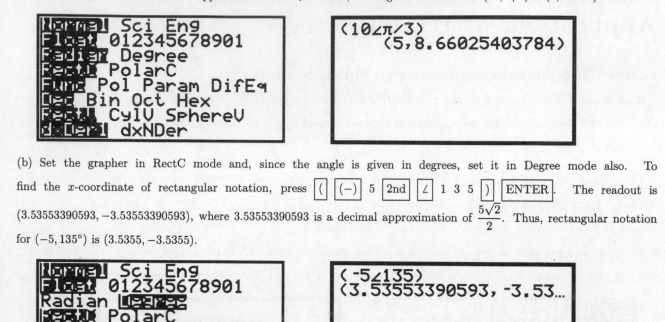

(b) Set the grapher in RectC mode and, since the angle is given in degrees, set it in Degree mode also. To find the x-coordinate of rectangular notation, press $\boxed{(}$ $\boxed{(-)}$ 5 $\boxed{\text{2nd}}$ $\boxed{\angle}$ 1 3 5 $\boxed{)}$ $\boxed{\text{ENTER}}$. The readout is (3.53553390593, −3.53553390593), where 3.53553390593 is a decimal approximation of $\dfrac{5\sqrt{2}}{2}$. Thus, rectangular notation for $(-5, 135°)$ is (3.5355, −3.5355).

GRAPHING POLAR EQUATIONS

Polar equations can be graphed in either Radian mode or Degree mode. The equation must be written in the form $r = f(\theta)$ and the grapher must be set in polar (Pol) mode. Typically we begin with a range of $[0, 2\pi]$ or $[0°, 360°]$, but it might be necessary to increase the range to ensure that sufficient points are plotted to display the entire graph.

Example 6, page 501: Graph: $r = 1 - \sin\theta$.

First set the grapher in Pol mode and in Radian mode.

The equation is given in $r = f(\theta)$ form. Press $\boxed{\text{GRAPH}}$ $\boxed{\text{F1}}$ to enter it on the "r(θ) =" screen. Clear any existing entries and, with the cursor beside "r1 =" press 1 $\boxed{-}$ $\boxed{\text{SIN}}$ $\boxed{\text{F1}}$. The keystroke $\boxed{\text{F1}}$ selects the variable θ. Now press

2nd | M2 | to select RANGE and enter the following settings:

θMin = 0   (Smallest value of θ to be evaluated)
θMax = 2π (Largest value of θ to be evaluated)
θStep = $\pi/24$ (Increment in θ values)
xMin = −6
xMax = 6
xScl = 1
yMin = −3.5
yMax = 3.5
yScl = 1

With these settings the grapher evaluates the function from $\theta = 0$ to $\theta = 2\pi$ in increments of $\pi/24$ and displays the graph in the square window $[-6, 6, -3.5, 3.5]$. Values entered in terms of π appear on the screen as decimal approximations. Press

F5 | to display the graph.

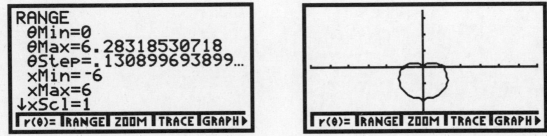

Although we have used a square window, the software used to produce the graph above causes some distortion. The graph produced on your grapher will not be distorted.

The curve can be traced with either rectangular or polar coordinates being displayed. The value of θ is also displayed when rectangular coordinates are selected. The choice of coordinates is made on the GRAPH FORMT screen. Press

MORE | F3 | to display this screen. Then position the blinking cursor over RectGC to select rectangular coordinates or over PolarGC to select polar coordinates.

Chapter 7/4
Systems and Matrices

This chapter corresponds to Chapter 7 in *ALGEBRA & TRIGONOMETRY: GRAPHS & MODELS* by Bittinger, Beecher, Ellenbogen, and Penna and to Chapter 4 in *COLLEGE ALGEBRA: GRAPHS & MODELS*. **The page number references show the** *ALGEBRA & TRIGONOMETRY* **page first followed by the** *COLLEGE ALGEBRA* **page.**

SOLVING SYSTEMS OF EQUATIONS

We can solve systems of up to 30 equations with 30 variables on the TI-85 using the SIMULT menu.

Example 2 (b), page 524/324: Solve the following system:

$$4x + 3y = 11,$$
$$-5x + 2y = 15.$$

Begin by pressing $\boxed{\text{2nd}}$ $\boxed{\text{SIMULT}}$ to display the SIMULT screen. (SIMULT is the second operation associated with the $\boxed{\text{STAT}}$ key.) The blinking cursor is positioned to the right of the notation "Number =." Because there are two equations, press 2 $\boxed{\text{ENTER}}$.

```
SIMULT
Number=2
```

The coefficient entry screen for the first equation will appear. Enter the coefficients and the constant term of the first equation by pressing 4 $\boxed{\text{ENTER}}$ 3 $\boxed{\text{ENTER}}$ 1 1 $\boxed{\text{ENTER}}$. Now the coefficient entry screen for the second equation appears. Enter the coefficients and the constant term of the second equation by pressing $\boxed{(-)}$ 5 $\boxed{\text{ENTER}}$ 2 $\boxed{\text{ENTER}}$ 1 5. The second equation's coefficient screen could also have been accessed by pressing $\boxed{\text{F2}}$ to select NEXT rather than by pressing $\boxed{\text{ENTER}}$ after 11, the constant in the first equation.

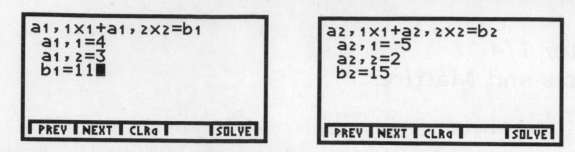

To see the solution of the system of equations, press $\boxed{\text{F5}}$ to select SOLVE. The solution $(-1, 5)$ is displayed as "$x1 = -1$" and "$x2 = 5$."

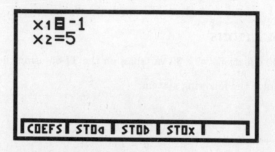

MATRICES AND ROW-EQUIVALENT OPERATIONS

Matrices with up to 255 rows and 255 columns can be entered on the TI-85. The number of matrices that can be entered is limited only by the memory available. Row-equivalent operations can be performed on matrices using the grapher.

Example 1, page 542/342: Solve the following system:

$$\begin{aligned} 2x - y + 4z &= -3, \\ x - 2y - 10z &= -6, \\ 3x + 4z &= 7. \end{aligned}$$

First we enter the augmented matrix

$$\begin{bmatrix} 2 & -1 & 4 & -3 \\ 1 & -2 & -10 & -6 \\ 3 & 0 & 4 & 7 \end{bmatrix}$$

on the grapher. Begin by pressing $\boxed{\text{2nd}}$ $\boxed{\text{MATRX}}$ to display the MATRX EDIT menu. (MATRX is the second operation associated with the $\boxed{7}$ key.) Then press $\boxed{\text{F2}}$ to select EDIT and name the matrix to be defined. We will name the matrix [**A**] by pressing $\boxed{\text{F1}}$ or by pressing A at the blinking cursor to the right of "Name =." Note that it is not necessary to press $\boxed{\text{ALPHA}}$ before pressing A in the MATRX EDIT screen. Now press $\boxed{\text{ENTER}}$.

The dimensions of the matrix are displayed on the top line of the next screen, with the cursor on the row dimension. Enter the dimensions of the augmented matrix, 3 x 4, by pressing 3 $\boxed{\text{ENTER}}$ 4 $\boxed{\text{ENTER}}$. Now the cursor moves to the element in the first row and first column of the matrix. Enter the elements of the first row by pressing 2 $\boxed{\text{ENTER}}$ $\boxed{(-)}$ 1 $\boxed{\text{ENTER}}$ 4 $\boxed{\text{ENTER}}$ $\boxed{(-)}$ 3 $\boxed{\text{ENTER}}$. The cursor moves to the element in the second row and first column of the matrix. Enter the elements of the second and third rows of the augmented matrix by typing each in turn followed by $\boxed{\text{ENTER}}$ as above. Note that the screen only displays the fourth column of the matrix at this point. The △ and ▽ keys can be used to move the cursor to any element at any time.

Row-equivalent operations are performed by making selections from the MATRX OPS menu. To view this menu press 2nd QUIT to leave the MATRX EDIT screen. Then press 2nd MATRX F4 . Now press MORE to see the menu with the four row-equivalent operations: rSwap, rAdd, multR, and mRAdd in locations F2 through F5 . These operations interchange two rows of a matrix, add two rows, multiply a row by a number, and multiply a row by a number and add it to a second row, respectively.

To view the matrix on the home screen press ALPHA A ENTER . We will use the grapher to perform the row-equivalent operations that were done algebraically in the text. First, to interchange row 1 and row 2 of matrix [A], with the MATRX OPS menu displayed , press F2 to select rSwap. Then press ALPHA A to select [A]. Follow this with a comma and the rows to be interchanged: , 1 , 2) ENTER .

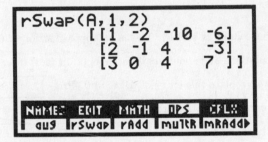

The grapher will not store the matrix produced using a row-equivalent operation, so when several operations are to be performed in succession it is helpful to store the result of each operation as it is produced. For example, to store the matrix resulting from interchanging the first and second rows of [A] as matrix [B] press STO▷ B ENTER immediately after interchanging the rows. Note that it is not necessary to press ALPHA before pressing B in this situation.

Next we multiply the first row of [B] by -2, add it to the second row and store the result as [B] again by pressing F5 (−) 2 , ALPHA B , 1 , 2) STO▷ B ENTER . These keystrokes select mRAdd from the MATRX OPS menu; then they specify that the value of the multiplier is -2, the matrix being operated on is [B], and that a multiple of row 1 is being added to row 2; finally they store the result as [B].

To multiply row 1 by -3, add it to row 3, and store the result as [B] press F5 (−) 3 , ALPHA B , 1 , 3) STO▷ B ENTER .

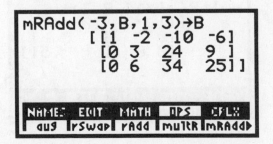

Now multiply the second row by 1/3 and store the result as [**B**] again. Press [F4] 1 [(÷)] 3 [,] [ALPHA] B [,] 2 [)] [STO▷] B [ENTER]. These keystrokes select multR from the MATRX OPS menu; then they specify that the value of the multiplier is 1/3, the matrix being operated on is [**B**], and row 2 is being multiplied; finally they store the result as [**B**]. The keystrokes 1 [(÷)] 3 could be replaced with 3 [2nd] [x^{-1}].

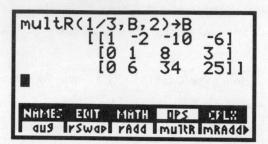

Multiply the second row by −6 and add it to the third row using mRAdd. Press [F5] [(−)] 6 [,] [ALPHA] B [,] 2 [,] 3 [)] [STO▷] B [ENTER].

The entry in the third row, second column is 1E−13. This is an approximation of 0 that occurs because of the manner in which the grapher performs calculations and should be treated as 0. In fact, it would be a good idea to return to the MATRX EDIT screen at this point to replace this entry of [**B**] with 0. Press [2nd] [M2] to select EDIT. Then press [F2] [ENTER] to display [**B**]. Move the cursor to the third row, second column and press 0 [ENTER]. Now press [2nd] [QUIT] to return to the home screen. Matrix **B** can be viewed by pressing [ALPHA] B [ENTER].

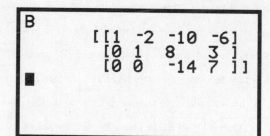

Finally, multiply the third row by −1/14 by pressing [2nd] [MATRX] [F4] [MORE] to view the row operations under the OPS menu. Then press [F4] [(−)] 1 [(÷)] 1 4 [,] [ALPHA] B [,] 3 [)] [ENTER]. The keystrokes [(−)] 1 [(÷)] 1 4 could be replaced with [(−)] 1 4 [2nd] [x^{-1}].

```
multR(-1/14,B,3)
     [[1  -2  -10  -6 ]
      [0  1   8    3  ]
      [0  0   1    -.5]]

NAMES  EDIT  MATH  OPS  CPLX
 aug  rSwap  rAdd  multR mRAdd▷
```

Write the system of equations that corresponds to the final matrix. Then use back-substitution to solve for x, y, and z as illustrated in the text.

Instead of stopping with row-echelon form as we did above, we can continue to apply row-equivalent operations until the matrix is in reduced row-echelon form as in Example 3 on page 544/344 of the text. Reduced row-echelon form of a matrix can be found directly by using the rref operation from the MATRX OPS menu. For example, to find reduced row-echelon form for matrix **A** in Example 1 above, after entering [**A**] and leaving the MATRX EDIT screen press | 2nd | | MATRX | | F4 | | F5 | | ALPHA | A | ENTER |. We can read the solution of the system of equations, $(3, 7, -0.5)$ directly from the resulting matrix.

```
rref A
            [[1  0  0  3   ]
             [0  1  0  7   ]
             [0  0  1  -.5]]
 ▮


 NAMES  EDIT  MATH   OPS   CPLX
  dim    Fill  ident  ref   rref ▶
```

MATRIX OPERATIONS

We can use the grapher to add and subtract matrices, to multiply a matrix by a scalar, and to multiply matrices.

Example 1 (a), page 549/349: Find $\mathbf{A} + \mathbf{B}$ for

a) $\mathbf{A} = \begin{bmatrix} -5 & 0 \\ 4 & \frac{1}{2} \end{bmatrix}$, $\mathbf{B} = \begin{bmatrix} 6 & -3 \\ 2 & 3 \end{bmatrix}$.

Enter **A** and **B** on the MATRX EDIT screen as [**A**] and [**B**] as described earlier in this chapter. Press | 2nd | | QUIT | to leave this screen. Then press | ALPHA | A | + | | ALPHA | B | ENTER | to display the sum.

```
A+B
              [[1  -3 ]
               [6  3.5]]
```

Example 2, page 550/350: Find $\mathbf{C} - \mathbf{D}$ for each of the following.

a) $\mathbf{C} = \begin{bmatrix} 1 & 2 \\ -2 & 0 \\ -3 & -1 \end{bmatrix}$, $\mathbf{D} = \begin{bmatrix} 1 & -1 \\ 1 & 3 \\ 2 & 3 \end{bmatrix}$ b) $\mathbf{C} = \begin{bmatrix} 5 & -6 \\ -3 & 4 \end{bmatrix}$, $\mathbf{D} = \begin{bmatrix} -4 \\ 1 \end{bmatrix}$

a) Enter **C** and **D** on the MATRX EDIT screen as [**C**] and [**D**]. Press | 2nd | | QUIT | to leave this screen. Then press | ALPHA | C | − | | ALPHA | D | ENTER | to display the difference.

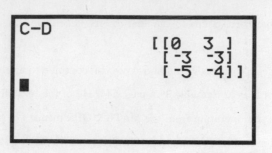

b) Enter **C** and **D** on the MATRX EDIT screen as [**C**] and [**D**]. Press 2nd QUIT to leave this screen. Then press ALPHA C − ALPHA D ENTER. The grapher returns the message ERROR 12 DIM MISMATCH, indicating that this subtraction is not possible. This is the case because the matrices have different orders.

```
ERROR 12 DIM MISMATCH




 GOTO              QUIT
```

Example 4, page 551/351: Find 3**A** and (−1)**A**, for $\mathbf{A} = \begin{bmatrix} -3 & 0 \\ 4 & 5 \end{bmatrix}$

Enter **A** on the MATRX EDIT screen as [**A**]. Press 2nd QUIT to leave this screen. Then to find 3**A** press 3 ALPHA A ENTER and to find (−1)**A** press (−) 1 ALPHA A ENTER. Note that (−1)**A** is the opposite, or additive inverse, of **A** and can also be found by pressing (−) ALPHA A ENTER.

```
3A
              [[-9  0 ]
               [12 15]]
-1A
              [[3   0 ]
               [-4  -5]]
```

Example 6 (a), (d), page 553/353: For

$$\mathbf{A} = \begin{bmatrix} 3 & 1 & -1 \\ 2 & 0 & 3 \end{bmatrix}, \mathbf{B} = \begin{bmatrix} 1 & 6 \\ 3 & -5 \\ -2 & 4 \end{bmatrix}, \text{ and } \mathbf{C} = \begin{bmatrix} 4 & -6 \\ 1 & 2 \end{bmatrix}$$

find each of the following.

a) **AB**   d) **AC**

First enter **A**, **B**, and **C** as [**A**], [**B**], and [**C**] on the MATRX EDIT screen. Press 2nd QUIT to leave this screen.

a) To find **AB** press ALPHA A × ALPHA B ENTER.

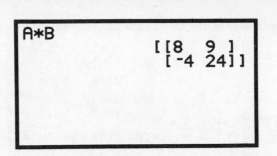

d) To find **AC** press $\boxed{\text{ALPHA}}$ A $\boxed{\times}$ $\boxed{\text{ALPHA}}$ C $\boxed{\text{ENTER}}$. The grapher returns the message ERROR 12 DIM MIS-MATCH, indicating that this multiplication is not possible. This is the case because the number of columns in **A** is not the same as the number of rows in **C**. Thus, the matrices cannot be multiplied in this order.

FINDING THE INVERSE OF A MATRIX

The inverse of a matrix can be found quickly on the grapher.

Example 3, page 562/362: Find $\mathbf{A}^{-1}$, where

$$\mathbf{A} = \begin{bmatrix} -2 & 3 \\ -3 & 4 \end{bmatrix}.$$

Enter **A** as [A] on the MATRX EDIT screen. Then press $\boxed{\text{2nd}}$ $\boxed{\text{QUIT}}$ to leave this screen. Now press $\boxed{\text{ALPHA}}$ A $\boxed{\text{2nd}}$ $\boxed{x^{-1}}$ $\boxed{\text{ENTER}}$.

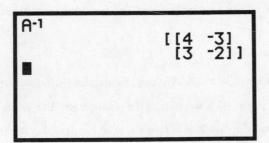

Exercise 9, page 564/364: Find $\mathbf{A}^{-1}$, where

$$\mathbf{A} = \begin{bmatrix} 6 & 9 \\ 4 & 6 \end{bmatrix}.$$

Enter **A** as [A] on the MATRX EDIT screen and then press $\boxed{\text{2nd}}$ $\boxed{\text{QUIT}}$ to leave this screen. Now press $\boxed{\text{ALPHA}}$ A $\boxed{\text{2nd}}$ $\boxed{x^{-1}}$ $\boxed{\text{ENTER}}$. The grapher returns the message ERROR 03 SINGULAR MAT, indicating that $\mathbf{A}^{-1}$ does not exist.

MATRIX SOLUTIONS OF SYSTEMS OF EQUATIONS

We can write a system of n linear equations in n variables as a matrix equation $\mathbf{AX} = \mathbf{B}$. If **A** has an inverse the solution of the system of equations is given by $\mathbf{X} = \mathbf{A}^{-1}\mathbf{B}$.

Example 4, page 563/363: Use an inverse matrix to solve the following system of equations:

$$x + 2y - z = -2,$$
$$3x + 5y + 3z = 3,$$
$$2x + 4y + 3z = 1.$$

Enter $\mathbf{A} = \begin{bmatrix} 1 & 2 & -1 \\ 3 & 5 & 3 \\ 2 & 4 & 3 \end{bmatrix}$ and $\mathbf{B} = \begin{bmatrix} -2 \\ 3 \\ 1 \end{bmatrix}$ on the MATRX EDIT screen as [**A**] and [**B**]. Press $\boxed{\text{2nd}}$ $\boxed{\text{QUIT}}$ to leave this screen. Then press $\boxed{\text{ALPHA}}$ A $\boxed{\text{2nd}}$ $\boxed{x^{-1}}$ $\boxed{\times}$ $\boxed{\text{ALPHA}}$ B $\boxed{\text{ENTER}}$. The result is the 3 x 1 matrix $\begin{bmatrix} 5 \\ -3 \\ 1 \end{bmatrix}$, so the solution is $(5, -3, 1)$.

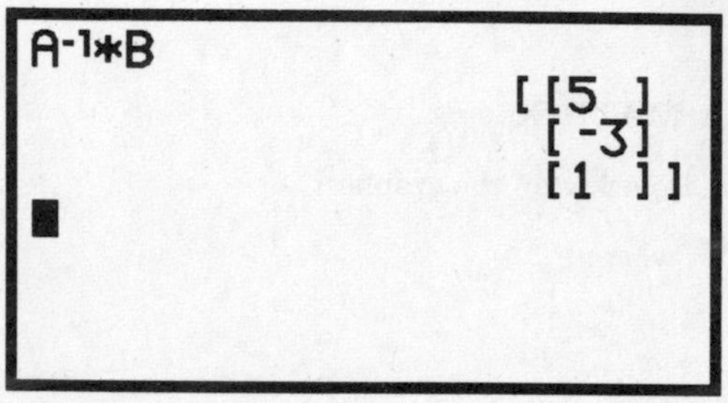

```
A-1*B

                    [ [5  ]
                      [-3]
                      [1  ] ]
■
```

GRAPHS OF INEQUALITIES

We can graph linear inequalities on the grapher, shading the region of the solution set. The grapher should be set in Func mode at this point.

Example 1, page 567/367: Graph: $y < x + 3$.

First we graph the related equation $y = x + 3$. We use the standard window $[-10, 10, -10, 10]$. Since the inequality symbol is $<$ we know that the line $y = x + 3$ is not part of the solution set. In a hand-drawn graph we would use a dashed line to indicate this. However, the only option here is to use a solid line, keeping in mind that it is not part of the solution set. After determining that the solution set of the inequality consists of all points below the line, we use the grapher's Shade operation to shade this region. Shade is accessed by pressing $\boxed{\text{MORE}}$ $\boxed{\text{F2}}$ to select DRAW and then $\boxed{\text{F1}}$ to select Shade.

Now enter a lower function and an upper function and the region between them will be shaded. We want to shade the area between the bottom of the window, $y = -10$, and the line $y = x + 3$ so we enter $\boxed{(-)}$ 1 0 $\boxed{,}$ $\boxed{x\text{-VAR}}$ $\boxed{+}$ 3 $\boxed{)}$ $\boxed{\text{ENTER}}$. We can also enter $x + 3$ as y_1 by typing $y1$. The result is shown below.

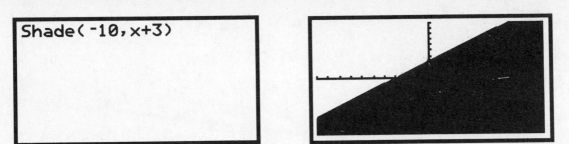

We can also use the Shade operation to graph a system of inequalities when the solution set lies between the graphs of two functions.

Exercise 37, page 574/374: Graph:

$$y \leq x,$$

$$y \geq 3 - x.$$

First graph the related equations $y = x$ and $y = 3 - x$ and determine that the solution set consists of all the points on or above the graph of $y = 3 - x$ and on or below the graph of $y = x$. We will shade this region by pressing $\boxed{\text{MORE}}$ $\boxed{\text{F2}}$ $\boxed{\text{F1}}$ $\boxed{3}$ $\boxed{-}$ $\boxed{x\text{-VAR}}$ $\boxed{,}$ $\boxed{x\text{-VAR}}$ $\boxed{)}$ $\boxed{\text{ENTER}}$. These keystrokes select the Shade operation from the DRAW menu and then enter $y = 3 - x$ as the lower function and $y = x$ as the upper function. We could also enter these functions as y_2 and y_1, respectively, by typing $y2$ and $y1$.

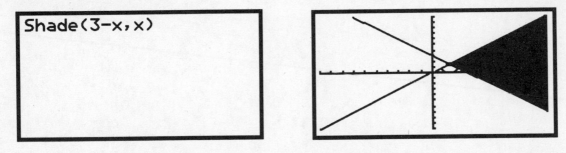

Chapter 8/5
Conic Sections

This chapter corresponds to Chapter 8 in *ALGEBRA & TRIGONOMETRY: GRAPHS & MODELS* by **Bittinger, Beecher, Ellenbogen, and Penna** and to Chapter 5 in *COLLEGE ALGEBRA: GRAPHS & MODELS*. **The page number references show the** *ALGEBRA & TRIGONOMETRY* **page first followed by the** *COLLEGE ALGEBRA* **page.**

Many conic sections are represented by equations that are not functions. Consequently, these equations must be entered on the TI-85 as two equations, each of which is a function. We have already done this for circles in Chapter G of this manual. Now we turn our attention to parabolas, ellipses, and hyperbolas.

GRAPHING PARABOLAS

To graph a parabola of the form $y^2 = 4px$ or $(y - k)^2 = 4p(x - h)$, we must first solve the equation for y.

Example 4, page 594/394: Graph the parabola $y^2 - 2y - 8x - 31 = 0$.

In the text we used the quadratic formula to solve the equation for y:
$$y = \frac{2 \pm \sqrt{32x + 128}}{2}.$$

One way to produce the graph of the parabola is to enter $y_1 = \dfrac{2 + \sqrt{32x + 128}}{2}$ and $y_2 = \dfrac{2 - \sqrt{32x + 128}}{2}$, select a window, and press $\boxed{\text{GRAPH}}$ to see the graph. Here we use $[-12, 12, -7, 7]$ since a square window gives the best representation of the shape of the parabola. The first equation produces the top half of the parabola and the second equation produces the lower half.

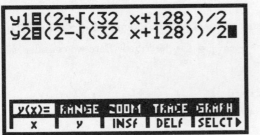 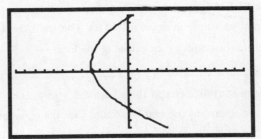

We can also enter $y_1 = \sqrt{32x + 128}$. Then use $y1$ to enter $y_2 = \dfrac{2 + y_1}{2}$ and $y_3 = \dfrac{2 - y_1}{2}$. For example, to enter $y_2 = \dfrac{2 + y_1}{2}$ position the cursor beside "y2 =" and press $\boxed{(}$ $\boxed{2}$ $\boxed{+}$ $\boxed{\text{F2}}$ $\boxed{1}$ $\boxed{)}$ $\boxed{\div}$ 2. Enter $y_3 = \dfrac{2 - y_1}{2}$ in a similar manner. Finally, deselect y_1 by moving the cursor to the right of the equals sign following y1 and pressing $\boxed{\text{F5}}$ to select SELCT. The top half of the graph is produced by y_2 and the lower half by y_3. The expression for y_1 was entered to avoid entering the square root more than once. By deselecting y_1 we prevent the graph of y_1 from appearing on the screen with the graph of the parabola.

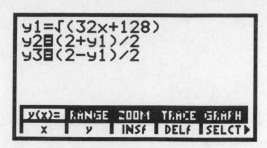

We could also use the standard equation of the parabola found in the text:

$$(y-1)^2 = 8(x+4).$$

Solve this equation for y.

$$y - 1 = \pm\sqrt{8(x+4)}$$
$$y = 1 \pm \sqrt{8(x+4)}$$

Then enter $y_1 = 1 + \sqrt{8(x+4)}$ and $y_2 = 1 - \sqrt{8(x+4)}$, or enter $y_1 = \sqrt{8(x+4)}$, $y_2 = 1 + y_1$, and $y_3 = 1 - y_1$, and deselect y_1 as above.

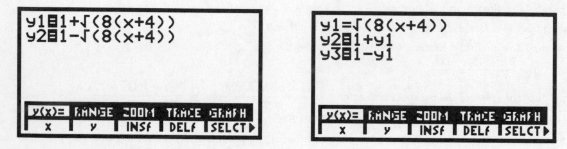

GRAPHING ELLIPSES

The equation of an ellipse must be solved for y before it can be entered on the TI-85. In Example 2 of Section 8.2 of the text the procedure for graphing an ellipse of the form $\dfrac{x^2}{a^2} + \dfrac{y^2}{b^2} = 1$ or $\dfrac{x^2}{b^2} + \dfrac{y^2}{a^2} = 1$ is described. Here we consider ellipses of the form $\dfrac{(x-h)^2}{a^2} + \dfrac{(y-k)^2}{b^2} = 1$ or $\dfrac{(x-h)^2}{b^2} + \dfrac{(y-k)^2}{a^2} = 1$

Example 4, page 604/404: Graph the ellipse $4x^2 + y^2 + 24x - 2y + 21 = 0$.

Completing the square in the text, we found that the equation can be written as

$$\frac{(x+3)^2}{4} + \frac{(y-1)^2}{16} = 1.$$

Solve this equation for y.

$$\frac{(x+3)^2}{4} + \frac{(y-1)^2}{16} = 1$$

$$\frac{(y-1)^2}{16} = 1 - \frac{(x+3)^2}{4}$$

$$(y-1)^2 = 16 - 4(x+3)^2 \qquad \text{Multiplying by 16}$$

$$y - 1 = \pm\sqrt{16 - 4(x+3)^2}$$

$$y = 1 \pm \sqrt{16 - 4(x+3)^2}$$

Now we can produce the graph in either of two ways. One is to enter $y_1 = 1 + \sqrt{16 - 4(x+3)^2}$ and $y_2 = 1 - \sqrt{16 - 4(x+3)^2}$, select a square window, and press $\boxed{\text{F5}}$ to select GRAPH. Here we use $[-12, 12, -7, 7]$. The first equation produces the top half of the ellipse and the second equation produces the lower half.

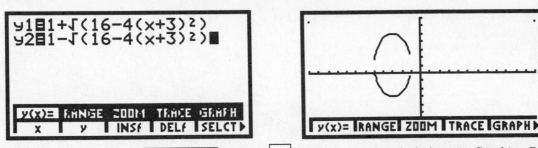

We can also enter $y_1 = \sqrt{16 - 4(x+3)^2}$ and use $\boxed{F2}$ to select y as described above in Graphing Parabolas to enter $y_2 = 1 + y_1$ and $y_3 = 1 - y_1$. Then deselect y_1, select a square window, and finally select GRAPH. As with parabolas, y_1 is used to eliminate the need to enter the square root more than once. Deselecting it prevents the graph of y_1 from appearing on the screen with the graph of the ellipse. The top half of the graph is produced by y_2 and the lower half by y_3.

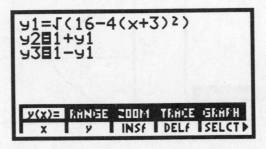

We could also begin by using the quadratic formula to solve the original equation for y.

$$4x^2 + y^2 + 24x - 2y + 21 = 0$$

$$y^2 - 2y + (4x^2 + 24x + 21) = 0$$

$$y = \frac{-(-2) \pm \sqrt{(-2)^2 - 4 \cdot 1 \cdot (4x^2 + 24x + 21)}}{2 \cdot 1}$$

$$y = \frac{2 \pm \sqrt{4 - 16x^2 - 96x - 84}}{2}$$

$$y = \frac{2 \pm \sqrt{-16x^2 - 96x - 80}}{2}$$

Then enter $y_1 = \dfrac{2 + \sqrt{-16x^2 - 96x - 80}}{2}$ and $y_2 = \dfrac{2 - \sqrt{-16x^2 - 96x - 80}}{2}$, or enter $y_1 = \sqrt{-16x^2 - 96x - 80}$, $y_2 = \dfrac{2 + y_1}{2}$, and $y_3 = \dfrac{2 - y_1}{2}$, and deselect y_1.

Select a square window and press $\boxed{F5}$ to display the graph.

GRAPHING HYPERBOLAS

As with equations of circles, parabolas, and ellipses, equations of hyperbolas must be solved for y before they can be entered on the TI-85.

Example 2, page 610/410: Graph the hyperbola $9x^2 - 16y^2 = 144$.

First solve the equation for y.

$$9x^2 - 16y^2 = 144$$

$$-16y^2 = -9x^2 + 144$$

$$y^2 = \frac{-9x^2 + 144}{-16}$$

$$y = \pm\sqrt{\frac{-9x^2 + 144}{-16}}, \text{ or } \pm\sqrt{\frac{9x^2 - 144}{16}}$$

It is not necessary to simplify further.

Now enter $y_1 = \sqrt{\frac{9x^2 - 144}{16}}$ and either $y_2 = -\sqrt{\frac{9x^2 - 144}{16}}$ or $y_2 = -y_1$, select a square window, and press $\boxed{F5}$ to select GRAPH. Here we use $[-12, 12, -7, 7]$. The top half of the graph is produced by y_1 and the lower half by y_2.

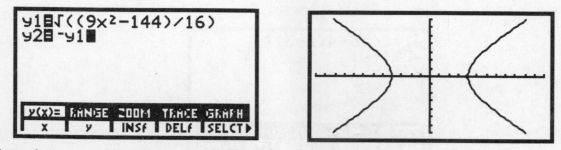

Example 3, page 613/413: Graph the hyperbola $4y^2 - x^2 + 24y + 4x + 28 = 0$.

In the text we completed the square to get the standard form of the equation. Now solve the equation for y.

$$\frac{(y + 3)^2}{1} - \frac{(x - 2)^2}{4} = 1$$

$$(y + 3)^2 = \frac{(x - 2)^2}{4} + 1$$

$$y + 3 = \pm\sqrt{\frac{(x - 2)^2}{4} + 1}$$

$$y = -3 \pm \sqrt{\frac{(x - 2)^2}{4} + 1}$$

As with ellipses, the graph can be produced in either of two ways. One way is to enter $y_1 = -3 + \sqrt{\frac{(x - 2)^2}{4} + 1}$ and $y_2 = -3 - \sqrt{\frac{(x - 2)^2}{4} + 1}$, select a square window, and press $\boxed{F5}$ to select GRAPH. Here we use $[-12, 12, -7, 7]$. The first equation produces the top half of the hyperbola and the second the lower half.

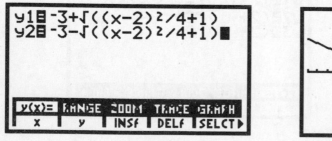
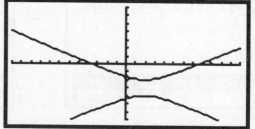

We can also enter $y_1 = \sqrt{\frac{(x - 2)^2}{4} + 1}$, $y_2 = -3 + y_1$, and $y_3 = -3 - y_1$. Then deselect y_1, select a square window, and press $\boxed{F5}$ to select GRAPH. As with parabolas and ellipses, y_1 is used to eliminate the need to enter the square root more than once. Deselecting it prevents the graph of y_1 from appearing on the screen with the graph of the hyperbola. The top half of the graph is produced by y_2 and the lower half by y_3.

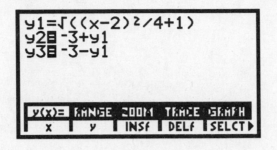

Chapter 9/6
Sequences, Series, and Combinatorics

This chapter corresponds to Chapter 9 in *ALGEBRA & TRIGONOMETRY: GRAPHS & MODELS* by Bittinger, Beecher, Ellenbogen, and Penna and to Chapter 6 in *COLLEGE ALGEBRA: GRAPHS & MODELS*. **The page number references show the** *ALGEBRA & TRIGONOMETRY* **page first followed by the** *COLLEGE ALGEBRA* **page.**

The computational capabilities of the grapher can be used when working with sequences, series, and combinatorics.

EVALUATING AND GRAPHING SEQUENCES

The grapher can be used to construct a list showing the terms of a sequence.

Example 3, page 633/433: Construct a list of values for the first 10 terms of the sequence whose general term is given by

$$a_n = \frac{n}{n+1}.$$

To construct the list of values for this sequence, press $\boxed{\text{2nd}}$ $\boxed{\text{MATH}}$ $\boxed{\text{F5}}$ to select MISC and then press $\boxed{\text{F3}}$ to select seq. Enter $x/(x+1)$ to the right of the statement "seq(" by pressing $\boxed{x\text{-VAR}}$ $\boxed{\div}$ $\boxed{(}$ $\boxed{x\text{-VAR}}$ $\boxed{+}$ $\boxed{1}$ $\boxed{)}$ $\boxed{,}$. This must be followed by four arguments: the first is the variable (x) in the expression $x/(x+1)$; the second is the first value of the variable, 1; the third is the last value of the variable, 10; and the fourth is the increment in the variable, 1. To enter these four arguments press $\boxed{x\text{-VAR}}$ $\boxed{,}$ $\boxed{1}$ $\boxed{,}$ $\boxed{1}$ $\boxed{0}$ $\boxed{,}$ $\boxed{1}$ $\boxed{)}$.

Note that x was used as the variable for ease of entry and because it is a real variable. Any real variable could have been used. To determine what letters are real variables inspect the list found by pressing $\boxed{\text{2nd}}$ $\boxed{\text{VARS}}$ $\boxed{\text{F2}}$ to select REAL. Press $\boxed{\text{2nd}}$ $\boxed{\text{QUIT}}$ to leave this list.

Press $\boxed{\text{ENTER}}$ to display the list of terms of the sequence. We see that when $n = 1$, $a_n = 0.5$; when $n = 2$, $a_n = 0.666666666667$; and so on. To see all of the terms press $\boxed{\triangleright}$ repeatedly.

```
seq(x/(x+1),x,1,10,1)
(.5 .666666666667 .7…
```

EVALUATING FACTORIALS, PERMUTATIONS, AND COMBINATIONS

Operations from the MATH PROB (probability) menu can be used to evaluate factorials, permutations, and combinations. Press $\boxed{\text{2nd}}$ $\boxed{\text{MATH}}$ $\boxed{\text{F2}}$ to display this menu.

Exercise 6, page 677/477: Evaluate 7!.

With the MATH PROB menu displayed, press 7 | F1 | | ENTER |. These keystrokes enter 7, select ! from the MATH PROB menu, and then cause 7! to be evaluated. The result is 5040.

Exercise 9, page 677/477: Evaluate $\dfrac{9!}{5!}$.

With the MATH PROB menu displayed, press 9 | F1 | | ÷ | 5 | F1 | | ENTER |. The result is 3024.

```
7!
                              5040
9!/5!
                              3024
■


 NUM  PROB  ANGLE  HYP  MISC
   !    nPr    nCr   rand
```

Example 6, page 674/474: Compute $_8P_4$.

With the MATH PROB menu displayed, press 8 | F2 | 4 | ENTER |. The result is 1680.

Example 3, page 682/482: Evaluate $\begin{pmatrix} 7 \\ 5 \end{pmatrix}$.

With the MATH PROB menu displayed, press 7 | F2 | 5 | ENTER |. The result is 21.

```
8 nPr 4
                              1680
7 nCr 5
                                21


 NUM  PROB  ANGLE  HYP  MISC
   !    nPr    nCr   rand
```

Programs For The TI-85
Graphics Calculator

PROGRAMS FOR THE TI-85 GRAPHICS CALCULATOR
(Created by Dave Slomer, Winton Woods High School, Cincinnati, OH.)

ATABLE

This program gives the TI-85 powerful TABLES (written by Marco Radzinschi, a freshman at Pikeville High School, Baltimore, MD), shortened and enhanced by Dave Slomer).

INPUT: Enter and/or select all functions to be included in the table and set the RANGE, keeping in mind that the table values will go from xMax to xMin in steps of xScl. Dimensions must be chosen so that all values from xMin to xMax are in the domains of all selected functions.

OUTPUT: Matrix T, viewed best in the MATRIX editor

```
:Func
:int((xMax-xMin)/xScl+1)→K
:dimL eval xMin
:{K,Ans}→dim T
:∅→K
:For(x,xMin,xMax,xScl)
:  K+1→K
: li▷vc (x+√-1*eval x)→T(K)
:End
```

QUADFORM

This program solves a quadratic equation of form $Ax^2 + Bx + C = 0$.

INPUT: A, B, C

OUTPUT: Real or complex solutions

```
:Prompt A,B,C
:Disp "ROOTS:"
:B²-4A*C→D
:Disp (-B+√D)/(2A)
:Disp (-B-√D)/(2A)
```

SYNDIV

This program does synthetic division to divide a polynomial by a linear factor with leading coefficient 1.

INPUT: List of coefficients of the dividend, enclosed in braces, in order of descending powers and the constant term of the linear divisor.

OUTPUT: The coefficients of the quotient, in order of descending powers, and remainder.

```
:Disp "ENTER {LIST} OF "
:Disp "DIVIDEND COEFFS:"
:Input L1
:Input "DIVISOR CONSTANT TERM:",C
:dimL (L1)→L
:L1(1)→S
:Disp "QUOTIENT COEFFS="
:For(I,1,L-1)
:Pause S
:C*S+L1(I+1)→S
:End
:Disp "REMAINDER=",S
```

LOGBASE
  This program computes logarithms of any base.
  INPUT: Number (X) and base (B)
  OUTPUT: $\log_B(X)$

```
:Prompt X
:Input "NEW BASE:",B
:log (X)/log (B)
```


TRISOL9Ø
  This program solves right triangles ABC in which legs L and M are opposite angles A and B, respectively.
  INPUT: One side and any other part (except the right angle, C)
  OUTPUT: First, the sides; then, the acute angles

```
:Degree
:Menu(1,"HA",P,2,"HL",Q,3,"LA",R,4,"LL",S)
:
:Lbl P
:Prompt H,A
:9Ø-A→B
:H*sin (A)→L
:H*sin (B)→M
:Goto X
:
:Lbl Q
:Prompt H,L
:√ (H^2-L^2)→ M
:sin⁻¹ (L/H)→A
:9Ø-A→ B
:Goto X
:
:Lbl R
:Prompt L,A
:9Ø-A→B
:L/tan (A)→M
:√‾ (L^2+M^2)→H
:Goto X
:
:Lbl S
:Prompt L,M
:√‾ (L^2+M^2)→H
:tan⁻¹ (L/M)→ A
:9Ø-A→B
:
:Lbl X
:Disp L,M,H,A,B
```

TRISOL

This program solves triangle ABC, in which sides L, M, and N are opposite angles A, B, and C, respectively. It covers the "no solution" case as well as the "two solutions" case.

INPUT: Three parts of a triangle, including at least one side

OUTPUT: First the sides, then the angles. The AAS case is not included, so in this case it is necessary to find the third angle by hand and then use ASA.

```
:Degree
:Disp "ANGLES A,B,C"
:Disp "SIDES L,M,N"
.Menu(1,"SSS",P,2,"SAS",Q,3,"(A)ASA",R,4,"SSA",S)
:
:Lbl P
:Prompt L,M,N
:cos⁻¹ ((M^2+N^2-L^2)/(2*M*N))→A
:cos⁻¹ ((L^2+N^2-M^2)/(2*L*N))→B
:18Ø-A-B→C
:Goto X
:
:Lbl Q
:Prompt L,C,M
:√‾‚(L^2+M^2-2*L*M*cos (C))→N
:cos⁻¹ ((M^2+N^2-L^2)/(2*M*N))→A
:18Ø-A-C→B
:Goto X
:
.Lbl R
:Prompt A,N,B
:18Ø-A-B→C
:sin (A)*N/(sin (C))→L
:sin (B)*N/(sin (C))→M
:Goto X
:
:Lbl S
:Prompt L,M,B
:L*sin (B)/M→Z
:If Z>1:Then:Disp "NO SOL":Stop:End
:sin⁻¹ (Z)→A
:18Ø-A-B→C
:sin (C)*M/(sin (B))→N
:Disp L,M,N,A,B,C
:If B≥A:Stop
:Disp "2ND SOL...":Pause
:18Ø-A→A
:18Ø-A-B→C
:sin (C)*M/(sin (B))→N
:
:Lbl X
:Disp L,M,N,A,B,C
```

DEMOIVRE

This program helps visualize Nth roots of a complex number $A + Bi$.

INPUT: A, B, N

OUPUT: Traceable graph of the N points (A, B) corresponding to the roots

```
:Param
:Degree
:Input "REAL PART:",A
:Input "IMAG PART:",B
:Input "INDEX:",N
:√‾(A²+B²)^(1/N)→R
:If A==Ø:Then
:  18Ø-sign (B)*9Ø
:Else
:  tan⁻¹ (B/A)+18Ø*(A<Ø)
:End
:Ans/N→H
:xt1=R*cos (t)
:yt1=R*sin (t)
:H→tMin
:H+36Ø→tMax
:36Ø/N→tStep
:1.5R→yMax
:-yMax→yMin
:1.7yMax→xMax
:-xMax→xMin
:Trace
```

SYSLINRR

This program solves systems of N linear equations in N variables, considered to be of the form $AX = B$, where A is the $N \times N$ matrix of coefficients of the variables, B is the $N \times 1$ matrix of coefficients of the right-hand side, and X is the $N \times 1$ matrix of unique solutions (if any). This works when SIMULT or multiplying by the inverse of the coefficient matrix fails.

INPUT: MATRIX A and MATRIX B

OUTPUT: MATRIX X or message "NO SOLUTION" or message "INFINITELY MANY SOLUTIONS"

```
:aug(A,B)→C
:Pause C
:rref C→R
:For(I,dim A(1),1,-1)
:  If R(I,I)==Ø:Then
:    If R(I,I+1)==Ø:Then
:      Disp "INF MANY SOL":
:    Else
:      Disp "NO SOL"
:  End
:    Return
:  End
:End
:Rᵀ
:Pause Ans(dim R(1))
```

The HP 38G
Graphic Calculator

Preliminaries

Press ON to turn on the HP 38G graphing calculator. (ON is the key at the bottom left-hand corner of the keypad.) To adjust the contrast, simultaneously press ON and + (or −) to increase (or decrease) the contrast. To turn the grapher off, press □ ON . (□ is the solid light green key.) The grapher will turn itself off automatically after several minutes without any activity.

It will be helpful to read the Getting Started section (pages 1-1 through 1-28) of your grapher User's Guide before proceeding.

To see a demonstration of some of the features of the HP 38G, type DEMO on the edit line in Home using the following keystrokes: HOME A...Z D A...Z E A...Z M A...Z O ENTER . (D, E, M, and O are the A...Z operations associated with the TAN , X, T, Θ , 9 , and 4 keys, respectively.) To stop the demonstration, press any key.

Press □ MODES to display the MODE settings. (MODES is the second operation associated withe the HOME key.)

```
▒▒▒▒▒▒▒ HOME MODES ▒▒▒▒▒▒▒
ANGLE MEASURE: ████████
NUMBER FORMAT: Standard
DECIMAL MARK:  Dot(.)
TITLE: HOME

CHOOSE ANGLE MEASURE
      CHOOS
```

To change a setting use ▽ or △ to move the cursor to the line of that setting. Then press the solid black key below the screen menu CHOOS, use ▽ or △ to highlight a setting, and press the black key below OK or press ENTER to select that setting. Throughout this manual we will use double braces to denote the solid black key below a screen menu. For example, {{CHOOS}} denotes the key below CHOOS and {{OK}} denotes the key below OK.

Press HOME to leave the MODE screen.

Chapter G
Introduction to Graphs and Graphers

SETTING THE VIEWING WINDOW

The viewing window is the portion of the coordinate plane that appears on the grapher's screen. XRNG specifies the minimum and maximum horizontal values, stored in Xmin and Xmax, respectively; YRNG specifies the minimum and maximum vertical values, stored in Ymin and Ymax, respectively. XRNG and YRNG are fields which are found in the Plot Setup, $\boxed{\square}$ $\boxed{\text{PLOT}}$. The notation [Xmin, Xmax, Ymin, Ymax] is used in the text to represent these window settings or dimensions. For example, [−12, 12, −8, 8] denotes a window that displays the portion of the x-axis from −12 to 12 and the portion of the y-axis from −8 to 8. In addition, the distance between tick marks on the axes is defined by the settings XTICK and YTICK. RES (resolution) allows for two different resolution values for plotting: "Faster" plots in every other column, and "More Detail" plots in every column. These values are chosen in Plot Setup. The window corresponding to the settings [−20, 30, −10, 20], XTICK = 5, YTICK = 2, is shown below.

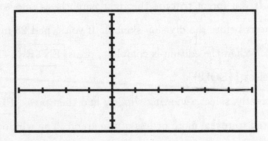

Press $\boxed{\square}$ $\boxed{\text{PLOT}}$ (for Plot Setup) to display the current window settings on your grapher. Additional settings may be accessed in Plot Setup by pressing the menu selection {{PAGE $\boxed{\triangledown}$}}.

```
▓▓▓▓FUNCTION PLOT SETUP▓▓▓▓
XRNG: -6.5        6.5
YRNG: -3.1        3.2
XTICK: 1      YTICK: 1
RES:  Faster

ENTER MINIMUM HORIZONTAL VALUE
 EDIT        PAGE ▼
```

To change a setting press $\boxed{\triangledown}$ or $\boxed{\triangleleft}$ to move the cursor to the setting you wish to change and enter the new value. For example, to change the settings to [−20, 30, −10, 20], Xtick = 5, Ytick = 2, press $\boxed{-x}$ 2 0 $\boxed{\text{ENTER}}$ (or {{OK}}) 3 0 $\boxed{\text{ENTER}}$ $\boxed{-x}$ 1 0 $\boxed{\text{ENTER}}$ 2 0 $\boxed{\text{ENTER}}$ 5 $\boxed{\text{ENTER}}$ 2 $\boxed{\text{ENTER}}$. You must use the $\boxed{-x}$ key on the fifth row of the keypad rather than the $\boxed{-}$ key in the right-hand column to enter a negative number. $\boxed{-x}$ represents "the opposite of" or "the additive inverse of" whereas $\boxed{-}$ is the subtraction key.

To return quickly to the default window setting $[-6.5,\ 6.5,\ -3.1,\ 3.2]$, Xtick = 1, Ytick = 1, press $\boxed{\square}$ $\boxed{\text{CLEAR}}$. (CLEAR is the second operation associated with the $\boxed{\text{DEL}}$ key.)

GRAPHING EQUATIONS

An equation must be solved for y before it can be graphed on the HP 38G.

Example 8 (a), page 8: To graph $2x + 3y = 18$, first solve for y, obtaining $y = \dfrac{18 - 2x}{3}$. Then press $\boxed{\text{LIB}}$ to open the Aplet Library. Use the $\boxed{\triangledown}$ or $\boxed{\triangle}$ key to highlight "Function" and press $\boxed{\text{ENTER}}$. If there are expressions present, they can be deleted by pressing $\boxed{\square}$ $\boxed{\text{CLEAR}}$ $\boxed{\text{ENTER}}$. Only the checkmarked expressions will be plotted. Thus, if you do not want to delete a particular checkmarked expression, scroll to it and uncheck it by selecting $\{\{\sqrt{\ } \text{CHK}\}\}$. Scroll to an empty line. Now press $\boxed{(}$ 18 $\boxed{-}$ 2 $\boxed{\text{X, T, }\Theta}$ $\boxed{)}$ $\boxed{/}$ 3 to enter the right-hand side of the equation. Press $\boxed{\text{ENTER}}$ to enter the equation. It is automatically checkmarked. Note that without the parentheses the expression $18 - \dfrac{2x}{3}$ would have been entered.

You can edit your entry if necessary. If, for instance, you pressed 5 instead of 8, use the $\boxed{\triangleleft}$ key to move the cursor to 5, press $\boxed{\text{DEL}}$, and then press 8. If you forgot to type the right parenthesis, move the cursor to the division symbol /; then press $\boxed{)}$ to insert the parenthesis before the division symbol. If you typed 25 instead of 2, move the cursor to 5 and press $\boxed{\text{DEL}}$. This will delete the 5. When the editing is complete, press $\boxed{\text{ENTER}}$. To edit after entering the expression, highlight it by scrolling to it and select $\{\{\text{EDIT}\}\}$.

Once the equation is entered correctly, select a viewing window and then press $\boxed{\text{PLOT}}$ to display the graph. You may change the viewing window as desired to reveal more or less of the graph. The window $[-10, 10, -10, 10]$ is shown here.

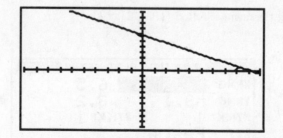

Example 8(c), page 8: To graph $x = y^2 + 1$, first solve the equation for y : $y = \pm\sqrt{x - 1}$. To obtain the entire graph of $x = y^2 + 1$, you must graph $y_1 = \sqrt{x - 1}$ and $y_2 = -\sqrt{x - 1}$ on the same screen. Be sure that the grapher is set in the Function aplet. Press $\boxed{\text{SYMB}}$ and clear any expressions that currently appear. With the cursor beside "F1(X) =" press $\boxed{\sqrt{x}}$ $\boxed{(}$ $\boxed{\text{X, T, }\Theta}$ $\boxed{-}$ 1 $\boxed{)}$ $\boxed{\text{ENTER}}$. Note that if the parentheses had not been used, the equation entered would have been F1(X) = $\sqrt{x} - 1$. The inclusion of a right parenthesis following 1 is optional, but we include it for completeness.

Now "F2(X) =" will be highlighted. There are two ways to enter F2(X) = $-\sqrt{x - 1}$. One is to enter the expression

$-\sqrt{x-1}$ directly by pressing $\boxed{-x}$ $\boxed{\sqrt{x}}$ $\boxed{(}$ $\boxed{\text{X, T, }\Theta}$ $\boxed{-}$ $\boxed{1}$ $\boxed{)}$ $\boxed{\text{ENTER}}$.

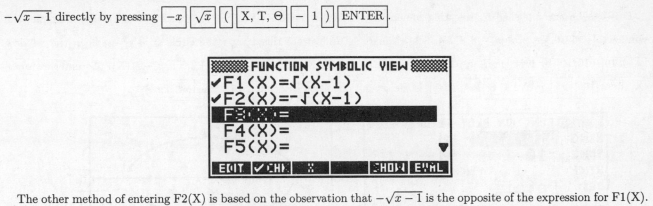

The other method of entering F2(X) is based on the observation that $-\sqrt{x-1}$ is the opposite of the expression for F1(X). That is, F2(X) = −F1(X). To enter this highlight "F2(X) =" and press $\boxed{-x}$ $\boxed{\text{A...Z}}$ F 1 $\boxed{(}$ $\boxed{\text{X, T, }\Theta}$ $\boxed{)}$ $\boxed{\text{ENTER}}$. This enters the opposite of F1(X) as the expression for F2(X).

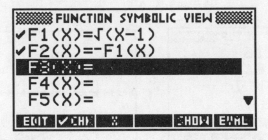

Select a viewing window and press $\boxed{\text{PLOT}}$ to display the graph. The window shown here is $[-2, 5, -5, 5]$, XTICK $= 1$, YTICK $= 1$.

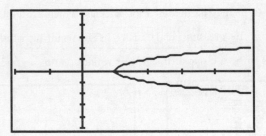

The top half is the graph of F1(X), the bottom half is the graph of F2(X), and together they yield the graph of $x = y^2 + 1$.

SQUARING THE VIEWING WINDOW

In the standard window, the distance between tick marks on the y-axis is $63/130$, or about $1/2$ the distance between tick marks on the x-axis. It is often desirable to choose window dimensions for which these distances are the same, creating a "square" window. Any window in which the ratio of the length of the y-axis to the length of the x-axis is $1/2$ will produce this effect.

This can be accomplished by selecting dimensions for which $\text{Ymax} - \text{Ymin} = \frac{1}{2}(\text{Xmax} - \text{Xmin})$. For example, the windows $[-16, 16, -8, 8]$ and $[-8, 8, -4, 4]$ are square. To illustrate this, graph the circle $x^2 + y^2 = 49$ in the window $[-10, 10, -10, 10]$ by first entering $\text{F1(X)} = \sqrt{49 - x^2}$ and $\text{F2(X)} = -\sqrt{49 - x^2}$ or $\text{F2(X)} = -\text{F1(X)}$. (To enter x^2 press $\boxed{\text{X, T, }\Theta}$ $\boxed{\square}$ $\boxed{x^2}$ or $\boxed{\text{X, T, }\Theta}$ $\boxed{x^y}$ 2. x^2 is the second operation associated with the $\boxed{x^y}$ key.)

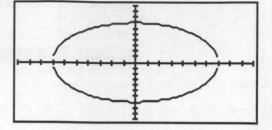

Note that the graph does not appear to be a circle.

Now change the window dimensions to $[-16, 16, -8, 8]$, Xtick = 1, Ytick = 1, and press $\boxed{\text{PLOT}}$.

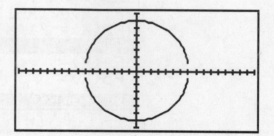

Observe that the distance between tick marks appears to be the same on both axes and that the graph appears to be a circle.

The window can also be squared by using the default Plot settings, which are $[-6.5, 6.5, -3.1, 3.2]$, Xtick = 1, Ytick = 1. Do this in the Function Plot Setup, by pressing $\boxed{\square}$ $\boxed{\text{CLEAR}}$. The resulting window dimensions and graph are shown below. Note that the graph appears to be a circle although this window is not a good choice for this particular graph.

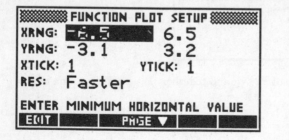
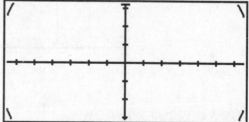

THE TABLE FEATURE

For an equation entered in the Function Symbolic view, a table of x-and y-values can be displayed. For example, enter $\text{F1(X)} = 3x^3 - 5x^2 + 2x - 1$ by pressing 3 $\boxed{\text{X, T, }\Theta}$ $\boxed{x^y}$ 3 $\boxed{-}$ 5 $\boxed{\text{X, T, }\Theta}$ $\boxed{\square}$ $\boxed{x^2}$ $\boxed{+}$ 2 $\boxed{\text{X, T, }\Theta}$ $\boxed{-}$ 1. Then press

□ NUM to display the Function Numeric Setup. A minimum value of x can be chosen along with an increment for the x-values. Press $-x$ 5 ENTER · 1 ENTER to select a minimum x-value of -5 and an increment of 0.1. The NUMTYPE setting should be Automatic. If it is not, use the arrow keys to move to the NUMTYPE field so that it is highlighted, select {{CHOOS}}, use the arrow keys to highlight Automatic, and press ENTER. To display the table press NUM.

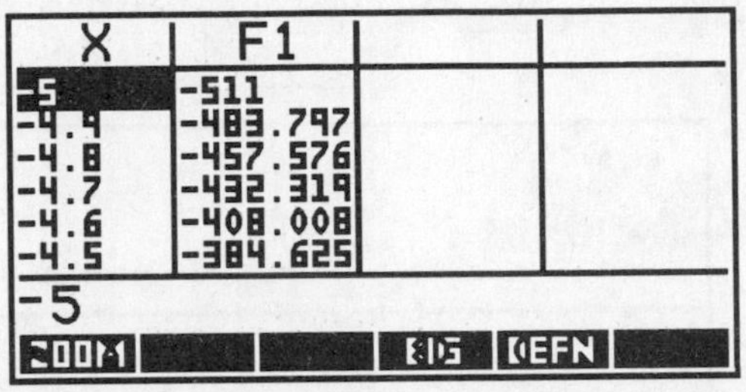

X	F1		
-5	-511		
-4.9	-483.797		
-4.8	-457.576		
-4.7	-432.319		
-4.6	-408.008		
-4.5	-384.625		

-5

ZOOM   BIG   DEFN

Use the arrow keys to scroll through the table. For example, by using ▽ to scroll down we can see that $y_1 = -212.968$ when $x = -3.6$. Using △ to scroll up, observe that $y_1 = -2529.76$ when $x = -8.9$.

THE SPLIT SCREEN

A vertically split screen can be used to display the graph of an equation along with a corresponding table of values. To produce a split screen, we first use the □ VIEWS menu. (VIEWS is the second operation associated with the LIB key.) For instance, for the equation $y = 3x^3 - 5x^2 + 2x - 1$ entered as above, select a viewing window. Then press □ VIEWS. Select Plot-Table and press ENTER. This selects the split screen option.

	Plot-Detail
XRN(	**Plot-Table**
YRN(	Overlay Plot
XTIC|	Auto Scale
RES:	Decimal ▼
ENTE|	UE

CANCL   OK

The graph is displayed on the left side of the screen with seven rows of the table to its right. The ◁ and ▷ keys move the crosshairs along the graph, and the table values adjust automatically to correspond to the location of the crosshairs. If more than one function is being graphed, use the △ and ▽ keys to move the crosshairs between graphs. In the table shown below, NUMSTEP is set to 0.3125.

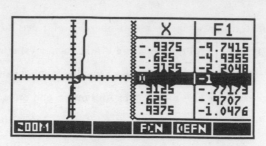

To return to a full Numeric or Plot view, press $\boxed{\text{NUM}}$ or $\boxed{\text{PLOT}}$, respectively.

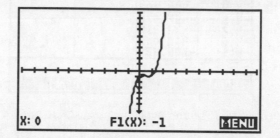

The NUMERIC feature can also be used to evaluate an expression. Enter F1(X) $= 5x^4 - 6x^2 + 4$ in the SYMBOLIC VIEW screen. Then press $\boxed{\square}$ $\boxed{\text{NUM}}$ $\boxed{\triangledown}$ $\boxed{\triangledown}$ {{CHOOS}} $\boxed{\triangledown}$ $\boxed{\text{ENTER}}$ to set the table in Build Your Own mode. In Build Your Own mode the grapher disregards the values of NUMSTART and NUMSTEP.

Press $\boxed{\text{NUM}}$ and an empty table is displayed. Now x-values can be entered in the X-column and the corresponding y-values will be displayed in the F1-column. For example, when $\boxed{-x}$ 9 $\boxed{\text{ENTER}}$ is pressed, -9 appears in the X-column and the grapher computes and enters 32323 in the Y_1-column. This is the value of $5x^4 - 6x^2 + 4$ when $x = -9$, or $5(-9)^4 - 6(-9)^2 + 4$. Press 16 $\boxed{\text{ENTER}}$ and 326148 appears in the F1-column. This is the value of the expression when $x = 16$. You can continue to enter x-values as desired.

IDENTITIES

An equation that is true for every possible real-number substitution for the variable is an identity. The grapher can be used to provide a partial check whether an equation is an identity. Either a graph or a table can be used to do this.

Example 9 (a), page 11: Determine whether $(x^2)^3 = x^6$ appears to be an identity.

To determine whether this equation appears to be an identity, graph $F1(X) = (x^2)^3$ and $F2(X) = x^6$. Examine the graphs in several viewing windows. The graphs appear to coincide no matter what the window. Thus, although there is a possibility that the graphs fail to coincide outside the windows that were examined, the equation appears to be an identity.

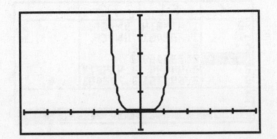

A table will also confirm this. Scroll through a table of values for F1 and F2 and observe that F1 and F2 appear to have the same value for a given value of x. Again, although the y-values could differ for an x-value that was not observed, the equation appears to be an identity.

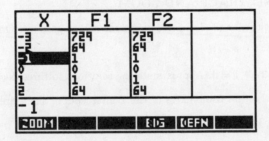

Example 9 (b), page 11: Determine whether $\sqrt{x + 4} = \sqrt{x} + 2$ appears to be an identity.

To determine whether this equation appears to be an identity, graph $F1(X) = \sqrt{x + 4}$ and $F2(X) = \sqrt{x} + 2$. Note that a left parenthesis must be used when entering $\sqrt{x + 4}$. Without the parenthesis the expression entered would be $\sqrt{x} + 4$. The inclusion of a right parenthesis following 4 is optional, but as usual we supply it for completeness: $\boxed{\sqrt{x}}$ $\boxed{(}$ $\boxed{\text{X, T, }\Theta}$ $\boxed{+}$ 4 $\boxed{)}$ $\boxed{\text{ENTER}}$.

Any window that includes a portion of the first quadrant will show that the graphs differ. Thus, the equation is not an identity.

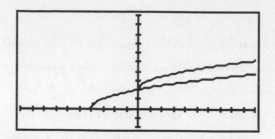

A table will also show that F1 and F2 do not always have the same value for a given x-value.

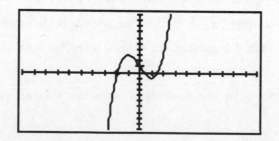

Note that F1 and F2 have the same value for $x = 0$ but not for the other possible substitutions shown. (The UNDEF. entries in the F2-column show that $x = -2$ and $x = -1$ cannot be substituted in $\sqrt{x} + 2$ to obtain a real number.)

Both the graph and the table demonstrate that the equation is not an identity.

SOLVING EQUATIONS USING TRACE AND ZOOM

There are several techniques that can be used to solve equations with a grapher. One such technique uses the grapher's Trace and Zoom features.

Example 10, page 13: Solve $x^3 - 3x + 1 = 0$. Approximate the solutions to three decimal places.

The solutions of this equation are the first coordinates of the x-intercepts of the graph of $y = x^3 - 3x + 1$. To find these coordinates we first graph $y = x^3 - 3x + 1$ in a viewing window that shows all of the x-intercepts. Here we use the window $[-10, 10, -10, 10]$.

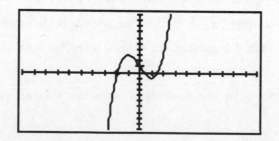

We see that x-intercepts occur near $x = -2$, $x = 0$, and $x = 2$. A portion of the viewing window can be enlarged near each of these values in order to find the desired three decimal place approximation. For example, let's examine the graph near $x = 0$.

Trace mode is the default when a plot has just been drawn. The Trace cursor appears on the graph at the middle x-value of the window, in this case at $x = 0$. The notation F1(X) appears in the bottom middle of the screen indicating that the cursor is on the graph of F1(X). The X- and F1(X)-values at the bottom of the screen indicate the coordinates of the point where the cursor is positioned, in this case at $x = 0$, $y = 1$. If there is more than one graph, use the ▵ and ▿ keys to move between graphs. When {{MENU}} and then {{DEFN}} are pressed, the grapher will display the equation of the curve being traced.

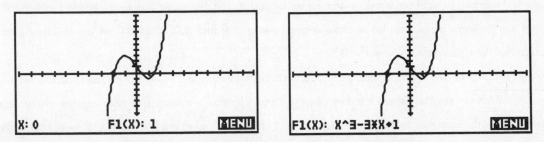

Pressing ◁ or ▷ moves the cursor to the left or right along the curve. Note that the TRACE cursor always remains on the curve. If the resolution in the Plot Setup view is set to Faster, the tracing might not appear to follow the curve precisely. This is because this resolution plots in every other column, but tracing always uses every column.

In order to find the middle x-intercept, we enlarge the portion of the graph near $x = 0$ by first positioning the cursor as close to this intercept as possible. That is, near $x = 0$, position the cursor as close as possible to $y = 0$. Then press {{MENU}} and then {{ZOOM}}. Highlight "In" and press ENTER. (If the zoom factors next to "In" are not set to 4×4, scroll down and highlight "Set Factors ....." Then set the zoom factors to 4, which we use in this example.) Press {{(X,Y)}} to display the crosshair coordinates again.

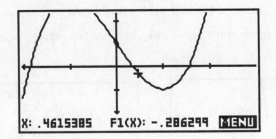

To enlarge this portion of the graph further move the cursor as close as possible to $y = 0$ near $x = 0$. Now press {{MENU}} {{ZOOM}}, select "In," and press {{(X,Y)}} .

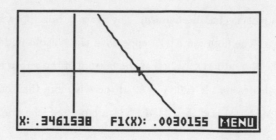

Continue tracing and zooming in until the x-values determined by positioning the cursor just to the left and just to the right of the x-intercept are the same when rounded to three decimal places. We find that $x \approx 0.347$ at the middle x-intercept. This is one solution of the equation $x^3 - 3x + 1 = 0$.

To find a second solution of the equation return to the Function Plot Setup and enter the original window settings, or simply press $\boxed{\square}$ $\boxed{\text{CLEAR}}$ to get the default window; then trace to a position on the curve near another x-intercept and zoom in as described above. Continue to trace and zoom in until the desired accuracy is obtained. Repeat this process to find the third solution. The other two solutions are about -1.879 and 1.532.

At any point in this process, we can zoom out to the previous window by pressing {{ZOOM}}, highlighting "Un-zoom," and pressing $\boxed{\text{ENTER}}$. Only the previous window is retained in memory, however, when using Un-zoom.

The BOX ZOOM operation can also be used to enlarge a portion of the viewing window. We select diagonally opposed corners of a box that defines the new window. For example, graph $y = x^3 - 3x + 1$ in the window $[-10, 10, -10, 10]$. If necessary, press {{MENU}} to activate the menu-key labels. Press {{ZOOM}} and choose "Box...." Then move the cursor from the center of the screen to any corner of the box to be defined. Note that the cursor used in this operation is a free-moving cursor. That is, it can be positioned at any point on the screen as opposed to the trace cursor whose position is restricted to points on the graph.

Press $\boxed{\text{ENTER}}$ to select the first corner. Now use $\boxed{\triangleleft}$, $\boxed{\triangleright}$, $\boxed{\triangle}$, and/or $\boxed{\triangledown}$ to move the cursor to the corner of the box diagonally opposite this one. As you move the cursor away from the first corner the boundaries of the box appear on the screen and change as the position of the cursor changes.

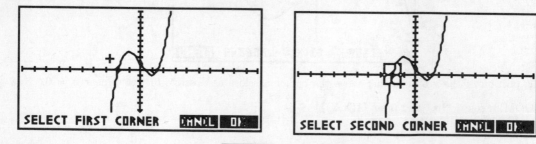

When the box is defined as you want it, press $\boxed{\text{ENTER}}$ to show only the portion of the graph in the box.

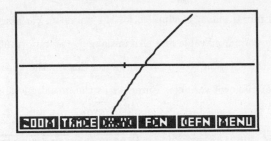

Now we can zoom in or use BOX ZOOM again to further enlarge a portion of the graph.

The Split Screen view gives two side-by-side views of the plot. To produce this press ☐ VIEWS and select "Plot-Detail." The same graph appears twice, but zoom can now be used on the right-hand side. The keystrokes ☐ ◁ and ☐ ▷ will move the cursor to the far left or the far right of the full plot, respectively. The menu selection {{<--}} will make the base plot (left-hand side) look just like the zoomed plot (right-hand side). It does this by resetting the variables in the Plot Setup.

SOLVING EQUATIONS USING SOLVE OR SOLVER

The Solve aplet can also be used to solve equations.

Example 10, page 13: Solve $x^3 - 3x + 1 = 0$. Approximate the solutions to three decimal places.

Begin as in the procedure described above for using Trace and Zoom by graphing $y = x^3 - 3x + 1$ in a window that shows all of the x-intercepts. Note again that the x-intercepts occur near $x = -2$, $x = 0$, and $x = 2$. We will first find the solution near $x = -2$.

Access the Solve aplet by pressing LIB and selecting Solve.

Up to 10 equations can be defined, named E1 through E0, and each equation can contain a maximum of 27 variables, named A through Z or θ. In the Solve Symbolic view, enter a complete equation with the equals sign (available as a menu selection). Although the equation in this example is written with 0 on one side of the equals sign, this form is not required on the HP 38G. For example, $7x - 5 = 6$ is a valid entry. Only one equation can be checkmarked at any time.

```
░░░░SOLVE SYMBOLIC VIEW░░░░
✓E1:X^3-3*X+1=0
 E2:
 E3:
 E4:
 E5:                      ▼
 EDIT ✓CHK   =     SHOW EVAL
```

Real-number variables must be assigned to all variables except one, which the calculator will solve for. To do this, press NUM to go to Numeric view, highlight each known variable, enter a value, highlight the unknown variable, and press {{SOLVE}}. The solution will appear in the unknown variable's field. A faster and perhaps more accurate solution can be obtained if an estimated value (an initial guess) is supplied for the unknown variable before pressing {{SOLVE}}. Solve will then look for a solution near the estimated value first. An initial guess is important in the event that there is more than one solution. Since we are seeking the solution near $x = -2$, we use this for the guess. In Solve Numeric view, note that x is the only variable, and it is the unknown variable. Enter -2 as the initial guess and press {{SOLVE}}. The grapher returns the value -1.87938524157. Thus one solution is about -1.879.

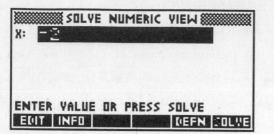
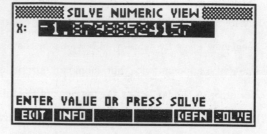

To find the solution near $x = 0$ enter 0. Then press {{SOLVE}} and the value $.347296355335$ is returned.

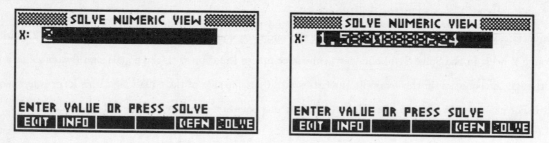

To find the solution near $x = 2$, repeat the previous process, entering 2.

Thus, as we saw before, the other two solutions are about 0.347 and 1.532.

After finding a solution with Solve, more information about the nature of the solution can be obtained by pressing {{INFO}} in the Numeric view. One of three messages will appear:

1) Zero. This indicates that Solve found a point, to an accuracy of 12 digits, where the equation's value is zero.

2) Sign Reversal. This indicates that Solve found two points where the value of the equation has opposite signs. However, it could not find a point between those two points where the value of the equation is zero. Either the two points are too close together (they differ by one in the twelfth digit) or the equation is not real-valued between the points. Solve returns the point where the equation's value is closer to zero.

3) Extremum. This indicates that Solve either found a point where the equation has a local maximum or minimum or it

stopped searching at the largest or smallest number the grapher can represent, $\pm9.99999999999\text{E}499$.

The message "Bad Guess(es)" means no solution was found because one or more of the initial guesses are not in the equation's domain, such as an initial guess of -1 for $\sqrt{x}$. The message "Constant?" means no solution was found because the equation has the same value at every point sampled.

The process of searching for a zero can be observed by pressing any key except $\boxed{\text{ON}}$ (which will cancel the operation) immediately after pressing {{SOLVE}}. Two intermediate guesses and, on the left, the signs of the equation's value when evaluated at those guesses, will be displayed. If no convergence in process is observed, cancel the operation by pressing $\boxed{\text{ON}}$ and start over but use a different initial guess.

Example 12, page 15: Solve: $\frac{2}{3}x - 7 = 5$.

Press $\boxed{\text{LIB}}$ and select "Solve" by pressing $\boxed{\text{ENTER}}$ or {{START}}. The Solve Symbolic view will appear. Enter the equation $\frac{2}{3}x - 7 = 5$.

```
░░░░░░░ SOLVE SYMBOLIC VIEW ░░░░░░░
✓E1:2/3*X-7=5
 E2:
 E3:
 E4:
 E5:                              ▼
 EDIT ✓CHK   =        SHOW EVAL
```

Use the Plot view to find an initial guess for x. First go to Plot Setup by pressing $\boxed{\square}$ $\boxed{\text{PLOT}}$ and set the viewing window. Here we use $[-5, 35, -10, 10]$, XTICK $= 5$, YTICK $= 2$. Now press $\boxed{\text{PLOT}}$, and note that $y = \frac{2}{3}x - 7$ and $y = 5$ are graphed. The x-coordinate of the point where they intersect is the solution. Move the cursor as close to the intersection as possible. The x-value at that point will be an initial guess for x.

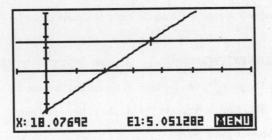

```
X: 18.07692    E1:5.051282  MENU
```

Now press $\boxed{\text{NUM}}$, and note that the initial guess from the plot has been entered in the unknown variable's field. Press {{SOLVE}}. The grapher returns the solution of the equation, 18.

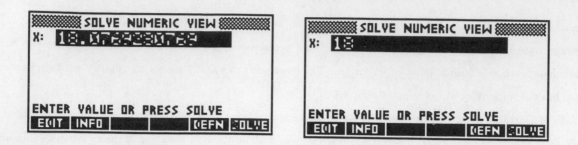

SOLVING EQUATIONS USING ROOT

A solution of an equation with 0 on one side is usually called a zero, but is sometimes called a root. We can find the zeros of an equation in the Plot view of the Function aplet which is accessed by first pressing $\boxed{\text{LIB}}$. The result will be saved in the variable Root so further computations can easily be done using it in the aplet or in Home.

Example 10, page 13: Solve $x^3 - 3x + 1 = 0$. Approximate the solutions to three decimal places.

In the Function aplet, graph $y = x^3 - 3x + 1$ in the standard window as before. Move the cursor as close to the x-intercept near $x = 0$ as possible. Press {{MENU}} and then {{FCN}}. Choose Root. The x-value that the grapher returns is the solution. We see again that the solution is about 0.347.

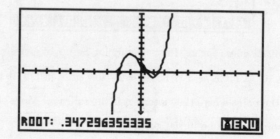

The other two solutions of the equation can be found by using the same procedure two more times.

FINDING POINTS OF INTERSECTION

There are several ways in which the grapher can be used to determine the point(s) of intersection of two graphs.

Example 11, page 14: Find the point of intersection of the graphs of the equations $y_1 = 3x^5 - 20x^3$ and $y_2 = 34.7 - 1.28x^2$. Approximate the coordinates to three decimal places.

First graph the equations as F1(X) and F2(X) in a window that shows all of the points of intersection. We use $[-4, 4, -80, 80]$, XTICK = 1, YTICK = 20 here.

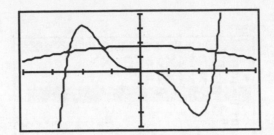

There are three points of intersection. One way to find their coordinates is to use Trace and Zoom. (See "Solving Equations Using Trace and Zoom" on page 166 of this manual.) Another method is to use the Intersection operation. We will illustrate its use by finding the point of intersection at the far left. After graphing F1(X) and F2(X) as above, move the cursor to the far left intersection point. We can use the $\triangle$ and $\triangledown$ keys to choose the curve that will be traced. Press {{MENU}} {{FCN}} and choose Intersection. A dialog box will appear. Choose the function, not the x-axis. The grapher returns the coordinates of the point of intersection. We see that they are about $(-2.463, 26.936)$. The x-coordinate of the point of intersection is saved in a variable named Isect.

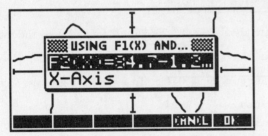
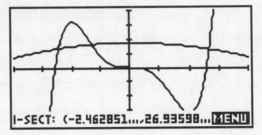

The coordinates of the other two points of intersection can be found by using the Intersection operation two more times.

The Solve aplet can also be used to find the x-coordinates of the points of intersection by finding solutions of F1(X) = F2(X), or F1(X) − F2(X) = 0.

Again it is necessary to graph F1(X) and F2(X) in order to find guesses for the solutions. To find the point of intersection on the far left, move the cursor to that point, or as close as possible to it. The x-coordinate will automatically be entered in the field of the unknown variable in the Solve Numeric view. Press $\boxed{\text{NUM}}$ to see this field. This is the initial guess. Press {{SOLVE}}. The grapher returns the value -2.46285103175. This is the first coordinate of the point of intersection.

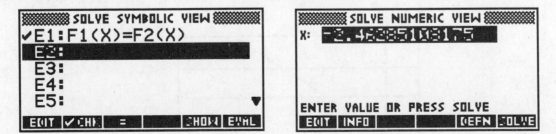

To find the second coordinate, press $\boxed{\text{SYMB}}$ to enter the Solve Symbolic view. Enter an equation, setting F1(X) = Y or F2(X) = Y. For example, enter F1(X) = Y. Press $\boxed{\text{NUM}}$ and note that the value we previously found for X has been entered.

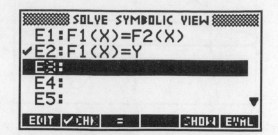

Highlight Y: and press {{SOLVE}}. The value 26.935986939 is returned.

Thus, we see that the coordinates of the point of intersection are about $(-2.463, 26.936)$. If we had used the rounded X-value of -2.463 in F1(X) to compute the corresponding Y-value, the result would have been 26.907983054. If we had used the rounded X-value in F2(X), the resulting Y-value would have been 26.93504768. To achieve the greatest accuracy, then, it is important to use the unrounded X-value in this computation.

SOLVING EQUATIONS USING INTERACTIVE INTERSECTION

The Intersection operation can also be used to solve equations.

Example 12, page 15: Solve: $\frac{2}{3}x - 7 = 5$.

The solution of this equation is the first coordinate of the point of intersection of the graphs of $F1(X) = \frac{2}{3}x - 7$ and $F2(X) = 5$. Thus, we graph these equations in a window that shows the point of intersection and use Intersection as described in "Finding Points of Intersection," page 172 of this manual. The x-coordinate of the point of intersection is 18. This is the solution of the equation.

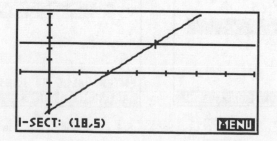

SELECTING DOT MODE

When graphing an equation in which a variable appears in a denominator, the CONNECT setting should not be used. Enter Plot Setup by pressing $\boxed{\square}$ $\boxed{\text{PLOT}}$. Then press {{PAGE $\triangledown$}}. If CONNECT has a checkmark, press $\boxed{\triangledown}$ to highlight that checkmark and press {{$\sqrt{}$ CHK}}. Now it is unchecked. This graphing mode is referred to as DOT mode on some graphers.

```
▓▓▓▓▓FUNCTION PLOT SETUP▓▓▓▓▓
✓SIMULT           _INV. CROSS
■CONNECT           _LABELS
✓AXES              _GRID


CONNECT PLOT POINTS?
   ✓CHK  ▲ PAGE
```

See page 16 in the text for further explanation of why DOT mode is used in certain cases and for an illustration of an equation graphed in both CONNECT and DOT modes.

Chapter R
Basic Concepts of Algebra

SCIENTIFIC NOTATION

To enter a number in scientific notation, first type the decimal portion of the number; then press $\boxed{\square}$ $\boxed{\text{EEX}}$ $\boxed{\text{ENTER}}$. (EEX is the second operation associated with the $\boxed{)}$ key.). Finally, type the exponent, which must be between -499 and 499. For example, to enter 1.789×10^{-11} in scientific notation, press 1 $\boxed{\cdot}$ 7 8 9 $\boxed{\square}$ $\boxed{\text{EEX}}$ $\boxed{-x}$ 1 1 $\boxed{\text{ENTER}}$. To enter 6.084×10^{23} in scientific notation, press 6 $\boxed{\cdot}$ 0 8 4 $\boxed{\square}$ $\boxed{\text{EEX}}$ 2 3 $\boxed{\text{ENTER}}$. The decimal portion of each number appears before an E while the exponent follows the E.

To use the grapher to convert from decimal notation to scientific notation, first select Scientific mode by pressing $\boxed{\square}$ $\boxed{\text{MODES}}$ $\boxed{\triangledown}$. This will highlight NUMBER FORMAT. Press {{CHOOS}} and select Scientific.

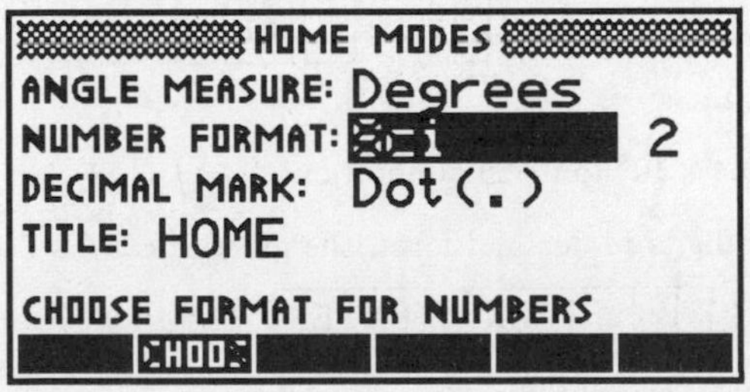

Note that a number appears to the right of Sci. This indicates the number of decimal places which the grapher will display and can be any integer from 0 to 11. For example, if 0 is set, 125 will be displayed as 1.E2; if 1 is set, it will be displayed as 1.3E2; if 5 is set, it will be displayed as 1.25000E2. To change this number use $\boxed{\triangleright}$ to highlight it and then enter the new choice.

Example 3, page 28: Convert 38,500,000,000 to scientific notation.

With the grapher in Scientific 2 mode, type 38500000000 followed by $\boxed{\text{ENTER}}$. The grapher returns 3.85E10, indicating that the scientific notation is 3.85×10^{10}.

Example 4, page 28: Convert 0.00000000000000000000000000167 to scientific notation.

With the grapher in Scientific 2 mode, type .00000000000000000000000000167 $\boxed{\text{ENTER}}$. The grapher returns 1.67E$-$27, indicating that the scientific notation is 1.67×10^{-27}.

```
┌─────────────────────────────────────┐
│ ▓CBS▓▓▓▓▓▓▓▓ HOME ▓▓▓▓▓▓▓            │
│ 38500000000                         │
│                        3.85E10      │
│ .00000000000000000000…              │
│                        1.67E-27     │
│                                     │
│ ─────────────────────────────────  │
│ ▓TO▶                                │
└─────────────────────────────────────┘
```

Even if Standard mode is selected for a computation, the grapher will display any number having more than 12 digits in scientific notation. Thus, the only numbers that can be converted to decimal notation using the HP 38G are those with 12 or fewer digits.

To use the grapher to convert from scientific notation to decimal notation, first set the grapher in Standard mode.

```
┌─────────────────────────────────────┐
│ ▓▓▓▓▓▓▓▓▓ HOME MODES ▓▓▓▓▓▓▓▓        │
│ ANGLE MEASURE: Degrees              │
│ NUMBER FORMAT: ▓Standard▓           │
│ DECIMAL MARK:  Dot(.)               │
│ TITLE: HOME                         │
│                                     │
│ CHOOSE FORMAT FOR NUMBERS           │
│      ▓CHOO▓                         │
└─────────────────────────────────────┘
```

We will consider an example similar to **Example 5 (a)**, page 28: Convert 7.632×10^{-10} to decimal notation.

Since 7.632×10^{-10} has more than 12 digits in decimal form, the grapher cannot be used for this conversion. To confirm this, with the grapher set in Standard mode, press 7 $\boxed{\cdot}$ 6 3 2 $\boxed{\square}$ $\boxed{\text{EEX}}$ $\boxed{-x}$ 1 0 $\boxed{\text{ENTER}}$. The grapher returns scientific notation rather than decimal notation.

Example 5 (b), page 28: Convert 9.4×10^5 to decimal notation.

Since 9.4×10^5 has fewer than 12 digits in decimal form, the grapher can be used to make this conversion. With the grapher set in Standard mode, press 9 $\boxed{\cdot}$ 4 $\boxed{\square}$ $\boxed{\text{EEX}}$ 5 $\boxed{\text{ENTER}}$. The grapher returns decimal notation, 940000.

```
┌─────────────────────────────────────┐
│ ▓CBS▓▓▓▓▓▓▓▓ HOME ▓▓▓▓▓▓▓            │
│ 7.632E-10                           │
│                     7.632E-10       │
│ 9.4E5                               │
│                        940000       │
│                                     │
│ ─────────────────────────────────  │
│ ▓TO▶                                │
└─────────────────────────────────────┘
```

To express the result of a computation in scientific notation, set the grapher in Scientific mode before performing the computation.

EXPRESSIONS WITH RATIONAL EXPONENTS

When using the HP 38G to find rational roots of the form $a^{m/n}$, where $a < 0$, m and n are natural numbers with no common factors other than 1, and $m > 1$, we must enter the expression as $((a)^m)^{1/n}$ or $(\sqrt[n]{a})^m$. If $m = 1$ and n is odd, use the keys $\boxed{\square}$ $\boxed{\sqrt[x]{x}}$. ($\sqrt[x]{x}$ is the second operation associated with the $\boxed{\sqrt{x}}$ key.) For example, $\sqrt[3]{-8}$ is entered with the key sequence 3 $\boxed{\square}$ $\boxed{\sqrt[x]{x}}$ $\boxed{-x}$ 8, and returns -2. It will appear as 3 NTHROOT -8 on the display.

To graph $y = x^{m/n}$, enter F1(X) $= ((x)^m)^{1/n}$ or F1(X) $= ((x)^{1/n})^m$. To illustrate this, first enter $(-8)^{4/3}$. The grapher returns an imaginary number. (Imaginary numbers will be introduced in Chapter 2 of the text.) Now enter $((-8)^4)^{1/3}$. The result is 16. Also enter $(\sqrt[3]{-8})^4$. The result is again 16.

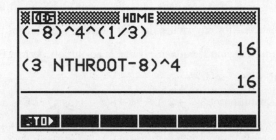

Now graph F1(X) $= x^{4/3}$. Notice that the graph contains no points corresponding to negative x-values.

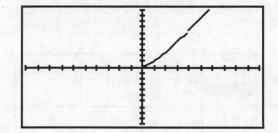

Then graph F1(X) $= (x^4)^{1/3}$. This graph includes negative as well as nonnegative x-values. The same result is obtained for F1(X) $= (\sqrt[3]{x})^4$.

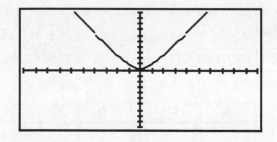

CHECKING SOLUTIONS USING A TABLE

The grapher's Numeric view feature can be used to check solutions of equations. In this situation it is most efficient to select Build Your Own for the NUMTYPE setting in the Numeric Setup screen. To do this, press $\boxed{\square}$ $\boxed{\text{NUM}}$ $\boxed{\triangledown}$ $\boxed{\triangledown}$ {{CHOOS}} $\boxed{\triangledown}$ $\boxed{\text{ENTER}}$. Recall that the values of NUMSTART and NUMSTEP are irrelevant in Build Your Own mode.

```
▓▓▓▓ FUNCTION NUMERIC SETUP ▓▓▓▓
NUMSTART: 3
NUM ┌──────────────────────┐
NUM │Automatic             │
NUM │Build Your Own        │
NUM └──────────────────────┘
CHOOSE TABLE FORMAT
                        CANCL  OK
```

```
▓▓▓▓ FUNCTION NUMERIC SETUP ▓▓▓▓
NUMSTART: 3
NUMSTEP:  1
NUMTYPE:  Build Your Own
NUMZOOM:  4
CHOOSE TABLE FORMAT
        CHOOS           PLOT▶
```

Now press $\boxed{\text{NUM}}$. The grapher displays a table that allows us to enter values for the independent variable. We can then enter the left-hand side of an equation as F1(X) and the right-hand side as F2(X) in the Function Symbolic view and use the table of numbers to evaluate each side for any values that are possible solutions of the equation. For a given value of x, when F1(X) = F2(X) the equation is true and the given x-value is a solution. When F1(X) $\neq$ F2(X) the equation is false and the given x-value is not a solution.

Example 1, page 59: The possible solution of $3(7 - 2x) = 14 - 8(x - 1)$ is 1/2. Use a table to check.

Enter F1(X) = $3(7 - 2x)$ and F2(X) = $14 - 8(x - 1)$ in the Function Symbolic view. Now, with the table set in Build Your Own mode, press $\boxed{\text{NUM}}$ to display the table. Press $\boxed{\square}$ $\boxed{\text{CLEAR}}$ $\boxed{\text{ENTER}}$ to clear the table if necessary. Then press 1 $\boxed{/}$ 2 $\boxed{\text{ENTER}}$ or $\cdot$ 5 $\boxed{\text{ENTER}}$. We see that F1 = F2 = 18, so the equation is true when X = 1/2 and thus the solution is 1/2.

```
┌──────┬──────┬──────┬──────┐
│  X   │  F1  │  F2  │      │
├──────┼──────┼──────┼──────┤
│ .5   │ 18   │ 18   │      │
│▓▓▓▓▓▓│      │      │      │
│      │      │      │      │
│      │      │      │      │
│      │      │      │      │
├──────┴──────┴──────┴──────┤
│ EDIT  INS  SORT  BIG  DEFN│
└───────────────────────────┘
```

Example 4, page 62: The possible solutions of $5 + \sqrt{x + 7} = x$ are 9 and 2. Use a table to check.

Enter F1(X) = $5 + \sqrt{x + 7}$ and F2(X) = x. With the table set in Build Your Own mode, display the table screen by pressing $\boxed{\text{NUM}}$ and press 9 $\boxed{\text{ENTER}}$ 2 $\boxed{\text{ENTER}}$. The table shows that F1 = F2 = 9 when X = 9, but F1 = 8 and F2 = 2 when X = 2. Thus, 9 is a solution of the equation, but 2 is not.

```
┌──────┬──────┬──────┬──────┐
│  X   │  F1  │  F2  │      │
├──────┼──────┼──────┼──────┤
│ 9    │ 9    │ 9    │      │
│ 2    │ 8    │ 2    │      │
│▓▓▓▓▓▓│      │      │      │
│      │      │      │      │
│      │      │      │      │
├──────┴──────┴──────┴──────┤
│ EDIT  INS  SORT  BIG  DEFN│
└───────────────────────────┘
```

CHECKING SOLUTIONS OF INEQUALITIES

Solutions of inequalities can be checked graphically.

Example 1 (b), page 67: The possible solution set of $13 - 7y \geq 10y - 4$ is $\{y|y \leq 1\}$. Check with a grapher.

Replace y with x and graph $F1(X) = 13 - 7x$ and $F2(X) = 10x - 4$ in a window that shows the point of intersection of the graphs. The window $[-10, 10, -10, 10]$ is shown here.

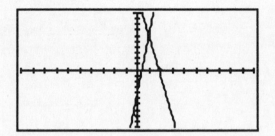

Now use Intersect or Trace and Zoom to find the first coordinate of the point of intersection, 1. Then observe that the graph of $F1(X)$ lies on or above the graph of $F2(X)$ at the point of intersection and to its left. (To see which graph the crosshairs are on, press $\{\{DEFN\}\}$.) That is, $F1(X) \geq F2(X)$, or $13 - 7x \geq 10x - 4$, for $\{x|x \leq 1\}$. Thus, the solution set of the original inequality, $13 - 7y \geq 10y - 4$, is $\{y|y \leq 1\}$.

Example 4, page 70: The possible solution set of $2x - 5 \leq -7$ or $2x - 5 > 1$ is $(-\infty, -1] \cup (3, \infty)$. Check with a grapher.

Graph $F1(X) = 2x - 5$, $F2(X) = -7$, and $F3(X) = 1$ in a window that shows the points of intersection of the graphs. The window $[-10, 10, -10, 10]$ is shown here.

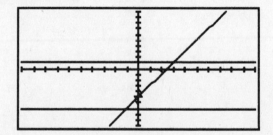

Now use Intersect or Trace and Zoom to find the first coordinates of the points of intersection. When $x = -1$, $F1(X)$ and $F2(X)$ intersect, and $F1(X)$ and $F3(X)$ intersect when $x = 3$. Now observe that the graph of $F1(X)$ lies on or below the graph of $F2(X)$ at their point of intersection and to its left. Thus, $F1(X) \leq F2(X)$, or $2x - 5 \leq -7$, on $(-\infty, -1]$. Also observe that the graph of $F1(X)$ lies above the graph of $F3(X)$ to the right of their point of intersection. That is, $F1(X) > F3(X)$, or $2x - 5 > 1$, on $(3, \infty)$. Then the solution set of the inequality is $(-\infty, -1] \cup (3, \infty)$.

Chapter 1
Graphs, Functions, and Models

FINDING FUNCTION VALUES

When a formula for a function is given, function values for real-numbered inputs can be found in several ways on a grapher.

Example 4 (a), (b), page 87: For $f(x) = 2x^2 - x + 3$, find $f(0)$ and $f(-7)$.

Method 1: Substitute the inputs directly in the formula. For example, to find $f(0)$ press 2 $\boxed{*}$ 0 $\boxed{\square}$ $\boxed{x^2}$ $\boxed{-}$ 0 $\boxed{+}$ 3 $\boxed{\text{ENTER}}$. (x^2 is the second function associated with the $\boxed{x^y}$ key.) To find $f(-7)$ press 2 $\boxed{(}$ $\boxed{-x}$ 7 $\boxed{)}$ $\boxed{\square}$ $\boxed{x^2}$ $\boxed{-}$ $\boxed{-x}$ 7 $\boxed{+}$ 3 $\boxed{\text{ENTER}}$.

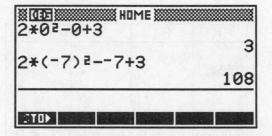

Method 2: Enter $F1(X) = 2x^2 - x + 3$ in Function Symbolic view. Then press $\boxed{\text{HOME}}$ to go to the home screen. Now to find $f(0)$, the value of $F1(X)$ when $x = 0$, press 0 {{STO ▷}} $\boxed{\text{X, T, }\Theta}$ $\boxed{\text{ENTER}}$ $\boxed{\text{A...Z}}$ F 1 $\boxed{(}$ $\boxed{\text{X, T, }\Theta}$ $\boxed{\text{ENTER}}$. This series of keystrokes stores 0 as the value of x and then substitutes it in the function $F1(X)$. To find the function value at $x = -7$, repeat this process, using -7 in place of 0.

Method 3: Enter $F1(X) = 2x^2 - x + 3$ in Function Symbolic view and press $\boxed{\text{HOME}}$ to go to the home screen. Then, to find $f(0)$ press $\boxed{\text{A...Z}}$ F 1 $\boxed{(}$ 0 $\boxed{)}$ $\boxed{\text{ENTER}}$. Note that these entries closely resemble function notation. To find $f(-7)$ repeat this process entering -7 in place of 0.

```
▒▓▒▒▒▒▒▒▒▒▒▒▒▒ HOME ▒▒▒▒▒▒▒▒▒▒▒▒
F1(0)
                                              3
F1(-7)
                                            108
─────────────────────────────────────────────
 STO▶
```

Method 4: The Solve aplet can be used to find function values. Press $\boxed{\text{LIB}}$ and choose Solve from the aplet library. Enter E1: $Y = 2X^2 - X + 3$ in the Solve symbolic view. Then press $\boxed{\text{NUM}}$ to go to Solve Numeric view, highlight the X: field, and press 0 $\boxed{\text{ENTER}}$ {{SOLVE}} to find $f(0)$. A similar procedure is performed to find $f(-7)$. The function value will appear in the Y: field after {{SOLVE}} is pressed.

Method 5: The Table feature can also be used to find function values. With $F1(X) = 2x^2 - x + 3$ entered in Function Symbolic view and the NUMTYPE set in Build Your Own mode, go to the table screen and press 0 $\boxed{\text{ENTER}}$ to find $f(0)$ and $\boxed{-x}$ 7 $\boxed{\text{ENTER}}$ to find $f(-7)$.

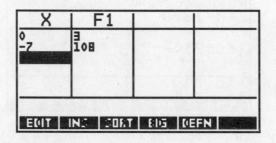

LINEAR REGRESSION AND SCATTERPLOTS

The linear regression operation of the grapher enables us to fit a linear function to a set of data.

Example 1, page 129: Fit a regression line to the data on life expectancy of women on page 128 of the text. Then predict the life expectancy of women in 2000.

First we enter the data from the table into the Numeric view of the Statistics aplet. Choosing Statistics in the aplet library will take us directly to the Numeric view. To clear any existing data press $\boxed{\square}$ $\boxed{\text{CLEAR}}$, choose "All columns," and press $\boxed{\text{ENTER}}$. For two-variable statistics, as in this example, be sure that {{2VAR□}} is on. If it is not, press {{1VAR□}} and then {{2VAR□}} will appear. Two-variable statistics require at least four data points, and one-variable statistics require at least two data points.

We will enter the x-values in C1 and the y-values in C2. The cursor should be at the top of the C1 column. To enter 0 press 0 $\boxed{\text{ENTER}}$. Continue typing the x-values 1 through 9, each followed by $\boxed{\text{ENTER}}$. Press $\boxed{\triangleright}$ to move to the top of the C2 column. Type the y-values in succession, each followed by $\boxed{\text{ENTER}}$.

To see a scatterplot of the data, first press $\boxed{\text{SYMB}}$ to go to the Statistics Symbolic view and clear any previous entries if necessary. In the default definition for S1, C1 is the previously entered independent data from the table and C2 is the dependent data. Since this reflects the conditions of our example, keep the default settings, and checkmark S1. "Fit 1" should be linear, $m * X + b$. If it is not, press ☐ SYMB to go to Statistics Symbolic Setup and use {{CHOOS}} to choose Linear for S1FIT.

```
▓█▓▓STATISTICS SYMBOLIC VIEW▓▓▓
✓S1: C1        C2
✓Fit1:▐m✳X+b▌
 S2:
 Fit2:a✳X^2+b✳X+c          ▼
ENTER USER DEFINED FIT
EDIT ✓CHK    ✗       SHOW EVAL
```

Press ☐ PLOT to go to Statistics Plot Setup and choose the type of mark that will be used for the points of the scatterplot. Highlight S1MARK, press {{CHOOS}}, and select a mark by highlighting it and pressing ENTER .

```
▓█▓▓▓STATISTICS PLOT SETUP▓▓▓▓
XRNG: .8         5.2
YRNG: 6.33333... 33.1
S1MARK:▣ S2MARK:✦ S3MARK::
S4MARK: : S5MARK:✖
CHOOSE MARK FOR SCATTER PLOT
    CHOOS PAGE ▼
```

```
▓█▓
XRN(   ✦                    ▲
YRN(   ✚
S1M    ▪▪              ::
       ✖
S4M(   ▪▪
       ▪             ▼
CHOO                CANCL OK
```

To see the scatterplot select a window and press PLOT . Instead of entering the window dimensions directly, we can press ☐ VIEWS and select Auto Scale. This automatically defines a viewing window that displays all the data points. The STAT lists and the scatterplot for these data are shown on page 129 of the text. {{FIT ☐}} should be on to find the regression curve and regression values. If it is not on, press {{MENU}} {{FIT}} to turn it on. To exit this screen press {{OK}}.

Press SYMB , highlight Fit1, and then press {{SHOW}} to display the regression expression. To see the correlation coefficient r, press NUM , choose {{STATS}}, and scroll down to CORR. This coefficient of correlation applies to the linear regression model only. To exit this screen press {{OK}}.

```
▓█▓▓STATISTICS SYMBOLIC VIEW▓▓▓
✓S1: C1        C2
✓Fit1:▐3.42787878788...▌
 S2:
 Fit2:a✳X^2+b✳X+c          ▼
ENTER USER DEFINED FIT
EDIT ✓CHK  ✗       SHOW EVAL
```

```

3.42787878788·X+50.654⁵


                            OK
```

2-VAR	S1		
ΣX2	285		
MEANY	66.08		
ΣY	660.8		
ΣY2	44662.54		
ΣXY	3256.4		
CORR	.9861248		

.986124753829

To predict the life expectancy of women in 2000 find the value of y when $x = 10$ in the following manner. Go to Home, press MATH A...Z S, and choose Stat-Two and PREDY on the command line. "PREDY(" will be displayed. Press 1 0 ENTER. Alternatively, this may be typed manually in Home's command line.

GRAPHING CIRCLES

Although the standard form of the equation of a circle cannot be entered in Function Symbolic view, circles can be graphed on the HP 38G. A square viewing window is required to give an accurate graph.

Example 5, page 138: Graph $x^2 + y^2 = 16$.

Solve the equation for y as shown on page 138 of the text, enter F1(X) $= \sqrt{16 - x^2}$ and F2(X) $= -\sqrt{16 - x^2}$, select a square window, and press PLOT. Note that we can enter F2(X) $= -$F1(X) instead of F2(X) $= -\sqrt{16 - x^2}$. The graph is shown on page 138 of the text.

THE ALGEBRA OF FUNCTIONS

The grapher can be used to evaluate and graph combinations of functions.

Example 1 (b), page 159: Given that $f(x) = x + 1$ and $g(x) = \sqrt{x + 3}$, find $(f + g)(6)$.

Choose the Function aplet. Press SYMB and enter F1(X) $= x + 1$, F2(X) $= \sqrt{x + 3}$, and F3(X) = F1(X) + F2(X). To enter F3(X) = F1(X) + F2(X) press A...Z F 1 (| {{x}} |) + A...Z F 2 (| {{x}} ENTER . Note that F3(X) $= f(x) + g(x)$, or $(f + g)(x)$. Use F3(X) to find $(f + g)(6)$ employing one of the methods for finding function values described on pages 183 and 184 of this manual. We find that $(f + g)(6) = 10$.

To view the graphs of $f(x)$, $g(x)$, and $(f + g)(x)$ enter F1(X), F2(X), and F3(X) as above, checkmark them, select a window, and press PLOT. These graphs appear on page 159 of the text. It is possible to deselect one or two of these functions and display the graph(s) of the remaining function(s). For example, to display only the graph of F3(X) without deleting the equations of F1(X) and F2(X), press $\boxed{\text{SYMB}}$. Then highlight F1(X) and press {{$\checkmark$ CHK}}. This deselects or turns off F1(X). Do the same for F2(X). Now press $\boxed{\text{PLOT}}$ and see only the graph of F3(X).

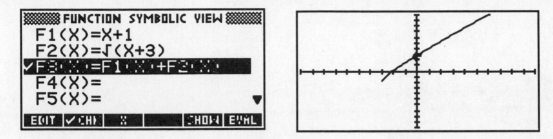

To select or turn on a function again, repeat this process. Note that a selected function has a checkmark.

Example 3 (a), page 162: Given that $f(x) = 2x - 5$ and $g(x) = x^2 - 3x + 8$, find $(f \circ g)(7)$ and $(g \circ f)(7)$.

In the Function aplet, press $\boxed{\text{SYMB}}$ and enter F1(X) = $2x - 5$, F2(X) = $x^2 - 3x + 8$, F3(X) = F1(F2(X)), and F4(X) = F2(F1(X)). Note that F3(X) = $(f \circ g)(x)$ and F4(X) = $(g \circ f)(x)$. Use F3(X) and F4(X) to find $(f \circ g)(7)$ and $(g \circ f)(7)$, respectively, employing one of the methods for finding function values described on pages 183 and 184 of this manual.

Chapter 2
Polynomial and Rational Functions

OPERATIONS WITH COMPLEX NUMBERS

Operations with complex numbers can be performed on the HP 38G. On this grapher complex numbers appear as ordered pairs (a, b) where a is the real part and b is the imaginary part. That is, $(a, b) = a + bi$. A complex number may be entered as an ordered pair, or in the form $a + bi$. The letter i can be obtained by pressing ☐ MATH ☐ and choosing it from the Constant menu, or it can be typed directly with the key sequence ☐ □ ☐ ☐ a...z ☐ I. (a...z is the second operation associated with the ☐ A...Z ☐ key. It is used to type lowercase letters.)

Example 4, page 176:

(a) Add: $(8 + 6i) + (3 + 2i)$.

To find this sum press ☐ (☐ 8 ☐ · ☐ 6 ☐) ☐ ☐ + ☐ ☐ (☐ 3 ☐ · ☐ 2 ☐) ☐ ☐ ENTER ☐. The result is $(11, 8)$, or $11 + 8i$.

(b) Subtract: $(4 + 5i) - (6 - 3i)$.

Press ☐ (☐ 4 ☐ · ☐ 5 ☐) ☐ ☐ − ☐ ☐ (☐ 6 ☐ · ☐ −x ☐ 3 ☐) ☐ ☐ ENTER ☐. The result is $(-2, 8)$, or $-2 + 8i$.

```
▓▓CAS▓▓▓▓▓▓▓▓▓ HOME ▓▓▓▓▓▓▓
(8,6)+(3,2)
                        (11,8)
(4,5)-(6,-3)
                        (-2,8)

▓STO▶
```

Example 5 (a), (b), (d), (e), page 177:

(a) Multiply: $\sqrt{-16} \cdot \sqrt{-25}$.

Press ☐ √x̄ ☐ ☐ −x ☐ 1 6 ☐ √x̄ ☐ ☐ −x ☐ 2 5 ☐ ENTER ☐. The result is $(-20, 0)$, or -20.

(b) Multiply: $\sqrt{-5} \cdot \sqrt{-7}$.

Press ☐ √x̄ ☐ ☐ −x ☐ 5 ☐ √x̄ ☐ ☐ −x ☐ 7 ☐ ENTER ☐. Note that this operation produces a decimal approximation of the product. That is, $\sqrt{-5} \cdot \sqrt{-7} \approx -5.91607978309$. The exact value of the product is $-\sqrt{35}$.

```
▓▓CAS▓▓▓▓▓▓▓▓▓ HOME ▓▓▓▓▓▓▓
√-16*√-25
                    (-20,0)
√-5*√-7
            (-5.91607978309,0)

▓STO▶
```

(d) Multiply: $(1 + 2i)(1 + 3i)$.

Press $\boxed{(}$ $\boxed{1}$ $\boxed{\cdot}$ $\boxed{2}$ $\boxed{)}$ $\boxed{(}$ $\boxed{1}$ $\boxed{\cdot}$ $\boxed{3}$ $\boxed{)}$ $\boxed{\text{ENTER}}$. The result is $(-5, 5)$, or $-5 + 5i$.

(e) Multiply: $(3 - 7i)^2$.

Press $\boxed{(}$ $\boxed{3}$ $\boxed{\cdot}$ $\boxed{-x}$ $\boxed{7}$ $\boxed{)}$ $\boxed{\square}$ $\boxed{x^2}$ $\boxed{\text{ENTER}}$. The result is $(-40, -42)$, or $-40 - 42i$.

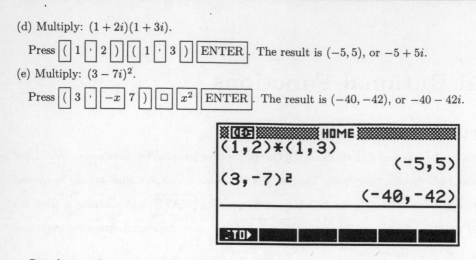

Complex numbers can also be divided. The real and imaginary parts of the quotient will be expressed in decimal form. For example, the quotient $(2 - 5i)/(1 - 6i)$ in Example 9, page 179 would be expressed as $(.864864864865, .18918....$ The initial display will not show the entire imaginary part of the quotient. To see the full quotient press $\boxed{\text{MATH}}$ and choose IM from the Complex menu. Then press $\boxed{\square}$ $\boxed{\text{ANSWER}}$ $\boxed{\text{ENTER}}$. (ANSWER is the second operation associated with the $\boxed{\text{ENTER}}$ key.) This will display the imaginary part of the previous answer. Alternatively, type IM(Ans) directly.

QUADRATIC AND CUBIC REGRESSION

In addition to the linear regression discussed earlier, second and third degree polynomial functions can be fit to data using the quadratic and cubic regression operations, respectively.

The operations of entering data, making scatterplots, and graphing and evaluating quadratic and cubic regression functions are the same as for linear regression functions. Before proceeding, reread the section on Linear Regression and Scatterplots beginning on page 184 of this manual.

Example 5, page 201: For the data on hours of sleep versus death rate on page 202 of the text, make a scatterplot for the data and determine which, if any, of the functions above fits the data. Then find the regression equation, graph the equation, and use it to make predictions.

Enter the data in C1 and C2 and make a scatterplot as described on page 184 of this manual. The scatterplot is shown in the text. It appears that a quadratic function fits the data. To find it press $\boxed{\square}$ $\boxed{\text{SYMB}}$, highlight S1FIT, and choose Quadratic. Then plot the data using the Auto Scale option ($\boxed{\square}$ $\boxed{\text{VIEWS}}$). If you do not see the regression curve being drawn, press {{MENU}} {{FIT}}. This must be done before the regression expression can be obtained. Then press $\boxed{\text{SYMB}}$ to go to the Statistics Symbolic view and select {{SHOW}} to see the expression. Use $\boxed{\triangleright}$ to scroll to the characters that do not appear on the initial screen. Note that at least three data points are required for quadratic regression.

To fit a cubic function to a set of data, enter the data in C1 and C2 as described earlier. Then use $\boxed{\square}$ $\boxed{\text{SYMB}}$ to go to the Statistics Symbolic Setup. Select cubic regression by highlighting S1FIT, or whichever is applicable, press {{CHOOS}}, and choose Cubic. It might be necessary to scroll up or down using the arrow keys. At least four data points are required for cubic regression.

Chapter 3
Exponential and Logarithmic Functions

EVALUATING e^x, **Log** x, and **Ln** x

Use the grapher's scientific keys to evaluate e^x, $\log x$, and $\ln x$ for specific values of x.

Example 6 (a), (b), page 270: Find the value of e^3 and $e^{-0.23}$. Round to four decimal places.

To find e^3 press $\boxed{\square}$ $\boxed{e^x}$ 3 $\boxed{\text{ENTER}}$. (e^x is the second operation associated with the $\boxed{+}$ key.) The grapher returns 20.0855369232. Thus, $e^3 \approx 20.0855$. To find $e^{-0.23}$ press $\boxed{\square}$ $\boxed{e^x}$ $\boxed{-x}$ $\cdot$ 2 3 $\boxed{\text{ENTER}}$. The grapher returns .794533602503, so $e^{-0.23} \approx 0.7945$.

Example 4 (a), (b), (c), page 279: Find the values of log 645,778, log 0.0000239, and log (-3). Round to four decimal places.

To find log 645,778 press $\boxed{\square}$ $\boxed{\text{LOG}}$ 6 4 5 7 7 8 $\boxed{\text{ENTER}}$. (LOG is the second operation associated with the $\boxed{/}$ key.) The grapher returns 5.81008324563. Thus, log $645,778 \approx 5.8101$. To find log 0.0000239 press $\boxed{\square}$ $\boxed{\text{LOG}}$ $\cdot$ 0 0 0 0 2 3 9 $\boxed{\text{ENTER}}$. The grapher returns -4.62160209905, so log $0.0000239 \approx -4.6216$. When we press $\boxed{\square}$ $\boxed{\text{LOG}}$ $\boxed{-x}$ 3 $\boxed{\text{ENTER}}$ we get a complex number (expressed as an ordered pair). This indicates that -3 is not in the domain of the function $\log x$.

Example 5 (a), (b), (c), page 279: Find the values of ln 645,778, ln 0.0000239, and ln (-5). Round to four decimal places.

To find ln 645,778 and ln 0.0000239 repeat the keystrokes used above to find log 645,778 and log 0.0000239 but press $\boxed{\square}$ $\boxed{\text{LN}}$ rather than $\boxed{\square}$ $\boxed{\text{LOG}}$. (LN is the second operation associated with the $\boxed{-}$ key.) We find that ln $645,778 \approx 13.3782$ and ln $0.0000239 \approx -10.6416$. When we press $\boxed{\square}$ $\boxed{\text{LN}}$ $\boxed{-x}$ 5 $\boxed{\text{ENTER}}$ we get a complex number (expressed as an ordered pair) indicating that -5 is not in the domain of the function $\ln x$.

USING THE CHANGE OF BASE FORMULA

To find a logarithm with a base other than 10 or e we use the change-of-base formula, $\log_b M = \dfrac{\log_a M}{\log_a b}$, where a and b are any logarithmic bases and M is any positive number.

Example 6, page 280: Find $\log_5 8$ using common logarithms.

We let $a = 10$, $b = 5$, and $M = 8$ and substitute in the change-of-base formula. Press $\boxed{\square}$ $\boxed{\text{LOG}}$ 8 $\boxed{)}$ $\boxed{/}$ $\boxed{\square}$ $\boxed{\text{LOG}}$ 5 $\boxed{\text{ENTER}}$. The result is about 1.2920.

Example 7, page 280: Find $\log_4 31$ using natural logarithms.

We let $a = e$, $b = 4$, and $M = 31$ and substitute in the change-of-base formula. Press $\boxed{\square}$ $\boxed{\text{LN}}$ 3 1 $\boxed{)}$ $\boxed{/}$ $\boxed{\square}$ $\boxed{\text{LN}}$ 4 $\boxed{\text{ENTER}}$. The result is about 2.4771.

Example 9, page 281: Graph $y = \log_5 x$.

To use a grapher we must first change the base to e or 10. Here we use e. Let $a = e$, $b = 5$, and $M = x$ and substitute in the change-of-base formula. Enter $F1(X) = \dfrac{\ln x}{\ln 5}$ in the Function Symbolic view screen, select a window, and press $\boxed{\text{PLOT}}$.

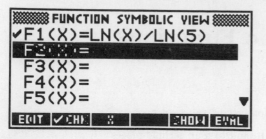
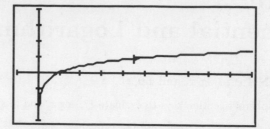

EXPONENTIAL, LOGARITHMIC, AND POWER REGRESSION

In addition to the types of polynomial regression discussed earlier, exponential, logarithmic, and power functions can be fit to data. The operations of entering data, making scatterplots, and graphing and evaluating these functions are the same as for linear regression functions. Before proceeding, reread the section on Linear Regression and Scatterplots beginning on page 184 of this manual.

Example 6 (a), page 310: Fit an exponential equation to the given data on cellular phones.

Enter the data in C1 and C2 as described on page 184 of this manual. Then press $\boxed{\square}$ $\boxed{\text{SYMB}}$ to view the Statistics Symbolic Setup. Highlight S1FIT, press {{CHOOS}}, and select Exponential. After plotting, we can see the exponential function by selecting {{SHOW}} in Statistics Symbolic view, but the coefficient of correlation r, found by pressing $\boxed{\text{NUM}}$ {{STATS}} and scrolling down to CORR, applies only to the linear regression model.

Exercise 26 (a), page 316: Fit a logarithmic function to the given data on forgetting.

After entering the data in C1 and C2 as described on page 184 of this manual, press $\boxed{\square}$ $\boxed{\text{SYMB}}$ to view the Statistics Symbolic Setup. Highlight S1FIT, press {{CHOOS}}, and select Logarithmic. After plotting, we can see the logarithmic function in Statistics Symbolic view, but the coefficient of correlation r, found by pressing $\boxed{\text{NUM}}$ {{STATS}} and scrolling down to CORR, applies only to the linear regression model.

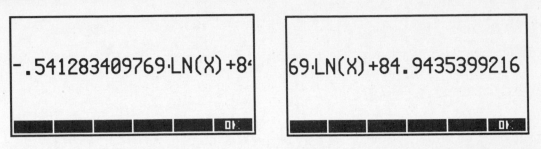

Example 7 (a), page 312: Fit a power function to the given data on cholesterol level and risk of heart attack.

Enter the data in C1 and C2 as described on page 184 of this manual. Then press $\boxed{\square}$ $\boxed{\text{SYMB}}$ to view the Statistics Symbolic Setup. Highlight S1FIT, press {{CHOOS}}, and select Power. After plotting, we can see the power function in Statistics Symbolic view, but the coefficient of correlation r, found by pressing $\boxed{\text{NUM}}$ {{STATS}} and scrolling down to CORR, applies only to the linear regression model.

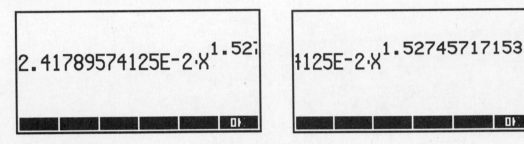

LOGISTIC REGRESSION

A logistic function can be fit to data using the HP 38G.

Exercise 28 (a), page 316: Fit a logistic function to the given data on the effect of advertising.

After entering the data in C1 and C2 as described on page 184 of this manual, press $\boxed{\square}$ $\boxed{\text{SYMB}}$ to view the Statistics Symbolic Setup. Highlight S1FIT, press {{CHOOS}}, and select Logistic. After plotting, we can see the logistic function in Statistics Symbolic view, but the coefficient of correlation r, found by pressing $\boxed{\text{NUM}}$ {{STATS}} and scrolling down to CORR, applies only to the linear regression model. Be sure that the variable L has the value of 0 before graphing. To ensure this, go to Home and press 0 {{STO ▷}} $\boxed{\text{A...Z}}$ L $\boxed{\text{ENTER}}$.

Chapter 4
The Trigonometric Functions

This chapter appears only in the text *ALGEBRA & TRIGONOMETRY: GRAPHS & MODELS* by **Bittinger,**
Beecher, Ellenbogen, and Penna and should be disregarded by students using the text *COLLEGE ALGEBRA:*
GRAPHS & MODELS.

CONVERTING BETWEEN D°M'S'' AND DECIMAL DEGREE MEASURE

The Real-Number functions HMS→ and →HMS can be used to convert D°M'S'' notation to decimal notation and vice

versa.

Example 5, page 328: Convert 5°42′30″ to decimal degree notation.

Press $\boxed{\text{MATH}}$, highlight Real, press $\boxed{\triangleright}$ $\boxed{\text{A...Z}}$ H to highlight HMS→, and then press $\boxed{\text{ENTER}}$. After highlighting Real

we could also use $\boxed{\triangleright}$ and $\boxed{\triangledown}$ $\boxed{\triangledown}$ $\boxed{\triangledown}$ $\boxed{\triangledown}$ $\boxed{\triangledown}$ to highlight HMS→. Now enter 5°42′30″ as the number of degrees followed

by a decimal point and then the remainder of the digits: 5.4230. Press $\boxed{\text{ENTER}}$. The grapher returns 5.708333333, so

5°42′30″ ≈ 5.71°.

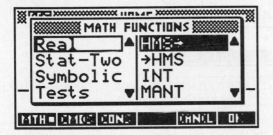

Example 6, page 328: Convert 72.18°to D°M'S'' notation.

Press $\boxed{\text{MATH}}$, highlight Real, press $\boxed{\triangleright}$ $\boxed{\text{A...Z}}$ H to skip to the entries beginning with the letter H. Then press $\boxed{\triangledown}$ to

highlight →HMS, and then press $\boxed{\text{ENTER}}$. After highlighting Real we could also use $\boxed{\triangleright}$ and $\boxed{\triangledown}$ $\boxed{\triangledown}$ $\boxed{\triangledown}$ $\boxed{\triangledown}$ $\boxed{\triangledown}$ $\boxed{\triangledown}$

to highlight →HMS. Now press 7 2 $\boxed{\cdot}$ 1 8 $\boxed{\text{ENTER}}$. The grapher returns 72.1048, where the digits in front of the decimal

point are degrees, the next two digits after the decimal point are minutes, and the two final digits are seconds. Thus we

have 72°10′48″.

The procedure for converting D°M'S" notation to decimal notation requires that both the minutes and the seconds be expressed using two digits. For example, enter 8°5'3" as 8.0503.

FINDING TRIGONOMETRIC FUNCTION VALUES

The grapher's SIN, COS, and TAN operations can be used to find the values of trigonometric functions. When angles are given in degree measure, the grapher must be set in Degree mode.

Example 7, page 328: Find the trigonometric function value, rounded to four decimal places, of each of the following.

a) tan 29.7°   b) sec 48°   c) sin 84°10'39"

a) Press $\boxed{\text{TAN}}$ 2 9 $\boxed{\cdot}$ 7 $\boxed{\text{ENTER}}$. We find that tan 29.7° ≈ 0.5704.

b) The secant, cosecant, and cotangent functions can be found by taking the reciprocals of the cosine, sine, and tangent functions, respectively. This can be done either by entering the reciprocal or by using the $\boxed{\Box}$ $\boxed{x^{-1}}$ keys. To find sec 48° we can enter the reciprocal of cos 48° by pressing 1 $\boxed{/}$ $\boxed{\text{COS}}$ 4 8 $\boxed{\text{ENTER}}$. To find sec 48° using the $\boxed{\Box}$ $\boxed{x^{-1}}$ keys press $\boxed{\text{COS}}$ 4 8 $\boxed{)}$ $\boxed{\Box}$ $\boxed{x^{-1}}$ $\boxed{\text{ENTER}}$. The result is sec 48° ≈ 1.4945.

```
░▒▓█ ▒▒▒▒▒▒▒▒ HOME ▒▒▒▒▒▒▒▒
1/COS(48)
                1.49447654986
COS(48)^-1
                1.49447654986
─────────────────────────────
 STO▶
```

c) First convert 84°10'39" to decimal form, and then press $\boxed{\text{SIN}}$ $\boxed{\Box}$ $\boxed{\text{ANSWER}}$ $\boxed{\text{ENTER}}$. We find that sin 84°10'39" ≈ 0.9948.

In addition to the sine, cosine, and tangent keys, the HP 38G has the following trigonometric functions built into the MATH menu: cotangent (COT), cosecant (CSC), and secant (SEC). These are accessed by first pressing $\boxed{\text{MATH}}$ and using $\boxed{\nabla}$ repeatedly to highlight Trig. on the left side of the menu. Then use $\boxed{\triangleright}$ to move to the right side of the menu and use $\boxed{\nabla}$ to scroll down. To find sec 48°, for instance, use the arrow keys as described to highlight SEC. Then press $\boxed{\text{ENTER}}$ 4 8 $\boxed{)}$ $\boxed{\text{ENTER}}$.

FINDING ANGLES

The inverse trigonometric function keys provide a quick way to find an angle given a trigonometric function value for that angle.

Example 8, page 329: Find the acute angle, to the nearest tenth of a degree, whose sine value is approximately 0.20113.

Although the Table feature can be used to approximate this angle, it is faster to use the inverse sine key. With the grapher set in Degree mode press $\boxed{\Box}$ $\boxed{\text{ASIN}}$ $\boxed{\cdot}$ 2 0 1 1 3 $\boxed{\text{ENTER}}$. (ASIN is the second operation associated with the

$\boxed{\text{SIN}}$ key.) We find that the desired acute angle is approximately 11.6°.

Exercise 63, page 332: Find the acute angle, to the nearest tenth of a degree, whose cotangent value is 2.127.

Angles whose secant, cosecant, or cotangent values are known can be found using the reciprocals of the cosine, sine, and tangent functions, respectively. Since $\cot\theta = \dfrac{1}{\tan\theta} = 2.127$, we have $\tan\theta = \dfrac{1}{2.127}$, or $(2.127)^{-1}$. To find θ press $\boxed{\square}$ $\boxed{\text{ATAN}}$ 1 $\boxed{/}$ 2 $\boxed{\cdot}$ $1\,2\,7$ $\boxed{\text{ENTER}}$ or $\boxed{\square}$ $\boxed{\text{ATAN}}$ 2 $\boxed{\cdot}$ $1\,2\,7$ $\boxed{\square}$ $\boxed{x^{-1}}$ $\boxed{\text{ENTER}}$. (ATAN is the second operation associated with the $\boxed{\text{TAN}}$ key.) We find that $\theta \approx 25.2°$.

CONVERTING BETWEEN DEGREE AND RADIAN MEASURE

We can use the grapher to convert from degree to radian measure and vice versa.

Example 3, page 363: Convert each of the following to radians.

a) 120°   b) −297.25°

a) Press $\boxed{\text{MATH}}$, highlight Real, and press $\boxed{\triangleright}$ $\boxed{\triangledown}$ $\boxed{\text{ENTER}}$. Then press $1\,2\,0$ $\boxed{\text{ENTER}}$. The grapher returns a decimal approximation of the radian measure. We see that $120° \approx 2.09$ radians.

b) Press $\boxed{\text{MATH}}$, highlight Real, and press $\boxed{\triangleright}$ $\boxed{\triangledown}$ $\boxed{\text{ENTER}}$. Then press $\boxed{-x}$ $2\,9\,7$ $\boxed{\cdot}$ $2\,5$ $\boxed{\text{ENTER}}$. We see that $-297.25° \approx -5.19$ radians.

```
▓▒▒▒▒▒▒▒▒▒ HOME ▒▒▒▒▒▒▒▒▒
DEG→RAD(120)
              2.09439510239
DEG→RAD(-297.25)
             -5.18799120155
_____
 STO▶
```

Example 4, page 363: Convert each of the following to degrees.

a) $\dfrac{3\pi}{4}$ radians   b) 8.5 radians

a) Press $\boxed{\text{MATH}}$, highlight Real, press $\boxed{\triangleright}$ $\boxed{\text{A...Z}}$ R to highlight RAD→DEG, and press $\boxed{\text{ENTER}}$. Then press 3 $\boxed{\square}$ $\boxed{\pi}$ $\boxed{/}$ 4 $\boxed{\text{ENTER}}$. (π is the second operation associated with the $\boxed{3}$ key.) The grapher returns 135, so $\dfrac{3\pi}{4}$ radians = 135°.

b) Press $\boxed{\text{MATH}}$, highlight Real, and press $\boxed{\triangleright}$ $\boxed{\text{A...Z}}$ R $\boxed{\text{ENTER}}$. Then press 8 $\boxed{\cdot}$ 5 $\boxed{\text{ENTER}}$. The grapher returns 487.014125861, so 8.5 radians $\approx 487.01°$.

```
▓▓▓DEG▓▓▓▓▓▓▓▓▓ HOME ▓▓▓▓▓▓▓▓▓
RAD→DEG(3*π/4)
                               135
RAD→DEG(8.5)
              487.014125861
─────────────────────────────
 STO▶
```

Chapter 5
Trigonometric Identities, Inverse Functions, and Equations

This chapter appears only in the text *ALGEBRA & TRIGONOMETRY: GRAPHS & MODELS* by Bittinger, Beecher, Ellenbogen, and Penna and should be disregarded by students using the text *COLLEGE ALGEBRA: GRAPHS & MODELS*.

FINDING INVERSE FUNCTION VALUES

We can use a grapher to find inverse function values in both radians and degrees.

Example 2 (a), (e), page 441: Approximate $\cos^{-1}(-0.2689)$ and $\csc^{-1} 8.205$ in both radians and degrees.

To find inverse function values in radians, first set the grapher in Radian mode.

```
▓▓▓▓▓▓▓ HOME MODES ▓▓▓▓▓▓▓
ANGLE MEASURE: Radians
NUMBER FORMAT: Standard
DECIMAL MARK:  Dot(.)
TITLE: HOME

CHOOSE ANGLE MEASURE
▓▓▓▓▓ CHOOS ▓▓▓▓▓▓▓▓▓▓▓▓▓
```

Then, from Home, to approximate $\cos^{-1}(-0.2689)$, press $\Box$ $\boxed{\text{ACOS}}$ $\boxed{-x}$ $\boxed{\cdot}$ 2 6 8 9 $\boxed{\text{ENTER}}$. The grapher returns 1.84304711148, so $\cos^{-1}(-0.2689) \approx 1.8430$ radians.

To find $\csc^{-1} 8.205$, recall the identity $\csc \theta = \dfrac{1}{\sin \theta}$. Then $\csc^{-1} 8.205 = \sin^{-1}\left(\dfrac{1}{8.205}\right)$. Press $\Box$ $\boxed{\text{ASIN}}$ 1 $\boxed{/}$ 8 $\boxed{\cdot}$ 2 0 5 $\boxed{\text{ENTER}}$ or $\Box$ $\boxed{\text{ASIN}}$ 8 $\boxed{\cdot}$ 2 0 5 $\Box$ $\boxed{x^{-1}}$ $\boxed{\text{ENTER}}$. The readout is .122180665346, so $\csc^{-1} 8.205 \approx 0.1222$ radians. Use $\boxed{\triangle}$ to scroll up the display in Home to see all three entries.

```
▓RAD▓▓▓▓▓ HOME ▓▓▓▓▓▓▼▓
ACOS(-.2689)
            1.84304711148
ASIN(1/8.205)
             .122180665346


STO▶        COPY SHOW
```

```
▓RAD▓▓▓▓▓ HOME ▓▓▓▓▓▓▲▓
ASIN(1/8.205)
             .122180665346
ASIN(8.205^-1)
             .122180665346


STO▶
```

To find inverse function values in degrees, set the grapher in degree mode.

```
▒▒▒▒▒▒▒▒ HOME MODES ▒▒▒▒▒▒▒▒
ANGLE MEASURE: Degrees
NUMBER FORMAT: Standard
DECIMAL MARK: Dot(.)
TITLE: HOME

CHOOSE ANGLE MEASURE
       CHOOS
```

Then use the keystrokes above to find that $\cos^{-1}(-0.2689) \approx 105.6°$ and $\csc^{-1} 8.205 \approx 7.0°$.

```
▒DEG▒▒▒▒▒▒ HOME ▒▒▒▒▒▒▒ ▼▒
ACOS(-.2689)
              105.598820932
ASIN(1/8.205)
              7.00043646244

STO▶          COPY SHOW
```

```
▒DEG▒▒▒▒▒▒ HOME ▒▒▒▒▒▒▒ ▲▒
ASIN(1/8.205)
              7.00043646244
ASIN(8.205^-1)
              7.00043646244

STO▶
```

We can also use reciprocal relationships to find function values for arcsecant and arccotangent. In addition, the HP 38G has the following inverse trigonometric functions built into the MATH menu: arccotangent (ACOT), arccosecant (ACSC), and arcsecant (ASEC). These are accessed by pressing MATH, using ▽ repeatedly to highlight Trig. on the left side of the menu, and then using ▷ and ▽ to highlight the desired inverse function on the right side of the menu. To find $\csc^{-1} 8.205$, for example, highlight Trig. on the MATH menu as described. Then press ▷ ▽ to move to the right side of the menu and highlight ACSC. Now press ENTER 8 · 2 0 5 ENTER to find the angle.

Chapter 6
Applications of Trigonometry

This chapter appears only in the text *ALGEBRA & TRIGONOMETRY: GRAPHS & MODELS* by Bittinger, Beecher, Ellenbogen, and Penna and should be disregarded by students using the text *COLLEGE ALGEBRA: GRAPHS & MODELS*.

CONVERTING FROM RECTANGULAR TO POLAR COORDINATES

The HP 38G can take rectangular coordinates and return the angle measure of the corresponding polar coordinates. The angle can be expressed in either degrees or radians. The grapher will supply an angle in the interval $(-180°, 180°]$, or $(-\pi, \pi]$.

Example 2 (a), page 498: Find the angle measure of the polar coordinates corresponding to the rectangular coordinates $(3,3)$.

To find θ in degrees, set the grapher in Degree mode and press $\boxed{\text{MATH}}$ $\boxed{\text{A}\ldots\text{Z}}$ C to skip to the entries beginning with the letter C. Then press $\boxed{\bigtriangledown}$ to highlight COMPLEX. Now press $\boxed{\triangleright}$ $\boxed{\text{ENTER}}$ $\boxed{(}$ 3 $\boxed{\cdot}$ 3 $\boxed{\text{ENTER}}$. The readout is 45, so $\theta = 45°$.

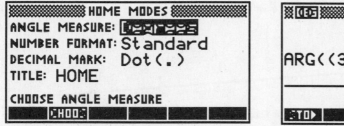

Set the grapher in Radian mode to find θ in radians. Repeat the keystrokes for finding θ above to find that $\theta \approx 0.7854$. This is a decimal approximation for $\pi/4$.

GRAPHING POLAR EQUATIONS

Polar equations can be graphed in either Radian mode or Degree mode. The equation must be written in the form $r = f(\theta)$, the Polar aplet must be activated, and the Polar Symbolic Setup should have ANGLE MEASURE set to the type of measure being used. Generally, we will use radian measure. We usually begin with a range of $[0, 2\pi]$ or $[0°, 360°]$, but it might be necessary to increase the range to ensure that sufficient points are plotted to display the entire graph.

Example 6, page 501: Graph: $r = 1 - \sin\theta$.

First press $\boxed{\text{LIB}}$ and select Polar. Then press $\boxed{\Box}$ $\boxed{\text{SYMB}}$ and choose Radians for angle measure. Press $\boxed{\text{SYMB}}$ to enter the Polar Symbolic view.

▓▓▓▓▓ APLET LIBRARY ▓▓▓▓▓ **Polar** Sequence Function Statistics Solve ▼ SAVE RESET SORT SEND RECV START	▓▓▓▓ POLAR SYMBOLIC SETUP ▓▓▓▓ ANGLE MEASURE: **Radians** CHOOSE ANGLE MEASURE CHOOS

The equation is given in $r = f(\theta)$ form. Clear any existing entries and highlight $R1(\theta) =$ and press 1 $\boxed{-}$ $\boxed{\text{SIN}}$ $\boxed{\text{X, T, }\Theta}$ $\boxed{\text{ENTER}}$. Now press $\boxed{\Box}$ $\boxed{\text{PLOT}}$ and enter the following settings:

θRNG: 0 2π	(Smallest value of θ to be evaluated)
θstep $= \pi/24$	(Increment in θ values)
XRNG: -4 4	
YRNG: -3 1	
({{PAGE ▽}})	
XTICK: 1 YTICK: $1 = -3$	
√ CONNECT	
√ AXES	

With these settings the grapher evaluates the function from $\theta = 0$ to $\theta = 2\pi$ in increments of $\pi/24$ and displays the graph in the square window $[-4, 4, -3, 1]$. Values entered in terms of π appear on the screen as decimal approximations. Press $\boxed{\text{PLOT}}$ to display the graph.

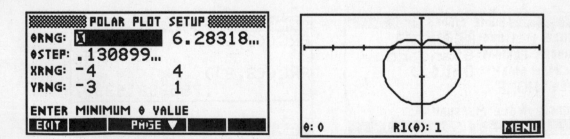

The curve can be traced with polar coordinates being displayed.

Chapter 7/4
Systems and Matrices

This chapter corresponds to Chapter 7 in *ALGEBRA & TRIGONOMETRY: GRAPHS & MODELS* by Bittinger, Beecher, Ellenbogen, and Penna and to Chapter 4 in *COLLEGE ALGEBRA: GRAPHS & MODELS*. The page number references show the *ALGEBRA & TRIGONOMETRY* page first followed by the *COLLEGE ALGEBRA* page.

MATRICES AND ROW-EQUIVALENT OPERATIONS

As many as ten matrices can be entered on the HP 38G at one time.

Example 1, page 542/342: Solve the following system:

$$\begin{aligned} 2x - y + 4z &= -3, \\ x - 2y - 10z &= -6, \\ 3x \phantom{{}- 2y} + 4z &= 7. \end{aligned}$$

The system can be represented by the following matrix equation:

$$\begin{bmatrix} 2 & -1 & 4 \\ 1 & -2 & -10 \\ 3 & 0 & 4 \end{bmatrix} \begin{bmatrix} x \\ y \\ z \end{bmatrix} = \begin{bmatrix} -3 \\ -6 \\ 7 \end{bmatrix}$$

The HP 38G cannot perform row-equivalent operations. However, there are two ways to solve this system of equations using the grapher.

Method 1: We refer to the first matrix on the left-hand side of the matrix equation above as the coefficient matrix and to the matrix on the right-hand side as the constants matrix. Using this method we "divide" the constants matrix by the coefficient matrix. We enter the constants matrix as a vector, press $\boxed{/}$, enter the coefficient matrix, and press $\boxed{\text{ENTER}}$.

On the HP 38G a matrix is defined as an array with at least two rows and two columns. A vector is an array with only one row or one column. Vectors are represented with single brackets, [2, 5, 6], and matrices are represented with nested brackets, [[2, 5, 6]].

There are two ways to enter vectors and matrices. We can use the matrix catalog or we can enter the matrix in Home.

First we solve the system using the matrix catalog. Press $\boxed{\square}$ $\boxed{\text{MATRIX}}$ to enter the catalog. (MATRIX is the second operation associated with the $\boxed{4}$ key.)

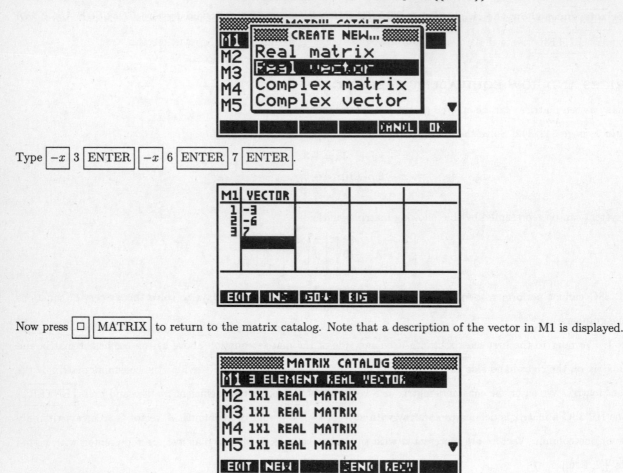

We will enter the constants vector in the matrix variable M1. To do this, press {{NEW}} and choose Real vector.

Type $-x$ 3 ENTER $-x$ 6 ENTER 7 ENTER.

Now press □ MATRIX to return to the matrix catalog. Note that a description of the vector in M1 is displayed.

Now highlight M2 and press {{NEW}} to enter the coefficient matrix. Choose Real matrix. Choose {{GO→}} if you prefer entering the coefficients row-by-row, or choose {{GO↓}} if you prefer entering the coefficients column-by-column. If you choose {{GO}}, the cursor will not automatically advance after a number is entered. Use the arrow keys to maneuver the cursor around the matrix, if necessary. Enter the coefficient matrix. When, done, the screen should look like this:

```
M2 │   1   │   2   │   3   │       │
─────────────────────────────────────
1 2│       │  -1   │   4   │       │
2 1│       │  -2   │ -10   │       │
3 3│███████│   0   │   4   │       │
─────────────────────────────────────
                                     │
─────────────────────────────────────
│ EDIT │ INS │ GO→ │ BIG │     │     │
```

Now press [HOME] to begin the actual computation. Enter the constants vector M1 by pressing [A...Z] M 1 or by pressing [VAR], highlighting Matrix and choosing M1. Then press [/] and follow that with the coefficient matrix M2. Finally press [ENTER]. Note that the coefficient matrix must be square in order to use this method.

```
▓OBS▓▓▓▓▓▓▓▓ HOME ▓▓▓▓▓▓▓
│                              │
│ M1/M2                        │
│                   [3,7,-.5]  │
│                              │
│ STO▶ │    │    │    │    │    │
```

If the solution is too large to fit on the screen, use [△] to highlight it and press {{COPY}} or {{SHOW}}, and then scroll through it with [▷]. {{COPY}} will place it in the edit line where it can be modified, if desired.

Now we solve the system again using the division method, but we will enter the matrices in Home. Press [□] [[[-x] 3] , [-x] 6] , [7] [□]]] / [□] [[□] [[2] , [-x] 1] , [4] [□]]] , [□] [[1] , [-x] 2] , [-x] 10 [□]]] , [□] [[3] , [0] , 4]]] [ENTER]. ([and] are the second operations associated with the [5] and [6] keys, respectively.

```
▓OBS▓▓▓▓▓▓▓▓ HOME ▓▓▓▓▓▓▓
│                              │
│ [-3,-6,7]/[[2,-1,4],[…       │
│                   [3,7,-.5]  │
│                              │
│ STO▶ │    │    │    │    │    │
```

Method 2: Another method of solving this system of equations on the HP 38G is find the reduced row-echelon form of the augmented matrix directly by using the RREF operation from the MATH menu in the MATRIX category. First we enter the augmented matrix

$$\begin{bmatrix} 2 & -1 & 4 & -3 \\ 1 & -2 & -10 & -6 \\ 3 & 0 & 4 & 7 \end{bmatrix}$$

in variable M1 through the matrix catalog. Press [HOME] to leave this screen. Now press [MATH] [A...Z] M to skip to Matrix. Press [▷] to go to the right-hand column followed by [A...Z] R to skip to the entries beginning with the letter

R. Press ▽ ▽ to go to RREF followed by ENTER A...Z M 1 ENTER. Use △ to highlight the result and press {{SHOW}} to view the augmented matrix in reduced row-echelon form Use ▷ to scroll to the right. We can read the solution of the system of equations, $(3, 7, -0.5)$ directly from the resulting matrix.

```
[[1,0,0,3],[0,1,0,7],[0,
```

```
,[0,1,0,7],[0,0,1,-.5]]
```

MATRIX OPERATIONS

We can use the grapher to add and subtract matrices, to multiply a matrix by a scalar, and to multiply matrices.

Example 1 (a), page 549/349: Find $\mathbf{A} + \mathbf{B}$ for

a) $\mathbf{A} = \begin{bmatrix} -5 & 0 \\ 4 & \frac{1}{2} \end{bmatrix}$, $\mathbf{B} = \begin{bmatrix} 6 & -3 \\ 2 & 3 \end{bmatrix}$.

Enter $\mathbf{A}$ and $\mathbf{B}$ in the Matrix Catalog as M1 and M2 as described earlier in this chapter. Press HOME to leave this screen. Then press A...Z M 1 + A...Z M 2 ENTER to display the sum.

```
▓▓▓▓▓▓▓▓ HOME ▓▓▓▓▓▓▓▓

M1+M2
         [[1,-3],[6,3.5]]

STO▶
```

Example 2, page 550/350: Find $\mathbf{C} - \mathbf{D}$ for each of the following.

a) $\mathbf{C} = \begin{bmatrix} 1 & 2 \\ -2 & 0 \\ -3 & -1 \end{bmatrix}$, $\mathbf{D} = \begin{bmatrix} 1 & -1 \\ 1 & 3 \\ 2 & 3 \end{bmatrix}$ b) $\mathbf{C} = \begin{bmatrix} 5 & -6 \\ -3 & 4 \end{bmatrix}$, $\mathbf{D} = \begin{bmatrix} -4 \\ 1 \end{bmatrix}$

a) Enter $\mathbf{C}$ and $\mathbf{D}$ in the Matrix Catalog as M3 and M4. Press HOME to leave this screen. Then press A...Z M 3 − A...Z M 4 ENTER to display the difference.

```
▓▓▓▓▓▓▓▓ HOME ▓▓▓▓▓▓▓▓

M3−M4
[[0,3],[-3,-3],[-5,-4…

STO▶
```

b) Enter **C** and **D** in the Matrix Catalog as M3 and M4. Press $\boxed{\text{HOME}}$ to leave this screen. Then press $\boxed{\text{A...Z}}$ M 3 $\boxed{-}$ $\boxed{\text{A...Z}}$ M 4 $\boxed{\text{ENTER}}$. The grapher returns the message Invalid Dimension, indicating that this subtraction is not possible. This is the case because the matrices have different orders.

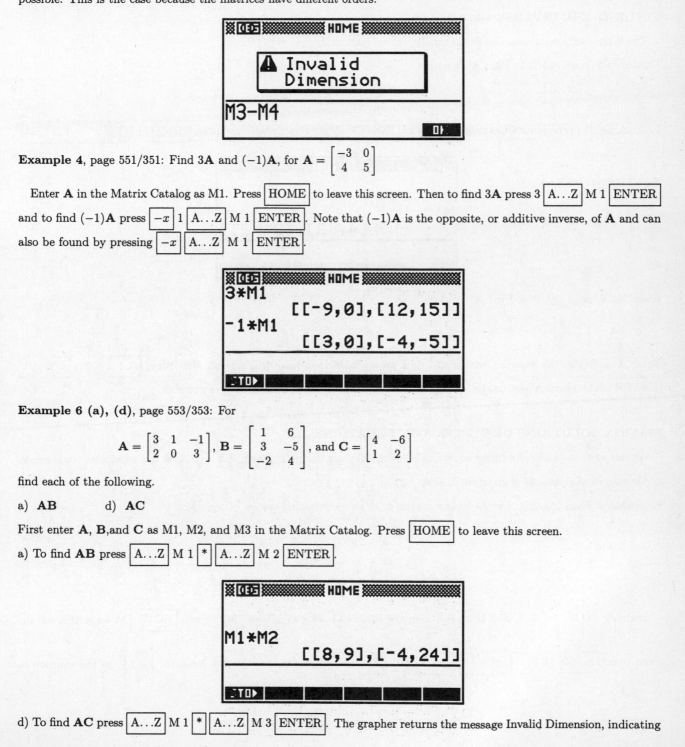

Example 4, page 551/351: Find 3**A** and (-1)**A**, for $\mathbf{A} = \begin{bmatrix} -3 & 0 \\ 4 & 5 \end{bmatrix}$

Enter **A** in the Matrix Catalog as M1. Press $\boxed{\text{HOME}}$ to leave this screen. Then to find 3**A** press 3 $\boxed{\text{A...Z}}$ M 1 $\boxed{\text{ENTER}}$ and to find (-1)**A** press $\boxed{-x}$ 1 $\boxed{\text{A...Z}}$ M 1 $\boxed{\text{ENTER}}$. Note that (-1)**A** is the opposite, or additive inverse, of **A** and can also be found by pressing $\boxed{-x}$ $\boxed{\text{A...Z}}$ M 1 $\boxed{\text{ENTER}}$.

Example 6 (a), (d), page 553/353: For

$$\mathbf{A} = \begin{bmatrix} 3 & 1 & -1 \\ 2 & 0 & 3 \end{bmatrix}, \mathbf{B} = \begin{bmatrix} 1 & 6 \\ 3 & -5 \\ -2 & 4 \end{bmatrix}, \text{ and } \mathbf{C} = \begin{bmatrix} 4 & -6 \\ 1 & 2 \end{bmatrix}$$

find each of the following.

a) **AB**   d) **AC**

First enter **A**, **B**, and **C** as M1, M2, and M3 in the Matrix Catalog. Press $\boxed{\text{HOME}}$ to leave this screen.

a) To find **AB** press $\boxed{\text{A...Z}}$ M 1 $\boxed{*}$ $\boxed{\text{A...Z}}$ M 2 $\boxed{\text{ENTER}}$.

d) To find **AC** press $\boxed{\text{A...Z}}$ M 1 $\boxed{*}$ $\boxed{\text{A...Z}}$ M 3 $\boxed{\text{ENTER}}$. The grapher returns the message Invalid Dimension, indicating that this multiplication is not possible. This is the case because the number of columns in **A** is not the same as the number of rows in **C**. Thus, the matrices cannot be multiplied in this order.

FINDING THE INVERSE OF A MATRIX

The inverse of a matrix can be found quickly on the grapher.

Example 3, page 562/362: Find $\mathbf{A}^{-1}$, where

$$\mathbf{A} = \begin{bmatrix} -2 & 3 \\ -3 & 4 \end{bmatrix}.$$

Enter **A** as M1 in the Matrix Catalog. Then press HOME to leave this screen. Now press A...Z M 1 ☐ x^{-1} ENTER.

```
▓ CES ▓▓▓▓▓▓ HOME ▓▓▓▓▓▓

M1^-1
            [[4,-3],[3,-2]]


 STO▶
```

Exercise 9, page 564/364: Find $\mathbf{A}^{-1}$, where

$$\mathbf{A} = \begin{bmatrix} 6 & 9 \\ 4 & 6 \end{bmatrix}.$$

Enter **A** as M1 in the Matrix Catalog and then press HOME to leave this screen. Now press A...Z M 1 ☐ x^{-1} ENTER. The grapher returns the message Infinite Result, indicating that $\mathbf{A}^{-1}$ does not exist.

MATRIX SOLUTIONS OF SYSTEMS OF EQUATIONS

We can write a system of n linear equations in n variables as a matrix equation $\mathbf{AX} = \mathbf{B}$. If **A** has an inverse the solution of the system of equations is given by $\mathbf{X} = \mathbf{A}^{-1}\mathbf{B}$.

Example 4, page 563/363: Use an inverse matrix to solve the following system of equations:

$$x + 2y - z = -2,$$
$$3x + 5y + 3z = 3,$$
$$2x + 4y + 3z = 1.$$

Enter $\mathbf{A} = \begin{bmatrix} 1 & 2 & -1 \\ 3 & 5 & 3 \\ 2 & 4 & 3 \end{bmatrix}$ and $\mathbf{B} = \begin{bmatrix} -2 \\ 3 \\ 1 \end{bmatrix}$ in the Matrix Catalog as M1 and M2. Press HOME to leave this screen. Then press A...Z M 1 ☐ x^{-1} * A...Z M 2 ENTER. The result is the 3 x 1 matrix $\begin{bmatrix} 5 \\ -3 \\ 1 \end{bmatrix}$, so the solution is $(5, -3, 1)$.

Chapter 8/5
Conic Sections

This chapter corresponds to Chapter 8 in *ALGEBRA & TRIGONOMETRY: GRAPHS & MODELS* **by Bittinger, Beecher, Ellenbogen, and Penna and to Chapter 5 in** *COLLEGE ALGEBRA: GRAPHS & MODELS.* **The page number references show the** *ALGEBRA & TRIGONOMETRY* **page first followed by the** *COLLEGE ALGEBRA* **page.**

Many conic sections are represented by equations that are not functions. Consequently, these equations must be entered on the HP 38G as two equations, each of which is a function. We have already done this for circles in Chapter G of this manual. Now we turn our attention to parabolas, ellipses, and hyperbolas.

GRAPHING PARABOLAS

To graph a parabola of the form $y^2 = 4px$ or $(y - k)^2 = 4p(x - h)$, we must first solve the equation for y.

Example 4, page 594/394: Graph the parabola $y^2 - 2y - 8x - 31 = 0$.

In the text we used the quadratic formula to solve the equation for y:
$$y = \frac{2 \pm \sqrt{32x + 128}}{2}.$$

One way to produce the graph of the parabola is to enter $F1(X) = \dfrac{2 + \sqrt{32x + 128}}{2}$ and $F2(X) = \dfrac{2 - \sqrt{32x + 128}}{2}$, select a window, and press $\boxed{\text{PLOT}}$ to see the graph. Here we use $[-12, 12, -8, 8]$. The first equation produces the top half of the parabola and the second equation produces the lower half.

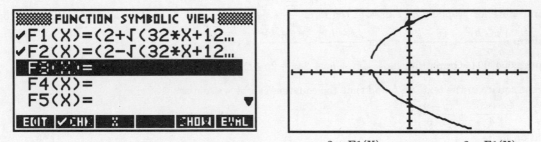

We can also enter $F1(X) = \sqrt{32x + 128}$. Then enter $F2(X) = \dfrac{2 + F1(X)}{2}$ and $F3(X) = \dfrac{2 - F1(X)}{2}$. For example, to enter $F2(X) = \dfrac{2 + F1(X)}{2}$, highlight "F2(X) =" and press $\boxed{(}$ 2 $\boxed{+}$ $\boxed{\text{A...Z}}$ F 1 $\boxed{(}$ $\boxed{\text{X, T, }\Theta}$ $\boxed{)}$ $\boxed{)}$ $\boxed{/}$ 2 $\boxed{\text{ENTER}}$. Enter $F3(X) = \dfrac{2 - F1(X)}{2}$ in a similar manner. Finally, deselect F1(X) by highlighting F1(X) and pressing {{√ CHK}}. The top half of the graph is produced by F2(X) and the lower half by F3(X). The expression for F1(X) was entered to avoid entering the square root more than once. By deselecting F1(X) we prevent its graph from appearing on the screen with the graph of the parabola.

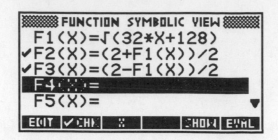

We could also use the standard equation of the parabola found in the text:

$$(y-1)^2 = 8(x+4).$$

Solve this equation for y.

$$y - 1 = \pm\sqrt{8(x+4)}$$
$$y = 1 \pm \sqrt{8(x+4)}$$

Then enter $F1(X) = 1 + \sqrt{8(x+4)}$ and $F2(X) = 1 - \sqrt{8(x+4)}$, or enter $F1(X) = \sqrt{8(x+4)}$, $F2(X) = 1 + F1(X)$, and $F3(X) = 1 - F1(X)$, and deselect $F1(X)$ as above.

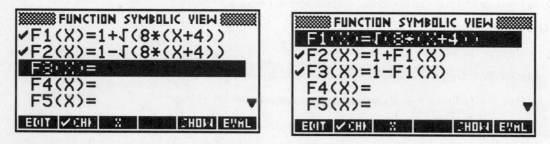

GRAPHING ELLIPSES

The equation of an ellipse must be solved for y before it can be entered on an HP 38G. In Example 2 of Section 8.2 of the text the procedure for graphing an ellipse of the form $\dfrac{x^2}{a^2} + \dfrac{y^2}{b^2} = 1$ or $\dfrac{x^2}{b^2} + \dfrac{y^2}{a^2} = 1$ is described. Here we consider ellipses of the form $\dfrac{(x-h)^2}{a^2} + \dfrac{(y-k)^2}{b^2} = 1$ or $\dfrac{(x-h)^2}{b^2} + \dfrac{(y-k)^2}{a^2} = 1$

Example 4, page 604/404: Graph the ellipse $4x^2 + y^2 + 24x - 2y + 21 = 0$.

Completing the square in the text, we found that the equation can be written as

$$\frac{(x+3)^2}{4} + \frac{(y-1)^2}{16} = 1.$$

Solve this equation for y.

$$\frac{(x+3)^2}{4} + \frac{(y-1)^2}{16} = 1$$
$$\frac{(y-1)^2}{16} = 1 - \frac{(x+3)^2}{4}$$
$$(y-1)^2 = 16 - 4(x+3)^2 \qquad \text{Multiplying by 16}$$
$$y - 1 = \pm\sqrt{16 - 4(x+3)^2}$$
$$y = 1 \pm \sqrt{16 - 4(x+3)^2}$$

Now we can produce the graph in either of two ways. One is to enter $F1(X) = 1 + \sqrt{16 - 4(x+3)^2}$ and $F2(X) = 1 - \sqrt{16 - 4(x+3)^2}$, select a square window, and press $\boxed{\text{PLOT}}$. Here we use $[-12, 12, -6, 6]$. The first equation produces the top half of the ellipse and the second equation produces the lower half.

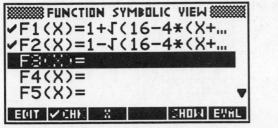 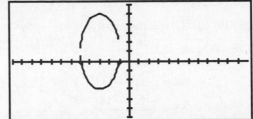

We can also enter $F1(X) = \sqrt{16 - 4(x+3)^2}$, $F2(X) = 1 + F1(X)$, and $F3(X) = 1 - F1(X)$. Then deselect $F1(X)$, select a square window, and press $\boxed{\text{PLOT}}$. As with parabolas, $F1(X)$ is used to eliminate the need to enter the square root more than once. Deselecting it prevents the graph of $F1(X)$ from appearing on the screen with the graph of the ellipse. The top half of the graph is produced by $F2(X)$ and the lower half by $F3(X)$.

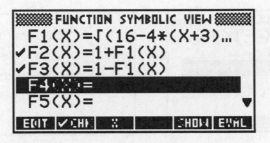

We could also begin by using the quadratic formula to solve the original equation for y.
$$4x^2 + y^2 + 24x - 2y + 21 = 0$$
$$y^2 - 2y + (4x^2 + 24x + 21) = 0$$
$$y = \frac{-(-2) \pm \sqrt{(-2)^2 - 4 \cdot 1 \cdot (4x^2 + 24x + 21)}}{2 \cdot 1}$$
$$y = \frac{2 \pm \sqrt{4 - 16x^2 - 96x - 84}}{2}$$
$$y = \frac{2 \pm \sqrt{-16x^2 - 96x - 80}}{2}$$

Then enter $F1(X) = \dfrac{2 + \sqrt{-16x^2 - 96x - 80}}{2}$ and $F2(X) = \dfrac{2 - \sqrt{-16x^2 - 96x - 80}}{2}$, or enter $F1(X) = \sqrt{-16x^2 - 96x - 80}$, $F2(X) = \dfrac{2 + F1(X)}{2}$, and $F3(X) = \dfrac{2 - F1(X)}{2}$, and deselect $F1(X)$.

Select a square window and press $\boxed{\text{PLOT}}$ to display the graph.

GRAPHING HYPERBOLAS

As with equations of ellipses, equations of hyperbolas must be solved for y before they can be entered on an HP 38G.

Example 2, page 610/410: Graph the hyperbola $9x^2 - 16y^2 = 144$.

First solve the equation for y.

$$9x^2 - 16y^2 = 144$$

$$-16y^2 = -9x^2 + 144$$

$$y^2 = \frac{-9x^2 + 144}{-16}$$

$$y = \pm\sqrt{\frac{-9x^2 + 144}{-16}}, \text{ or } \pm\sqrt{\frac{9x^2 - 144}{16}}$$

It is not necessary to simplify further.

Now enter $F1(X) = \sqrt{\dfrac{9x^2 - 144}{16}}$ and either $F2(X) = -\sqrt{\dfrac{9x^2 - 144}{16}}$ or $F2(X) = -F1(X)$, select a square window, and press $\boxed{\text{PLOT}}$. Here we use $[-12, 12, -6, 6]$. The top half of the graph is produced by $F1(X)$ and the lower half by $F2(X)$.

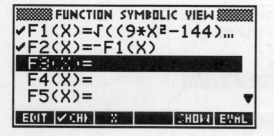
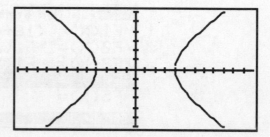

Example 3, page 613/413: Graph the hyperbola $4y^2 - x^2 + 24y + 4x + 28 = 0$.

In the text we completed the square to get the standard form of the equation. Now solve the equation for y.

$$\frac{(y + 3)^2}{1} - \frac{(x - 2)^2}{4} = 1$$

$$(y + 3)^2 = \frac{(x - 2)^2}{4} + 1$$

$$y + 3 = \pm\sqrt{\frac{(x - 2)^2}{4} + 1}$$

$$y = -3 \pm\sqrt{\frac{(x - 2)^2}{4} + 1}$$

As with ellipses, the graph can be produced in either of two ways. One is to enter $F1(X) = -3 + \sqrt{\dfrac{(x - 2)^2}{4} + 1}$ and $F2(X) = -3 - \sqrt{\dfrac{(x - 2)^2}{4} + 1}$, select a square window, and press $\boxed{\text{PLOT}}$. Here we use $[-18, 18, -9, 9]$. The first equation produces the top half of the hyperbola and the second the lower half.

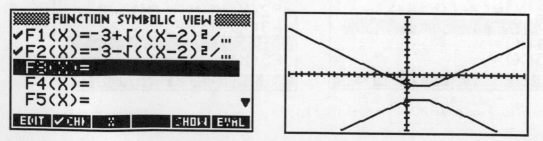

We can also enter $F1(X) = \sqrt{\dfrac{(x-2)^2}{4} + 1}$, $F2(X) = -3+ F1(X)$, and $F3(X) = -3- F1(X)$. Then deselect $F1(X)$, select a square window, and press $\boxed{\text{PLOT}}$. As with parabolas and ellipses, $F1(X)$ is used to eliminate the need to enter the square root more than once. Deselecting it prevents the graph of $F1(X)$ from appearing on the screen with the graph of the hyperbola. The top half of the graph is produced by $F2(X)$ and the lower half by $F3(X)$.

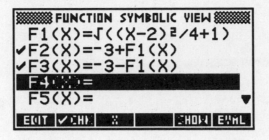

Chapter 9/6
Sequences, Series, and Combinatorics

This chapter corresponds to Chapter 9 in *ALGEBRA & TRIGONOMETRY: GRAPHS & MODELS* by Bittinger, Beecher, Ellenbogen, and Penna and to Chapter 6 in *COLLEGE ALGEBRA: GRAPHS & MODELS*. The page number references show the *ALGEBRA & TRIGONOMETRY* page first followed by the *COLLEGE ALGEBRA* page.

Both the graphing capabilities and the computational capabilities of the grapher can be used when working with sequences, series, and combinatorics.

EVALUATING AND GRAPHING SEQUENCES

The grapher can be used to construct a table showing the terms of a sequence and to graph a sequence.

Example 3, page 633/433: Construct a table of values and a graph for the first 10 terms of the sequence whose general term is given by

$$a_n = \frac{n}{n+1}.$$

Begin by pressing $\boxed{\text{LIB}}$ and selecting the Sequence aplet. The Sequence Symbolic view will appear. Press $\boxed{\triangledown}$ $\boxed{\triangledown}$ to highlight "U1(N) =" and enter $\frac{n}{n+1}$ by pressing $\boxed{\text{X, T, }\Theta}$ $\boxed{/}$ $\boxed{(}$ $\boxed{\text{X, T, }\Theta}$ $\boxed{+}$ 1 $\boxed{)}$ $\boxed{\text{ENTER}}$. Note that the values for U1(1) and U1(2) are entered automatically.

To construct the table of values for this sequence, press $\boxed{\square}$ $\boxed{\text{NUM}}$ and set NUMSTART: 1, NUMSTEP: 1, and NUM-TYPE: Automatic. Now press $\boxed{\text{NUM}}$ to display the table.

We see that when $n = 1$, a_n, or U1 = 0.5; when $n = 2$, a_n, or U1 = 0.6666667; and so on. We can scroll through the table to find additional sequence values. To find a specific term of the sequence, set NUMTYPE to Build Your Own and then enter the desired value of n on the Table screen as described in Chapter G of this manual.

To graph the sequence first press $\boxed{\square}$ $\boxed{\text{PLOT}}$. Choose SEQPLOT: Stairstep. Now set NRNG: 1   10 to set the values of n at which plotting begins and ends at 1 and 10, respectively. Set XRNG: 0   10, YRNG: 0   1, press {{PAGE$\boxed{\triangledown}$}}, set XTICK: 1 and YTICK: 1 to define the window dimensions and the spacing between tick marks. Now press $\boxed{\text{PLOT}}$ to display the graph of the first 10 terms of the sequence.

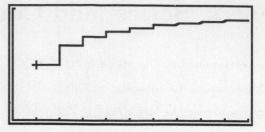

Recursively defined sequences can also be entered on the grapher.

Example 7, page 636/436: Find the first 5 terms of the sequence defined by

$$a_1 = 5, \ a_{k+1} = 2a_k - 3, \text{ for } k \geq 1.$$

Press $\boxed{\text{SYMB}}$ to enter Sequence Symbolic view and enter the recursive function beside "U1(N) =" by pressing 2 {{U1}} {{(N − 1)}} $\boxed{-}$ 3 $\boxed{\text{ENTER}}$. Beside "U1(1) =" and "U1(2) =" enter the first and second terms of the sequence, 5 and 7, respectively. Press $\boxed{\square}$ $\boxed{\text{NUM}}$ to display the Sequence Numeric Setup, press {{PLOT $\boxed{\triangleright}$}} {{OK}}, and set NUMTYPE: Automatic. Now press $\boxed{\text{NUM}}$ to display the table of values.

We see that $a_1 = 5$, $a_2 = 7$, $a_3 = 11$, $a_4 = 19$, and $a_5 = 35$.

EVALUATING FACTORIALS, PERMUTATIONS, AND COMBINATIONS

Operations from the MATH Prob. (probability) menu can be used to evaluate factorials, permutations, and combinations.

Exercise 5, page 677/477: Evaluate 5!.

Press 5 $\boxed{\text{MATH}}$ $\boxed{\triangle}$ $\boxed{\triangleright}$ $\boxed{\triangledown}$ $\boxed{\text{ENTER}}$ $\boxed{\text{ENTER}}$. These keystrokes enter 5, display the MATH menu, select Prob., select ! from that menu, and then cause 5! to be evaluated. The result is 120.

Exercise 9, page 677/477: Evaluate $\dfrac{9!}{5!}$.

Press 9 $\boxed{\text{MATH}}$ $\boxed{\triangle}$ $\boxed{\triangleright}$ $\boxed{\triangledown}$ $\boxed{\text{ENTER}}$ $\boxed{/}$ 5 $\boxed{\text{MATH}}$ $\boxed{\triangle}$ $\boxed{\triangleright}$ $\boxed{\triangledown}$ $\boxed{\text{ENTER}}$ $\boxed{\text{ENTER}}$. The result is 3024.

```
▓▒▓ HOME ▓▒▓▒▓
5!
                              120
9!/5!
                             3024

▓TO▶
```

Example 6, page 674/474: Compute $_8P_4$.

Press [MATH] [△] [▷] [▽] [▽] [ENTER] 8 , 4 [ENTER]. These keystrokes display the MATH menu, select Prob., select PERM from that menu, enter 8 for 8 objects, enter 4 for 4 objects taken at a time, and then cause the calculation to be performed. The result is 1680.

Example 3, page 682/482: Evaluate $\binom{7}{5}$.

Press [MATH] [△] [▷] [ENTER] 7 , 5 [ENTER]. These keystrokes display the Math menu, select Prob., select COMB from that menu, enter 7 for 7 objects, enter 5 for 5 objects taken at a time, and then cause the calculation to be performed. The result is 21.

```
▓▒▓ HOME ▓▒▓▒▓
PERM(8,4)
                             1680
COMB(7,5)
                               21

▓TO▶
```

Programs For The HP 38G
Graphic Calculator

PROGRAMS FOR THE HP 38G GRAPHICS CALCULATOR
Created by Mike Rosenborg

QUADFORM

This program solves a quadratic equation of the form $Ax^2 + Bx + C = O$.

INPUT: A, B, C

OUTPUT: Real or complex solutions

```
INPUT A; "QUADRATIC"; "A"; "ENTER NUMBER"; O:
INPUT B; "QUADRATIC"; "B"; "ENTER NUMBER"; O:
INPUT C; "QUADRATIC"; "C"; "ENTER NUMBER"; O:
DISP 1; "ROOTS:":
B^2-4*A*C --> D:
IF D≥O THEN DISP 2; (-B+√(D))/(2A):
DISP 3; (-B-√(D))/(2A):
ELSE DISP 2; -B/(2A) "+/-" √(-D)/(2A) "i":
END:
FREEZE
```

SYNDIV

This program does synthetic division to divide a polynomial by a linear factor with leading coefficient 1.

INPUT: List of coefficients of the dividend, enclosed in braces, in order of descending powers and the constant term of the linear divisor

OUTPUT: The coefficients of the quotient, in order of descending powers, and remainder

NOTE: If, for example, the divisor is $x - 3$, enter 3 as the divisor constant term. This program outputs list $L1 = \{x_1, x_2, ..., x_{n-1}, r\}$, where n is the size of the original dividend coefficient list and r is the remainder. This list can be viewed in the HP 38G's list editor.

```
INPUT L1; "SYNDIV"; "COEFF {LIST}"; "ENTER LIST"; O:
INPUT C; "SYNDIV"; "DIVISOR"; "ENTER NUMBER"; O:
SIZE(L1) --> L:
L1(1) --> S:
FOR I=1 TO L-1 STEP 1; S --> L1(I):
C*S+L1(I+1) --> S:
END:
S --> L1(L):
DISP 1; "LIST L1:" L1:
FREEZE
```

LOGBASE

This program computes logarithms of any base.

INPUT: Number (X) and base (B)

OUTPUT: $\log_B(X)$

```
INPUT X; "LOGBASE"; "X"; "ENTER NO."; O:
INPUT B; "LOGBASE"; "B"; "NEW BASE"; O:
MSGBOX LN(X)/LN(B)
```

TRISOL90

This program solves right triangles *ABC* in which legs *L* and *M* are opposite angles *A* and *B*, respectively. It consists of the main program, TRISOL90, and four subroutines: HA, HL, LA, and LL. It is activated by running TRISOL90 and following the prompts. In the programs below, "ANG" represents the angle-measure symbol available in the character catalog of the HP 38G.

INPUT: One side and any other part (except the right angle, *C*)
OUTPUT: First, the sides; then, the acute angles

TRISOL90
```
1 --> Angle:
1 --> Z:
CHOOSE Z; "TRISOL90"; "HYP-ANG"; "HYP-LEG"; "LEG-ANG"; "LEG-LEG":
CASE IF Z==1 THEN RUN HA END IF Z==2 THEN RUN HL END IF Z==3 THEN RUN LA END
IF Z==4 THEN RUN LL END END:
MSGBOX "L1 =" L " " "L2=" M " " "HYP=" H " " "ANG 1 =" A " " "ANG 2=" B
```

HA
```
INPUT H; "HYP-ANG"; "HYPOTENUSE"; "ENTER LENGTH"; 0:
INPUT A; "HYP-ANG"; "ANGLE"; "ENTER DEGREES"; 0:
90-A --> B:
H*SIN(A) --> L:
H*SIN(B) --> M
```

HL
```
INPUT H; "HYP-LEG"; "HYPOTENUSE"; "ENTER LENGTH"; 0:
INPUT L; "HYP-LEG"; "LEG"; "ENTER LENGTH"; 0:
√(H^2-L^2) --> M:
ASIN(L/H) --> A:
90-A --> B
```

LA
```
INPUT L; "LEG-ANG"; "LEG"; "ENTER LENGTH"; 0:
INPUT A; "LEG-ANG"; "ANGLE"; "ENTER DEGREES"; 0:
90-A --> B:
L/TAN(A) --> M:
√(L^2+M^2) --> H
```

LL
```
INPUT L; "LEG-LEG"; "LEG 1"; "ENTER LENGTH"; 0:
INPUT M; "LEG-LEG"; "LEG 2"; "ENTER LENGTH"; 0:
√(L^2+M^2) --> H:
ATAN(L/M) --> A:
90-A --> B
```

TRISOL

This program solves triangle ABC, in which sides L, M, and N are opposite angles A, B, and C, respectively. It covers the "no solution" case as well as the "two solutions" case. The program consists of the main program, TRISOL, and six subroutines: INIT, SSS, SAS, AAS, ASA, and SSA. It is activated by running TRISOL and following the prompts. It covers the "no solution" case as well as the "two solutions" case.

INPUT: Three parts of a triangle, including at least one side
OUTPUT: First the sides, then the angles

```
TRISOL
RUN INIT:
IF Z==5 THEN IF B≥A THEN STOP:
ELSE MSGBOX"2nd SOLN. TO FOLLOW...":
180-A --> A:
180-A-B --> C:
M*SIN(C)/(SIN(B))--> N:
MSGBOX"SIDE a=" L " SIDE b=" M " SIDE c=" N:
MSGBOX "ANG A=" A " ANG B=" B " ANG C=" C:
END:
ELSE STOP:
END
```

```
INIT
1 --> Angle:
1 --> Z:
CHOOSE Z; "TRISOL"; "SSS"; "SAS"; "AAS"; "ASA"; "SSA":
CASE IF Z==1 THEN RUN SSS END IF Z==2 THEN RUN SAS END IF Z==3 THEN RUN AAS
END IF Z==4 THEN RUN ASA END IF Z==5 THEN RUN SSA END END:
MSGBOX "SIDE a=" L " SIDE b=" M " SIDE c=" N:
MSGBOX "ANG A=" A " ANG B=" B " ANG C=" C
```

```
SSS
INPUT L; "SSS"; "SIDE a"; "ENTER LENGTH"; 0:
INPUT M; "SSS"; "SIDE b"; "ENTER LENGTH"; 0:
INPUT N; "SSS"; "SIDE c"; "ENTER LENGTH"; 0:
ACOS((M^2+N^2-L^2)/(2*M*N)) --> A:
ACOS((L^2+N^2-M^2)/(2*L*N)) --> B:
180-A-B --> C
```

```
SAS
INPUT L; "SAS"; "SIDE a"; "ENTER LENGTH"; 0:
INPUT C; "SAS"; "ANG C"; "ENTER DEGREES"; 0:
INPUT M; "SAS"; "SIDE b"; "ENTER LENGTH"; 0:
√(L^2+M^2-2*L*M*COS(C)) --> N:
ACOS((M^2+N^2-L^2)/(2*M*N)) --> A:
180-A-C --> B
```

```
AAS
INPUT A; "AAS"; "ANG A"; "ENTER DEGREES"; 0:
INPUT B; "AAS"; "ANG B"; "ENTER DEGREES"; 0:
INPUT L; "AAS"; "SIDE a"; "ENTER LENGTH";0:
180-A-B --> C:
L*SIN(B)/(SIN(A)) --> M:
L*SIN(C)/(SIN(A)) --> N
```

ASA
```
INPUT A; "ASA"; "ANG A"; "ENTER DEGREES"; 0:
INPUT N; "ASA"; "SIDE c"; "ENTER LENGTH"; 0:
INPUT B; "ASA"; "ANG B"; "ENTER DEGREES"; 0:
180-A-B --> C:
N*SIN(A)/(SIN(C)) --> L:
N*SIN(B)/(SIN(C)) --> M
```

SSA
```
INPUT L; "SSA"; "SIDE a"; "ENTER LENGTH"; 0:
INPUT M; "SSA"; "SIDE b"; "ENTER LENGTH"; 0:
INPUT B; "SSA"; "ANG B"; "ENTER DEGREES"; 0:
L*SIN(B)/M --> X:
IF X>1 THEN MSGBOX "NO SOLN.":
STOP:
ELSE ASIN(X) --> A:
180-A-B --> C:
M*SIN(C)/(SIN(B)) --> N:
END
```

DEMOIVRE

This program helps visualize Nth roots of a complex number $A + Bi$.

INPUT: A, B, N

OUPUT: Traceable graph of the N points (A, B) corresponding to the roots

```
INPUT A; "COMPLEX NUMBER"; "REAL PART"; "ENTER NO."; 0:
INPUT B; "COMPLEX NUMBER"; "IMAGINARY PART"; "ENTER NO."; 0:
INPUT N; "INDEX OF ROOT"; "INDEX"; "ENTER NO."; 2:
√(A^2+B^2)^(1/N) --> R:
IF A==0 THEN 180-ABS(B)/B*90:
ELSE ATAN(B/A)+180*(A<0):
END:
Ans/N --> H:
'R*COS(T)' --> X1(T):
'R*SIN(T)' --> Y1(T):
H --> Tmin:
H+360 --> Tmax:
360/N --> Tstep:
1.5*R --> Ymax:
-1*Ymax --> Ymin:
1.5*Ymax --> Xmax:
-1*Xmax --> Xmin:
SELECT Parametric:
CHECK 1:
1 --> Connect
```

AP

This program finds the Nth term of an arithmetic sequence $a_N = A + (N-1)*D$.

INPUT: A, N, D

OUTPUT: a_N

```
INPUT A; "AP"; "A"; "ENTER NO."; 0:
INPUT D; "AP"; "D"; "ENTER NO."; 0:
INPUT N; "AP"; "N"; "ENTER NO."; 0:
MSGBOX A+D*(N-1)
```

GP

This program finds the Nth term of a geometric sequence $a_N = A * R^{N-1}$.

INPUT: A, R, N

OUTPUT: a_N

```
INPUT A; "GP"; "A"; "ENTER NO."; 0:
INPUT R; "GP"; "R"; "ENTER NO."; 0:
INPUT N; "GP"; "N"; "ENTER NO."; 0:
MSGBOX A*R^(N-1)
```